Future Perspectives on Human-Computer Interaction Research

Sergio Sayago · Montserrat Sendín · Mercè Teixidó
Editors

Future Perspectives on Human-Computer Interaction Research

Towards the Year 2030

Springer

Editors
Sergio Sayago
Computer Science and Digital Design
Universitat de Lleida—Campus Igualada
Igualada, Barcelona, Spain

Montserrat Sendín
Computer Science and Digital Design
Universitat de Lleida
Lleida, Spain

Mercè Teixidó
Computer Science and Digital Design
Universitat de Lleida
Lleida, Spain

ISBN 978-3-031-71696-6 ISBN 978-3-031-71697-3 (eBook)
https://doi.org/10.1007/978-3-031-71697-3

This Springer imprint is published by the registered company Springer Nature Switzerland AG
The registered company address is: Gewerbestrasse 11, 6330 Cham, Switzerland

Foreword

As we approach the year 2030, the field of HCI continues to expand and adapt, driven by rapid advancements in digital technology and the evolving needs of users. Integrating these technologies into every aspect of our lives demands new design, evaluation, and implementation approaches. This book, *Future Perspectives on Human-Computer Interaction Research: Towards the Year 2030* offers a comprehensive look at the forefront of HCI research, highlighting innovative methodologies and emerging topics that will shape our future.

This book is derived from the outstanding contributions presented at the XXIII International Conference on Human-Computer Interaction 2023 (Interacción 2023), organized by the prominent GRIHO research group at the University of Lleida, Spain, and supported by the Association of Human-Computer Interaction (AIPO). The conference gathered a diverse community of researchers and practitioners who shared their latest findings and insights. The selected papers underwent a rigorous peer-review process and have been expanded into the chapters in this book. Each chapter showcases cutting-edge work being conducted across various domains of HCI, from human-centred artificial intelligence to virtual and augmented reality. The chapters have been meticulously curated and expanded by distinguished editors and experts in their respective fields of HCI, ensuring the highest quality and relevance of the content.

The breadth of topics covered in this book underscores the interdisciplinary nature of HCI. It addresses the critical questions and challenges that arise as we design and interact with increasingly sophisticated technologies. Authored by leading experts in their areas, the chapters delve into creating trustworthy AI systems, developing user-centred approaches in agile environments, and designing digital media that support cognitive development in children. These explorations are essential as we strive to build technologies that are functional, efficient, accessible, usable, intuitive, and beneficial for a diverse user base.

AIPO has always been committed to advancing the field of HCI by fostering collaboration and innovation. The Interacción 2023 conference exemplified this commitment, bringing together experts from various regions and levels of academic seniority. This book directly results from that collaborative spirit, showcasing the best contemporary HCI research and providing a platform for future advancements.

Moving forward, the field of HCI must adapt continually to technological advancements and shifting user requirements. This book provides valuable insights and guidance for researchers, practitioners, and students, encouraging them to push the boundaries of the next frontiers in HCI. By embracing new challenges and opportunities, we can continue improving our interactions with technology, ensuring it enhances human capabilities and experiences.

I am honoured to introduce this book and highly recommend it to anyone interested in the future directions of HCI research. It is a testament to the dedication and ingenuity of the HCI community and a valuable resource for understanding the next steps in our journey towards the year 2030.

Lourdes Moreno
Chair of the Spanish Society
of Human-Computer Interaction
(AIPO)
Universidad Carlos II de Madrid
Madrid, Spain

Preface

This book brings together an extended and curated version of the most outstanding papers presented at the XXIII International Conference on Human-Computer Interaction, held at the University of Lleida (Spain) in September 2023. The authors of these distinguished papers were invited to deepen and widen their discussions, enabling this volume to explore the "past, present, and future" of the areas addressed in each paper. Each chapter is rooted in rigorous research and has gone through two rounds of peer-review. As a rough guideline, at least 50 per cent of the chapters are original and not published elsewhere. Thus, this book is not just a conference proceedings.

Human-Computer Interaction (HCI) is a field characterized by rapid evolution and continuously expanding boundaries. As we look towards the future, it is crucial to reflect on the paths that have led us here and see where we are going. This book serves as a crucial nexus for such reflections, offering a comprehensive overview of current research and future directions in HCI. This book addresses important topics such as Human-Centred Artificial Intelligence, Augmented and Virtual Reality, and User-Centred Design, providing insights into how these areas will continue to influence and transform our interaction with technology. The chapters are enriched with case studies and examples that illustrate the practical application of theoretical approaches and ideas. This not only enriches our understanding of HCI but also illustrates how these innovations can significantly enhance (or worsen) our everyday lives.

This book is mostly aimed at researchers, at different levels of academic seniority, and students within the HCI community. Yet, it also offers valuable insights for anyone interested in the future of technology and its interface with humans, whether he or she is looking to deepen his or her understanding of current trends or inspiration for future projects. This publication also encourages a multidisciplinary dialogue, bridging gaps between technological development, psychological understanding, and design principles. By integrating perspectives from different disciplines, the book fosters an approach to developing technology that is both innovative and user-friendly. This cross-disciplinary collaboration is crucial in addressing the complex challenges that arise at the intersection of humans and technology, ensuring that advancements in HCI continue to be ethical, inclusive, and effective.

We wish to acknowledge the support and assistance from all contributors and collaborators who made this project possible. Your dedication and expertise enriches this publication and contributes to moving forward the entire field of HCI. Thank you for your invaluable contributions and for ensuring that the potential of HCI continues to be thoughtfully explored and realized.

Igualada, Spain — Sergio Sayago
Lleida, Spain — Montserrat Sendín
Lleida, Spain — Mercè Teixidó

Contents

Introduction 1
Sergio Sayago, Montserrat Sendín, and Mercè Teixidó

Past, Present and Future of User-Centred Design Methodologies that Empathise with the User and Generate Better Accessible Experiences. From Theory to Practice 17
Afra Pascual Almenara, Jose Humanes Elich, and Toni Granollers Saltiveri

An Analysis of Videogames to Compose an Adapted Heuristic Evaluation 45
Roger Larriba Baudilio, Toni Granollers Saltiveri, and Juan Enrique Garrido Navarro

Towards Trustworthy and Human-Centred AI Explanations 69
Cristina Manresa-Yee, Silvia Ramis, F. Xavier Gaya-Morey, and Jose Maria Buades Rubio

Interactive Human-in-the-Loop Topic Modeling 93
Laura Ham and Luis A. Leiva

Mobile Augmented Reality Gamification Strategies to Promote Social Skills: Case Studies and Future Challenges 119
Lissette López-Faican, Javier Jaen, and Jorge Montaner

From Past to Present: Human–Machine Interfaces Evolve Toward Adaptivity 151
Angela Carrera-Rivera, Felix Larrinaga, Ganix Lasa, Daniel Reguera-Bakhache, and Gorka Unamuno

The Future of Midwife Training: Towards a Virtual Reality Haptic Obstetric Simulator with Two Points of Contact 187
Fernando Luján Millán, Pascual González López,
Ana Belén García Bravo, Jonatan Martínez Muñoz,
Arturo S. García Jiménez, and José Pascual Molina Massó

Flipping the Reality of Young Children's Technology Through the 4Cs: Create, Connect, Communicate, and Control 207
Juan Pablo Hourcade and Flannery Currin

Conclusion 231
Sergio Sayago, Montserrat Sendín, and Mercè Teixidó

Introduction

Sergio Sayago, Montserrat Sendín, and Mercè Teixidó

Abstract This book provides some future perspectives on Human–Computer Interaction research towards the year 2030. This introductory chapter aims to situate this edited collection in a broader context, hoping to show some of the general contributions this book makes to the field. This chapter also gives an overview of the contents of the book.

1 Overview

This book provides some future perspectives on Human–Computer Interaction (HCI) research towards the year 2030. It brings together an extended and curated version of the best papers published in the XXIII International Conference on Human–Computer Interaction 2023 (https://interaccion2023.udl.cat/). The authors of these papers were invited to submit a book chapter. We asked them to discuss past, present, and future research on the topic of the papers. The resulting chapters, which are summarized in Sect. 7, provide an overview of research in areas including Human-Centred Artificial Intelligence, Augmented and Virtual Reality, Usability, and User-Centred Design. The chapters also address research issues and questions that we consider are of relevance now and in the years to come, e.g. how should we design trustworthy and human-centred explanations (in AI-enabled technologies)? How do we adopt a user-centred approach in agile software development methodologies and in an ecosystem wherein digital technologies are active agents? Which heuristics

S. Sayago (✉)
Department of Computer Science and Digital Design, University of Lleida, Campus Universitari Igualada-UdL, Avinguda Pla de la Massa, 08, 08700 Igualada, Spain
e-mail: sergio.sayago@udl.cat

M. Sendín · M. Teixidó
Department of Computer Science and Digital Design, University of Lleida, Escola Politècnica Superior, Jaume II, 69, 25001 Lleida, Spain
e-mail: montse.sendin@udl.cat

M. Teixidó
e-mail: merce.teixido@udl.cat

S. Sayago et al. (eds.), *Future Perspectives on Human-Computer Interaction Research*,
https://doi.org/10.1007/978-3-031-71697-3_1

should be followed to conduct a usability evaluation of a digital game, and why? How can digital media be designed to have a positive impact young children's cognitive development?

In this introductory chapter, we situate this edited collection in a broader context, hoping to show some of the general contributions this book makes to the field of HCI. We also give an overview of the contents of the book. The contributions made to each specific area are discussed in the chapters. Within HCI, which is a burgeoning field that is evolving rapidly, taking stock of the past and the present helps us to envisage and discuss new directions and research agendas. This is an important task because the very structure of life is increasingly computational and networked [9, 20]. Several HCI works have already reflected on the history, achievements, gaps, and evolution of the field. We provide an overview of several of them[1] in Sect. 2, as this edited collection also reflects on the past and thinks about future perspectives, and doing so allows us to show the extent to which this book extends and widens previous works. Section 3 focuses on usability, which has taken on a fundamental role in the inception and evolution of HCI. This section engages in a discussion on whether usability is (and will be) dead or alive in contemporary (future) HCI research. We consider that this discussion is timely and important since the current focus on UX might encourage HCI researchers and designers to overlook usability. Section 4 is about going beyond user-centred design. While placing the user at the centre of design is widely regarded as a good HCI practice, most of today's AI-enabled digital technologies are active agents in our interactions with them, and this challenges the pivotal and classical role of the user in user-*centred* design. Section 5 focuses on human-centred AI, which represents an innovative approach consequent on the growing emphasis on integrating human needs and capabilities into the design and development of AI-powered systems. Finally, Sect. 6 provides an overview of user interfaces evolution and Sect. 7 presents an outline of the chapters.

2 A Guided Overview of HCI Evolution(s) and How This Book Contributes to Them

Myers [32] provides a brief history of HCI technology. This history shows that many of the most famous HCI successes, such as direct manipulation and the mouse pointing device, which were developed by companies, are deeply rooted in university research. Myers [32] also considers that the interfaces of the future (this paper was published in 1998) will use gesture and speech recognition, intelligent agents, and adaptive interfaces. It might be worth noting that we are already using these user interfaces nowadays. This book addresses them. [7, 9, 18, 41] trace back the beginning

[1] Any overview emphasizes some things while de-emphasizing or omitting others. This overview covers topics, and therefore cites publications, that we regard as relevant within the context of this book. Publications that might also be of importance can therefore either be missed or receive less attention than another overview might provide.

of HCI as an academic discipline in the early 1980s. As discussed in [7], at the inception of HCI, the notion that computer systems and software should be designed and developed with explicit consideration of the needs, abilities and preferences of their ultimate users was not a dominant view, since the users were primarily engineers, operators, and technicians. With the advent of the personal computer and the mass use of it, HCI began to be concerned about the study and practice of usability [34], as there was a significant change in the users and the purposes the systems were developed and used for [9, 18]. Over time, this focus on usability and human factors or ergonomics has shifted towards what is known as "user experience" (UX) [23], as our relationship with digital technologies goes beyond instrumental aspects to include non-instrumental ones, like emotions [40] and cultures [42], and the users are not only a collection of human factors but social actors [2]. HCI now covers all aspects of human life, through all manner of computing [41]. This increasing evolution has encouraged HCI researchers to reflect on waves of HCI research [5] or paradigm changes [21], as the research objectives, ways of doing research, and underlying metaphor of interaction change. Other works have reflected on what HCI will be like in the 2020 [20]. According to [20], any new direction for HCI would need to place human values at its core, because the new computing is about supporting human relationships [45], and there is an ongoing transition from machine-oriented to human-oriented systems [30]. Further research has addressed the important question of what HCI is [31]. For some, HCI is a mix of disciplines [41] and the place where humans and computers communicate and change each other [39]. Others see HCI as an inter-discipline [4] or problem-solving [38]. Liu et al. [30] argues that the big hole in HCI research (based on an analysis of CHI papers) is a lack of motor or mainstream themes, which, as discussed in [8], can be taken as an indication of a lack of coherence and a strong focus on innovation.

This edited collection reinforces the fact that the only constant element in HCI research (and I the evolutions of this field) is change. It is our conviction that this feature of HCI is unlikely to disappear in the future. HCI changes because computer technology, the user landscape, and the reasons or purposes for using all manners of computers, change. These changes encourage HCI researchers to adapt or find new (or different) ways to study, design, create, and evaluate the interactions between people and computers. The chapters of this book are just an example. The transition from machine-oriented to human-oriented systems [19]—or the new computing, as discussed by Shneiderman in [45], which is about what people can do rather than what computers can do, is addressed in all the chapters of this book. This encourages us to suggest that future HCI research will continue to be heavily human-oriented. Whereas [28] argues that "the only tradition in HCI is that of having no tradition in terms of research topics", which reinforces the "(a) lack of coherence" discussed in [8] and that "anything goes" in HCI [41], this book addresses, among other topics, usability evaluation and user-centred design methodologies, which have been, are, and will be motor themes (perhaps, under different names) in HCI. Usability is not dead and designing technologies that are not only easy and obvious to use but also make our lives better in the era of rapid technological developments (e.g. AI) calls for new or different methodologies. This book also addresses topics which are receiving increasing research attention, such as explainability, and discusses research with an ever-increasing diverse use base, from children and media broadcasting professionals to nurses. Addressing a wide spectrum of research and application areas related to our interaction with computer technologies has been [19] a distinguishing feature of HCI. We expect to see even more diversity in (technologies, users, and contexts of interaction) in the future, as computer technologies are more pervasive in multiple facets of the lives of most of us, with every day that goes by. HCI research as problem-solving [38], i.e. HCI is about solving problems related to human use of computing, cuts across this book. Yet, the chapters of this publication show that HCI research (both past, present, and future is not only about solving problems but also about creating new opportunities. Most of the chapters are eminently practical, the theoretical component is either missing or weak. This reinforces a systematic weakness of HCI, which is unlikely to be improved soon unless more efforts are made in the future: conceptual or theoretical contributions are also needed.

3 Usability: Dead or Alive?

Usability has traditionally served as a cornerstone in software development, emphasizing the creation of digital products that are effective, efficient, and satisfying for users within specific contexts. Nielsen [34] outlined usability heuristics that emphasize key principles like consistency, error prevention, and user control, shaping how we assess product quality. Early usability research focussed on ensuring that digital interfaces met the practical needs of users, facilitating ease of use, reducing learning curves, and increasing overall satisfaction with the product's interface.

The field matured significantly in the 1980s and 1990s, with seminal works such as [34, 37] shaping the foundational principles of usability. The former introduced the concept of User-Centred System Design, advocating for the iterative inclusion of user feedback throughout the design process. The latter provided practical guidelines and heuristics for usability engineering, emphasizing that digital interfaces should minimize user errors, provide clear system feedback, and remain consistent in design and terminology.

However, the broader concept of User Experience (UX) has gradually expanded the focus of design beyond usability to encompass emotional and aesthetic aspects of user interaction. Norman [36] emphasized the importance of visceral, behavioural, and reflective design, highlighting how products must evoke positive emotions in addition to being functional. This shift marks a significant evolution in design, moving from task-oriented criteria like efficiency, effectiveness, and satisfaction to a holistic view of the user's emotional responses, beliefs, and preferences.

Usability is now considered an integral component of UX, which includes a broader spectrum of user-product interactions. Hassenzahl [23] elaborated on this by noting that UX recognizes the value of aesthetics, emotions, and experiences that go beyond traditional usability goals. Despite this evolution, usability remains crucial in ensuring that digital products are accessible and usable.

Accessibility has become a growing concern as the digital divide continues to impact individuals with disabilities and special needs. The concept of inclusive design, as outlined by [29], advocates for digital products and services that cater to diverse user groups from the outset. The Web Content Accessibility Guidelines (WCAG), developed by the World Wide Web Consortium (W3C), provide comprehensive recommendations to ensure web content is accessible to individuals with visual, auditory, cognitive, and motor impairments.

Vigo et al. [46] extended the conversation on accessibility by identifying the challenges developers face in incorporating accessibility features into their designs. They highlighted the need for better tools and educational resources to help developers understand and implement accessibility guidelines effectively. Moreover, [1] emphasized the importance of conducting usability testing with individuals with disabilities to identify and address specific barriers they encounter.

Overall, the transition from usability to UX has brought a broader and more inclusive perspective to digital design. While usability remains essential for creating effective and efficient products, UX emphasizes the importance of emotional and aesthetic aspects, ensuring that digital interactions are not only functional but also enjoyable and meaningful. Thus, and although the current focus on UX and the evolution(s) of HCI (see Sect. 2 of this chapter) might lead us to believe that usability is "dead"—what is the point of improving the usability of a system (e.g. removing problems) if its value extends beyond its utility?—This edited collection argues that usability is alive. Making digital technologies which are easy and obvious to use is still both important and a challenge, and this is unlikely to change in the future, as new technologies bring further usability issues. Ignoring usability (errors, efficiency, efficacy, time…) is ignoring too much, and puts some people, especially those with low tech literacy and general literacy, at a further risk of digital exclusion.

4 Beyond User-Centred Design: The User Is No Longer at the Centre

User-Centred Design (UCD) has long been a framework that places the user at the heart of the design and development process. Foundational texts like [37] have shaped the UCD philosophy, advocating for designs that align seamlessly with user expectations and provide intuitive, satisfying experiences. UCD prioritizes iterative design processes, user feedback, and usability testing, ensuring that products meet functional requirements while delivering a satisfying user experience.

However, the traditional UCD methodology faces critiques as digital interactions grow more complex. Technologies are increasingly becoming active agents capable of learning, adapting, and making decisions. The classic UCD approach that positions the user strictly at the centre may no longer suffice. Norman [35] noted that AI-enabled systems challenge the central role of the user in design, suggesting that designers consider the reciprocal interactions between users and intelligent systems.

Recent developments in AI and machine learning have accelerated the shift towards what [3] describe as a "post-user-centred" design philosophy. In this approach, technology is not merely a passive tool awaiting human command but an active participant that shapes user experiences and outcomes. This partnership model recognizes the increasing agency of technology in HCI, suggesting a new framework where humans and intelligent systems collaborate to achieve common goals.

Shneiderman [44] introduced the concept of Human-Centred AI (HCAI), emphasizing the need to design AI systems that complement human capabilities rather than replace them. This collaborative intelligence approach acknowledges that humans and AI bring different strengths to the table, leading to innovative solutions that neither could achieve independently. In healthcare, for example, AI can analyse vast amounts of data to identify patterns and suggest diagnoses, while human professionals provide contextual understanding and empathetic patient care.

In creative industries, AI can offer novel inspirations and ideas, while humans refine and contextualize these inputs to produce original works. Dove et al. [11] explored this collaborative dynamic in design processes, noting that designers increasingly rely on AI tools for ideation and problem-solving. However, they emphasized the importance of maintaining a balance between human creativity and technological influence.

The rise of AI-enabled systems also challenges traditional UCD principles like control and transparency. Eiband et al. [12] highlighted the importance of providing users with meaningful explanations of AI decisions, enabling them to understand and trust the system's recommendations. This transparency is crucial for fostering trust in AI-enabled technologies, especially as they become more autonomous and capable of making critical decisions on behalf of users.

Moreover, [27] discussed the ethical implications of AI in decision-making, emphasizing the need for frameworks that ensure fairness, accountability, and transparency. As AI systems increasingly shape user experiences, designers must consider not only the technical aspects of HCI but also the broader social and ethical implications of these interactions.

In conclusion, as we move beyond traditional User-Centred Design, which is likely to be the road to follow in the future in HCI design and research, the challenge lies in balancing technology's agency with humans' needs, interests, values, and agency. This evolving landscape calls for a collaborative approach to design, where the synergy between human creativity and AI's analytical prowess leads to breakthrough innovations and experiences that are both meaningful and empowering. This edited collection explores these issues by looking into human-centred AI applications and the interplay of agile software development, accessibility and UCD.

5 From Human Factors to Human–Computer Interaction to Human-Centred AI

As a natural progression of a growing emphasis on understanding and integrating human needs and capabilities into the design and development of technological systems, this section intends to depict this specific evolution. This progression reflects a shift from simply fitting technology to humans to creating a collaborative relationship between humans and AI.

Human Factors primary goals were to reduce human error, increase productivity and system availability, and enhance safety, health and comfort with a specific focus on the interaction between the human and equipment [48]. It was the result of applying physiological principles to the design of processes, and systems. It provides a multidisciplinary discipline aimed at studying the design of equipment, devices, and processes that fit the human body and its cognitive abilities, based on the human behaviour. A popular example is the design of airplane cockpits with clear controls and displays to minimize pilot fatigue and error.

By building upon Human Factors, HCI recognizes the interactive nature of technology and the importance of communication between humans and computers. That involves an open-ended dialogue between the user and the computer, which is a crucial analogy in the field. The focus is, thus, on the interfaces between people (users) and computers. These "user" interfaces are crucial to facilitating this interaction. The main goals are usability, user experience (UX) and at the end designing interfaces for human use, which are intuitive, easy to learn, and enjoyable. The term was popularized by Stuart K. Card, Allen Newell, and Thomas P. Moran in their 1983 book, The Psychology of HCI. The first known use was in 1975 by Carlisle [6]. The growth in human–computer interaction field has resulted in many new areas of research. Additionally, it has led to an increase in the quality of interaction, as final users obtain a greater satisfaction and a better experience with interactive systems, while reducing human–computer misunderstandings. A classic example is the Three Mile Island accident, a nuclear meltdown accident, where investigations concluded that the design of the user interface was at least partly responsible for the disaster [13].

Finally, Human-Centred AI (HCAI, and HAI) [24] is a growing field within AI development that emphasizes designing and developing AI systems that prioritize human needs, values, and capabilities. It is acknowledged the increasing complexity of AI systems and the need for them to be not just focussed on user experience, but also ethical (considering potential ethical issues such as bias, fairness, and privacy), transparent in their decision-making processes, and aligned with human values [14]. In other words, it considers the social and ethical implications of AI alongside usability, reducing thus the potential risks of its implementation. The goal is to develop AI systems that are beneficial, trustworthy, and that empower human decision-making. In other words, HCAI goes beyond usability and builds on the foundation of user-centred design principles while incorporating ethical considerations and a focus on societal well-being.

As example, we could select infinite cases, as long as AI systems today embraces any field. To mention some of them, recommendation engines on e-commerce platforms, adaptive learning platforms, smart assistants, can be representative ones. A significant example can be an AI-powered healthcare diagnostics that provides transparency in their decision-making and supports human doctors in providing better care. AI is employed in medical imaging to assist radiologists in identifying anomalies in X-rays, MRIs, and CT scans. Companies like Aidoc use AI to detect abnormalities in medical images, potentially improving diagnostic accuracy and speed.

Within the Human-centred AI (HCAI) area, Human-in-the-loop AI (HITL) is a particular approach to developing AI that prioritizes ongoing human involvement. This approach ensures that humans actively participate continuously, on different aspects of the AI development process, aligning thus this method with the User-Centred Design. Just like on the HCI field, HITL focuses on integrating human input and feedback throughout the complete AI lifecycle. This includes design, training, and deployment. Human's oversight plays a crucial role in ensuring accuracy, mitigating bias, and improving user experience, what ensures trustworthiness.

Examples of HITL AI applications can be self-driving cars, medical diagnosis and fraud detection. All of them need human action in some situation (to take control in case of unexpected situations), and expertise is still crucial for making final decisions.

Finaly, a subfield within HCAI is eXplainable AI (XAI), which focuses on making the decision-making processes of AI models more understandable and transparent to humans, which is addressed in (Chapter-Cristina). On the last step, we can mention that Human-centred Explainable Artificial Intelligence (HCXAI) takes the principles of both Human-Centred AI (HCAI) and Explainable AI (XAI) to create AI systems that are not only user-friendly and ethical, but also transparent and understandable for humans.

6 Evolution of "User" Interfaces

Because almost every type of computer technology involves interaction between people and computers in some form, it is hard not to engage in a discussion about the evolution of the notion of user interfaces in a book that aims to provide some future perspectives on HCI research towards 2030. As discussed in [17], the location of the user interface has been pushed farther and farther out from the computer itself, deeper into the user and the work (in a broad sense) environment. Initially, the user interface was located on the hardware itself, as most users were engineers working directly with the hardware. When computers reached out of laboratory settings, and for a long time since then, it seemed as if the human–computer interface was to be limited to working on a desktop computer, using a mouse and a keyboard to interact with windows, icons, menus, and pointers (WIMP) [43]. More recently, however, we can interact with computers in several (and different) ways. Tangible computing and voice-based interaction are some examples. There has been a continuity, i.e.

from hardware to software to increasingly higher-level cognitive capabilities and finally to social processes [17], to the outward movement of the computer's interface to its external environment. Ubiquitous computing [10] is an example. We expect to see more of this integration of user interfaces in our everyday lives in the future. Whether this will be in the terms suggested by [47] or not is uncertain [10]. This book contributes to this evolution of user interfaces by discussing virtual and augmented reality in several scenarios, such as medicine and education, and adaptive user interfaces, which aim to provide personalized user experiences.

By considering this succinct and general overview of the evolution of the user interface, along with technological developments and the role that user interfaces play in HCI, there are no reasons to think that user interfaces will not be relevant in the future. We agree with [32] on "(we believe that) user interface design is poised for a radical change in the near future". However, it might be worth reflecting on the term "user interface". The spark for writing about this issue comes from working on this edited collection and [16], which challenges us to think about the extent to which "our terminology and habits of speech kept us with the changes, or do they perpetuate an outmoded perspective that holds us back?" (ibid., p. 112). As discussed in [16], the term "user interface" originated in the engineering environment in the late 1970s. In engineering environments, a computer's architecture includes many internal "interfaces". Since the interface to the users was one of many interfaces that had to be discussed, labelling it "the user interface" was an obvious and noncontroversial choice. However, this terminology obscures changes that have occurred in how interfaces are developed and used. Why do we talk about "user" interface and not "users" when most computer technologies are not only used by a single person? Why do we keep using the term "user", which is semantically poorer than, for instance, "student", "teacher", or "nurse"? What exactly counts as the "interface" in computer technologies which are increasingly becoming ubiquitous, embedded in everyday objects, and more transparent? Is the interface software, hardware, a metaphor…or, as Negroponte suggests, "the place where bits and people meet? [33]. Little work has been published on the history and evolution of user interfaces at large [26]. This is not the objective of this section, and this book does not engage in this discussion either, yet we hope it can contribute to fostering further reflection and future research on this issue.

7 Overview of the Chapters

The first two chapters are methodological. Chapter "Past, Present and Future of User-Centred Design Methodologies that Empathise with the User and Generate Better Accessible Experiences. From Theory to Practice" contributes to the discussion on going beyond user-centred design by discussing a novel process model of usability and accessibility engineering within the context of agile software development. Chapter "An Analysis of Videogames to Compose an Adapted Heuristic Evaluation" focuses on usability evaluation, argues that we are still far from knowing how to carry out heuristic evaluation of digital games, and shows that usability is not dead at all in the era of UX.

Chapter "Past, Present and Future of User-Centred Design Methodologies that Empathise with the User and Generate Better Accessible Experiences. From Theory to Practice" provides an overview of past, present, and future research on User-Centred Design (UCD). Initially, the efforts focussed on the development of technology. Over time, the focus shifted towards considering people's characteristics to design and develop useful and easy-to-use systems. This overview also discusses software development, which has shifted from the classical waterfall model to agile methodologies. This chapter notes that incorporating practices related to UCD into an Agile framework is a major challenge. To address it, Chapter "Past, Present and Future of User-Centred Design Methodologies that Empathise with the User and Generate Better Accessible Experiences. From Theory to Practice" discusses the process of adapting Agile methodologies and the MPIu+a model (Process Model of Usability and Accessibility Engineering) [15], which results in the MPIu+aX methodology. The chapter presents a case study in which this methodology was successfully followed to create a professional conference website [25]. It also discusses present and future challenges in UCD in three areas: (a) an increasingly diverse user base; (b) new wearable devices and the Internet of Things (IoT), which involve new habits, needs, and lifestyles of people; and (c) current AI-enabled interactive systems, which have evolved from being an application aimed at an end user to an integral service where understanding the needs of the different agents involved is fundamental.

Chapter "An Analysis of Videogames to Compose an Adapted Heuristic Evaluation" argues that heuristic evaluation is a valid method to evaluate the usability and user experience of video games. Yet, it requires adaptation. This chapter presents an adapted version of a pre-existing heuristic evaluation to evaluate the usability and user experience of video game interfaces. This chapter provides an overview of heuristic evaluation. This overview highlights that the initial set of heuristics, which were proposed by Nielsen and Molich in the 1990s, were deemed too general, which encouraged HCI scholars to provide more specific ones, depending on the object of study. This chapter focuses on video games, which play a key role in today's society, and argues that usability, engage-ability, motivation, emotion, immersion, and commitment are crucial elements of their UX. This chapter also discusses the process followed to adapt the heuristic evaluation technique to video games. The starting point is an existing technique for usability evaluation created at the University of Lleida. This technique combines two sets of heuristic principles: Nielsen's and Tognazzini's lists. An analysis of heuristics applied to video games is provided and form the basis of the new heuristic evaluation, which, as discussed in the chapter, provides HCI practitioners with an effective tool to calculate a quantitative value of the usability and user experience of video games.

Chapters "Towards Trustworthy and Human-Centred AI Explanations and Interactive Human-in-the-Loop Topic Modelling" focus on Artificial Intelligence (AI). Chapter "Towards Trustworthy and Human-Centred AI Explanations" focuses on how human-centred techniques are applied to the design and evaluation of explanations with end-users and how the explanations influence the users' trust. Chapter

"Interactive Human-in-the-Loop Topic Modelling" delves into the interplay of AI systems and humans by focussing on human-in-the-loop approaches, which seem to be one of the most promising and effective solutions to handle this interplay between humans and systems as optimally as possible. Both chapters contribute to the increasing turn to human-centred AI.

Chapter "Towards Trustworthy and Human-Centred AI Explanations" addresses the challenge of building AI technologies that are human-centred, that is, AI technologies that are designed responsibly, respect privacy or follows human-centred design principles. Towards this end, this chapter focuses on explainability, provide an overview of past, present and future research on human-centred explainable AI (XAI), and present a case study which explores explanations' impact on users for facial expression recognition specifically regarding trust and understanding. This chapter argues that although the concept of explainable AI is not a novel idea, the past few years have seen a growth in efforts on explainability across the academic and industry landscapes, and that the design space of XAI along with other factors, from the adoption of usability principles to conceptual frameworks remain largely unexplored. In this line, open research questions for the integration of human-centred approaches to XAI are outlined.

The case study addresses the research question of whether a local or global visual explanation invokes a different level of trust and understanding in an automatic facial expression recognition system than no explanation at all. By analysing the results of an experimental study, Manresa and colleagues stress the need of offering explanations to increase transparency and make AI systems more accountable to users and stakeholders, to build proper mental models on how the system works, and to achieve more trustworthy and effective AI systems. Added to that, we cannot forget the legal and ethical imperatives [14] for providing explanations, which call for interdisciplinary work.

Chapter "Interactive Human-in-the-Loop Topic Modelling" discusses a real-world use case of human-in-the-loop AI to support broadcasting companies in the production of audiovisual contents. The goal is to understand the interplay of AI systems and humans, such that they can cooperate towards a common goal, acknowledging their weaknesses and leveraging their strengths.

Broadcasting companies produce large amounts of text and audiovisual content. Extracting meaningful insights from these sources is important. Yet, doing so requires efficient analysis methods, which are often only palatable to data scientists. To bridge this gap, this chapter focuses on interactive topic modelling (ITM), which requires efficient analysis methods and techniques for automatic theme discovery. In an overview of past, present and future research in this area, this chapter points out that classical topic models have important shortcomings, such as the difficulty in interpreting topics, and models being prone to extracting too many or few topics. Contemporary, ITM address these shortcomings by incorporating human expertise in the process. Yet, most ITM applications are designed for data scientists and NLP (Natural Language Processing) experts. This chapter introduces INTEX, an interactive topic modelling application that bridges the gap between NLP and domain experts. A user evaluation shows that INTEX enables domain experts to extract and explore topics in an intuitive and efficient manner. This encourages this chapter to argue that INTEX overcomes past challenges in topic modelling, representing the future of interactive applications in in the field of broadcasting companies.

Chapters "Mobile Augmented Reality Gamification Strategies to Promote Social Skills: Case Studies and Future Challenges, From Past to Present: Human-Machine Interfaces Evolve Towards Adaptivity, The Future of Midwife Training: Towards a Virtual Reality Haptic Obstetric Simulator with Two Points of Contact and Flipping the Reality of Young Children's Technology through the 4Cs: Create, Connect, Communicate, and Control" deal with different types of "users" interfaces. Chapter "Mobile Augmented Reality Gamification Strategies to Promote Social Skills: Case Studies and Future Challenges" discusses current trends in Mobile Augmented Reality (MAR) research intended to promote social skills and empathy, given that in this context to promote social skills there are few proposals that integrate MAR technology into their design. Chapter "From Past to Present: Human-Machine Interfaces Evolve Towards Adaptivity" discusses adaptive user interfaces within the context of Human–Machine Interfaces (HMI). Chapter "The Future of Midwife Training: Towards a Virtual Reality Haptic Obstetric Simulator with Two Points of Contact" focuses on medicine, namely, on intrapartum care. Compared to current practice with silicon models or pregnant women, virtual simulators can offer many advantages. Chapter "Flipping the Reality of Young Children's Technology through the 4Cs: Create, Connect, Communicate, and Control" argues that it is timely and important to rethink technologies for children. As more of children's time is spent using computers, this use, according to a system's perspective on human development, could impact on their behaviour, neural activity, and gene expression. As a counter to these concerning developments in computing, this chapter builds on the 3Cs approach to young children's technologies (create, connect, and communicate), and proposes a 4th C: control. These chapters contribute to the increasing evolution of "user" interfaces.

Chapter "Mobile Augmented Reality Gamification Strategies to Promote Social Skills: Case Studies and Future Challenges" examines several strategies for developing social skills with augmented reality and presents two case studies with location-based mobile augmented reality to promote social skills among students. Lissette and colleagues argue that Augmented Reality allows for the creation of immersive and stimulating learning experiences through enriched teaching environments. However, a great deal of research is focussed on single-user environments and few applications benefit from Mobile Augmented Reality (MAR) with markerless and location-based experiences. This chapter is a step forward towards location-based gamified MAR strategies for social skills development. One of the case studies explores the positioning of virtual content in the real world designed by "spatial anchors", which implements multi-user scenarios for identification and manipulation of basic emotional states for emotional intelligence and social skills evaluated with primary school children. The other case study is designed with GPS at a single-user and multi-user level, which implements help scenarios and narratives aimed at a target character to promote empathy in terms of prosocial behaviour among secondary students. This chapter also puts forward several guidelines to consider in the design of interactive MAR systems for the promotion of social skills in students in the future.

Chapter "From Past to Present: Human-Machine Interfaces Evolve Towards Adaptivity" discusses adaptive user interfaces within the context of Human–Machine Interfaces (HMI). Over the years, HMI have evolved significantly, from common-line interfaces to graphical user interfaces, voice interfaces, touchscreens and augmented reality displays, just to mention just a few. Angela et al. argue that a lack of adaptivity of HMI can lead to a steep learning curve, reduced efficiency, and a poor User Experience. To fill (partially) this gap, this chapter introduces a framework for the development of adaptive HMI, since adaptive user interfaces hold the potential of altering interface characteristics and functionality based on user requirements. A case study is presented with a hands-on development approach to demonstrate the practical implementation of the framework in an industrial environment, considering technological aspects and utilizing appropriate tools. The case study demonstrates the possibilities of implementation in a real-world scenario with multiple user roles, including researchers, testers, and maintenance operators. The chapter discusses technical aspects of the development of adaptive user interfaces in the case study, including a dashboard, APIs (Application Programming Interface) and databases. The chapter also puts forward some future perspectives, including human–robot collaboration, ethical and social implications, such as human autonomy, job displacement and automation.

Chapter "The Future of Midwife Training: Towards a Virtual Reality Haptic Obstetric Simulator with Two Points of Contact" addresses the future of midwife training. One of the techniques that midwives use in their profession is the digital vaginal examination. The teaching and learning of this technique is based on theoretical knowledge of the anatomy of the woman and the foetus. It is also based on practice with silicone obstetric simulators and real practice with pregnant women. Silicone models, even the simplest, are expensive and provide only a limited number of cases to practice. Molina et al argue that Virtual Reality (VR) solutions based on tactile and kinaesthetic feedback devices (haptic devices) can offer many advantages, such as the possibility of recreating an unlimited number of cases, personalized monitoring of the student, and carrying out examinations under the supervision of a teacher or facilitating self-assessment. Working towards this goal, this chapter explores how a vibrating device can contribute to the obstetric simulator. Driven by an exploratory method, the limits of vibrotactile haptic feedback technology are explored in constructing an obstetric simulator to train this technique. This chapter also discusses future perspectives, which call for bringing together an ecosystem of technologies to aid and assist midwives through their careers, from student to professional practice, accelerating learning and reducing the likelihood of misjudgement in real labour.

Chapter "Flipping the Reality of Young Children's Technology through the 4Cs: Create, Connect, Communicate, and Control" is concerned with child–computer interaction. This chapter argues that activities supported by digital technologies for children should involve creativity, communication, connection, and control. This 4Cs approach should enable us to address challenges not only related to the social and physical environment but also with privacy and a compulsive use of technologies. Key characteristics of this 4C approach, especially those related to control, on which the chapter focuses, include removing dependence on technology and better control over time and data. To situate this approach in a broader context, this chapter provides historical context for the latest changes in computing, in which computer use by 2–5-year-olds is regarded as recent and with benefits unclear for them. The chapter provides examples of current 4Cs technologies. The chapter also discusses child development, wherein computers are increasingly mediating children's interactions with the environment, and how it could be affected by dark patterns in computing, such as incentives for compulsive use. This chapter encourages us to rethink technologies for children in the future. Current trends involve dark patterns leading to isolation, passive consumption, unimaginative uses, and threats to privacy. The 4Cs provide a guide to a different approach.

References

1. Babu R, Singh R, Ganesh J (2010) Understanding blind users' web accessibility and usability problems. AIS Trans Human–Comput Interaction 2(3):73–94
2. Bannon LJ (1995) From human factors to human actors: the role of psychology and human–computer interaction studies in system design. In: Readings in human–computer interaction. Morgan Kaufmann, pp 205–214
3. Benyon D, Turner P, Turner S (2014) Designing interactive systems: people, activities, contexts, technologies. Pearson
4. Blackwell AF (2015) HCI as an inter-discipline. In: Proceedings of the 33rd annual ACM conference extended abstracts on human factors in computing systems, 503–516. https://doi.org/10.1145/2702613.2732505
5. Bødker S (2006) When second wave HCI meets third wave challenges. In: Proceedings of the 4th Nordic conference on human–computer interaction: changing roles, pp 1–8
6. Carlisle JH (1976) Evaluating the impact of office automation on top management communication. In: Proceedings of the June 7–10, 1976, national computer conference and exposition on—AFIPS'76. Proceedings of the 7–10 June 1976, national computer conference and exposition, pp 611–616
7. Carroll J (2002) Human–computer interaction in the new millennium. ACM Press
8. Chignell M, Wang L, Zare A, Li J (2023) The evolution of HCI and human factors: integrating human and artificial intelligence. ACM Trans Comput–Human Interact 30(2):1–30. https://doi.org/10.1145/3557891
9. Dix A (2017) Human–computer interaction, foundations and new paradigms. J Vis Lang Comput 42:122–134. https://doi.org/10.1016/j.jvlc.2016.04.001
10. Dourish P, Bell G (2011) Divining a digital future: mess and mythology in ubiquitous computing. MIT Press
11. Dove G, Halskov K, Forlizzi J, Zimmerman J (2017) UX design innovation: challenges for working with machine learning as a design material. In: Proceedings of the 2017 CHI conference on human factors in computing systems, 278–288
12. Eiband M, Schneider H, Bilandzic M, Fazekas-Connelly K, Hussmann H (2018) Bringing transparency design into practice. In: Proceedings of the 23rd international conference on intelligent user interfaces, 211–223
13. Ergoweb (2011) What is cognitive ergonomics? Ergoweb.com. Archived from the original on September 28

14. European Commission (2019) High-level expert group on AI. Ethics guidelines for trustworthy AI
15. Granollers T (2003) User centred design process model. Integration of usability engineering and software engineering. In: Interact 2003. ISBN: 978-1-58603-363-7
16. Grudin J (1993) Interface: an evolving concept. Commun ACM 36(4):110–119
17. Grudin J (1990) The computer reaches out: the historical continuity of interface design. In: Proceedings of the SIGCHI conference on human factors in computing systems, pp 261–268
18. Grudin J (2017) From tool to partner: the evolution of human–computer interaction. synthesis lectures on human-centered interaction. Morgan and Claypool Publishers
19. Gurcan F, Cagiltay NE, Cagiltay K (2021) Mapping human–computer interaction research themes and trends from its existence to today: a topic modeling-based review of past 60 years. Int J Human–Comput Interaction 37(3):267–280. https://doi.org/10.1080/10447318.2020.1819668
20. Harper R, Rodden T, Rogers Y, Sellen A (2008) Being human: human–computer interaction in the year 2020. Microsoft Research Ltd.
21. Harrison S, Tatar D, Sengers P (2007) The three paradigms of HCI. In: Alt. Chi. session at the SIGCHI Conference on human factors in computing systems San Jose, California, USA, pp 1–18
22. Hassenzahl M, Tractinsky N (2006) User experience-a research agenda. Behaviour Inf Technol 25(2):91–97
23. Hassenzahl M (2008) User experience (UX): towards an experiential perspective on product quality. In: Proceedings of the 20th international conference of the association francophone d'Interaction Homme-Machine, 11–15
24. IBM Research (2024). https://research.ibm.com/topics/human-centered-ai
25. Interacción (2023) https://interaccion2023.udl.cat/
26. Jørgensen AH, Myers BA (2008) User interface history. CHI'08 extended abstracts on human factors in computing systems, 2415–2418. https://doi.org/10.1145/1358628.1358696
27. Kleinberg J, Mullainathan S, Raghavan M (2018) Inherent trade-offs in the fair determination of risk scores. In: Proceedings of the 8th innovations in theoretical computer science conference, 1–23
28. Kostakos V (2015) The big hole in HCI research. Interactions 22(2):48–51. https://doi.org/10.1145/2729103
29. Lazar J, Goldstein DG, Taylor A (2015) Ensuring digital accessibility through process and policy. Morgan Kaufmann
30. Liu Y, Goncalves J, Ferreira D, Xiao B, Hosio S, Kostakos V (2014) CHI 1994–2013: mapping two decades of intellectual progress through co-word analysis. In: Proceedings of the SIGCHI conference on human factors in computing systems, 3553–3562. https://doi.org/10.1145/2556288.2556969
31. Long J, Dowell J (n.d.) Conceptions of the discipline of HCI: craft, applied science, and engineering
32. Myers BA (1998) A brief history of human–computer interaction technology. Interactions 5(2):44–54. https://doi.org/10.1145/274430.274436
33. Negroponte N (2015) Being digital. Vintage
34. Nielsen J (1994) Usability engineering. Academic Press
35. Norman DA (1998) The invisible computer: why good products can fail, the personal computer is so complex, and information appliances are the solution. MIT Press
36. Norman DA (2004) Emotional design: why we love (or hate) everyday things. Basic Books
37. Norman DA, Draper SW (1986) User-centered system design: new perspectives on human–computer interaction. Lawrence Erlbaum Associates
38. Oulasvirta A, Hornbæk K (2016) HCI research as problem-solving. In: Proceedings of the 2016 CHI conference on human factors in computing systems, 4956–4967. https://doi.org/10.1145/2858036.2858283
39. Petrick ER (2020) A historiography of human–computer interaction. IEEE Ann Hist Comput 42(4):8–23. https://doi.org/10.1109/MAHC.2020.3009080

40. Picard RW (2000) Affective computing. MIT Press
41. Rogers Y (2012) HCI Theory. classical, modern, and contemporary. synthesis lectures on human-centered interaction. Morgan and Claypool Publishers
42. Sayago S (2023) Cultures in human–computer interaction. Synthesis lectures on human-centered interaction. Springer Nature
43. Shaer O (2009) Tangible user interfaces: past, present, and future directions. Foundations Trends® Human–Comput Interaction 3(1–2):1–137. https://doi.org/10.1561/1100000026
44. Shneiderman B (2020) Human-centered AI. Oxford University Press
45. Shneiderman B (2003) Leonardo's laptop: human needs and the new computing technologies. MIT Press
46. Vigo M, Brown J, Conway V (2014) Benchmarking web accessibility evaluation tools: measuring the harm of sole reliance on automated tests. In: Proceedings of the 13th web for All conference, 1–10
47. Weiser M (1991) The computer for the 21st century. Sci Am 265(3):94–105
48. Wickens, Gordon, Liu (1997) An introduction to human factors engineering (PDF), archived from the original (PDF) on 19 June 2018

Past, Present and Future of User-Centred Design Methodologies that Empathise with the User and Generate Better Accessible Experiences. From Theory to Practice

Afra Pascual Almenara, Jose Humanes Elich, and Toni Granollers Saltiveri

Abstract User-Centred Design (UCD) is a set of technological design methodologies that places the user at the centre of development. Initially, developers focused solely on technology. Over time, they gradually began to consider people more seriously in their designs. In 2004, the UCD methodology, Usability and Accessibility Engineering Process Model (MPIu+a) ("Modelo de Proceso de la Ingeniería de la Usabilidad y Accesibilidad", MPIu+a in Spanish), was developed. Over time, Agile development methodologies emerged, which sought to identify system requirements through collaborative efforts with end-user involvement. However, Agile methodologies can be difficult to implement due to their incompatibility with DCU tenets. This chapter outlines the process of adapting agile methodologies to the MPIu+a model for the development of current interactive systems. This research work has a twofold objective: firstly, to improve the MPIu+a methodology by incorporating previously studied empathic techniques that enhance the Accessible User eXPerience (AUX)—this variant will be referred to as MPIu+aX. Secondly, to apply our MPIu+aX proposal to a case study, which focuses on the creation of the Interaccion 2023 conference website, to observe its real-world application. At the end of this document, we present the new challenges faced by UCD in adapting to the changing lifestyles and needs of users.

A. P. Almenara (✉) · J. H. Elich · T. G. Saltiveri
Departamento de Ingeniería Informática y Diseño Digital, Universitat de Lleida, Escola Politècnica Superior, Jaume II, 69, 25001 Lleida, Catalunya, Spain
e-mail: afra.pascual@udl.cat

J. H. Elich
e-mail: jhe3@alumnes.udl.cat

T. G. Saltiveri
e-mail: toni.granollers@udl.cat

S. Sayago et al. (eds.), *Future Perspectives on Human-Computer Interaction Research*,
https://doi.org/10.1007/978-3-031-71697-3_2

1 Introduction

Human–Computer Interaction practitioners understand User-Centred Design (UCD) as technology design methodologies where the user is the focus of every development [1–3]. They consider the user in the whole process of ideation, design and development of an interactive system and its User Interface (UI) with the aim to adapt it to their mental model, their needs and their desires. The final goal is to make the system easier to use and generate more satisfaction for the end-users. Usability is an internal quality of interactive systems defined as "the ability of software to be understood, learned, used and enjoyed by the user under specific conditions of use" [4]. Web accessibility is a practice that "ensures that websites, technologies and tools are designed to be usable by people with disabilities" [5]. User eXperience (UX) is defined by ISO 9241-210 [6] as the perceptions and responses of people resulting from the use or anticipated use of a product, system or service. Related to this, Accessible User Experience (AUX) [7] is a practice that ensures that websites are designed to provide a better user experience for all, beyond accessibility for people with disabilities. In this context, it must be considered that the population is ageing [8], a person may be temporarily unable to move, see or hear [9], and according to various surveys [10], between 15 and 20% of the world's population lives with some kind of disability. The laws and regulations [11] that websites must comply with in terms of digital accessibility are based on the Web Content Accessibility Guidelines (WCAG) [12]. However, several studies indicate that these principles are complex to understand for designers [13, 14] and non-technical content creators [15–17]. However, despite these standard-setting efforts, less than 10% of websites are accessible [18, 19] worldwide. Public administrations and benchmarking companies should develop high-quality products, paying careful attention to Accessible User Experience (AUX) aspects, as they are organisations that reflect the state of technology in society and can have a very direct impact on people's perceptions.

This chapter discusses the process of adapting Agile methodologies and the MPIu+a model [20] (Modelo de Proceso de la Ingenieria de la Usabilidad y Accesibilidad, MPIu+a in Spanish) to update it to current interactive systems development methodologies. The main objective of this research work is twofold: on the one hand, to work on an improvement of the MPIu+a methodology to include empathic techniques previously studied [21] to improve the Accessible User eXPerience (AUX) (we will call this variant MPIu+aX) and, on the other hand, the experimental follow-up of our own MPIu+aX proposal to a real case study, the creation of the Interaction 2023 conference website (https://interaccion2023.udl.cat/), to observe its application in a real context. In the different phases of the methodology, Design Thinking and Design Sprint strategies were combined to drive the project forward [22]. Techniques associated with UI development that allow visual information to be organised and input to be provided on graphical elements. User eXperience and Accessible User eXperience [7] have been considered in all phases of the process to create a website with a high interactive quality, and, as that we understand a web that empathises with the real needs of its users and generates satisfactory user experiences for all. Information on the development of the system can be found on the project summary website: https://interaccion2023.udl.cat/desarrollo-del-proyecto-web-interaccion2023.

The chapter is structured firstly with this introduction. Next, the related work is presented, in which the past and present of UCD is addressed. Afterwards, the new contributions made to the MPIu+a methodology to become the MPIu+aX methodology are explained. The case study section is included with an explanation of the process carried out in the development of the Interacción2023 conference website, and then the advances towards new UCD methodologies are showed. Finally, the conclusions are presented.

2 Related Works

In the early days of computing, in the 1960s and 1970s, systems were not user-friendly. There was a very technology-centric approach, where it was important to develop systems that could do complex tasks that people could not do. Although the technology worked, the problem was that users often had to study complex manuals or take specialised courses to understand what they could do with the applications. However, users often made mistakes because they did not understand how to use the system. In this period Methodologies like User-Centred Design (UCD) did not exist.

From the 1980s, personal computers became popular and were widely used in homes and offices. It was then that the problems associated with the usability of systems and applications became more apparent, and a new, more user-centred view of the system began to emerge. Disciplines such as software ergonomics or human factors [23, 24] were considered. Software ergonomics is the science that studies the interaction between humans and the elements of a system, with the ultimate goal of making software use comfortable and healthy for the user. It was Donald Norman at the University of California at San Diego who developed the interdisciplinary field of cognitive science [25]. This area studies human intelligence and behaviour, focusing on how the nervous system represents, processes and transforms information. This has led to a new approach that considers user characteristics to make interactive systems easier to use for all people. UCD emerged in this period to extend usability engineering by including an early focus on involving users in pre-design activities to understand user needs, then continuing to include users in iterative evaluations of design prototypes. Later, in the 1990s and 00s, concepts, principles and methodologies were developed to find out what the user's needs were with respect to the system. The concept of usability emerged [26], Nielsen's heuristic principles [27], techniques such as usability testing [28], personas [29] and scenarios [30] or card sorting [31], among others. These aspects laid the foundation for future UCD methodologies.

Also, around this time, work began on a rapid application development methodology for effective and efficient development and delivery of a task. The main focus was on developing high-quality systems with a relatively low investment cost.

Common to these methodologies was the use of iterative development and prototyping to drive the development of a system. But it was not until the early 00s that the Agile Manifesto was born, when a group of experts met to see how they could better meet the needs of their customers, reduce delivery times and avoid rigidity in the face of change. Agile methodologies propose a new way of thinking and interacting based on the following premises: (a) people come first, (b) development teams must be multidisciplinary, (c) create systems interactively and incrementally, (d) respond quickly to changes that may occur during the development of the system, (e) collaborate with the client so that they are present throughout the system development process [32].

With these characteristics, agile development methodologies [33] applied to the development of interactive systems offer opportunities to overcome the problems presented by traditional development methods.

2.1 Methodologies Related with UCD

In this context, the methodology of the Process Model of Usability and Accessibility Engineering (*Modelo de Proceso de la Ingenieria de la Usabilidad y Accesibilidad*, MPIu+a in Spanish) was published in the early 00s [20]. This methodology enables the development of usable and accessible systems by working iteratively in the phases of requirements analysis, design, prototyping, evaluation and implementation. Subsequently, in 2010, a theoretical research paper was developed, in which agile methodologies such as (SCRUM, XP, Crystal Family and FDD) were integrated into the MPIu+a user-centred process model, called MPIu+a Agile [34], but no practical application of the methodology was carried out.

Incorporating practices related to User eXperience (UX) into an Agile framework is a major challenge for many organisations, mainly because Agile methods describe the activity or project management while UX design methods describe activities to design product and/or user interface interactions [35–37]. Related to this, AgileUX methodologies [38] group User eXperience (UX) design within the Agile development methodology with the aim of unifying developers and designers in the agile process of advancing iterations and product delivery.

Design Thinking (DT) [39–41] is an agile methodology that works with techniques related to empathy. It aims to elicit the concrete needs of users with respect to the system. It is divided into five steps [42, 43] that help developers to put themselves in the user's shoes and think about designing solutions from a more human point of view. The Design Sprint (DS) [44] follows a temporalisation in development, mixing agile methodologies such as Design Thinking (DT) in order to obtain a five-day process or iteration in which to validate ideas and advance in the product development stages [45]. Each 5-day iteration is called a "sprint". A sprint is a short, fixed period of time in which a team works to complete a set amount of work.

2.2 *Techniques of Design and Interaction*

User Interface (UI) and User eXperience (UX) are related concepts: UI defines the overall design, look and feel of the product; UX defines interaction models, tasks, flows and creates communication scenarios. In this context, User Interface (UI) design techniques [46] focus on the design/creation of everything in the system that people come into contact with, either physically, perceptually or conceptually. The development of a design system [47] offers several advantages that facilitate the creation of consistent user interfaces (UIs). Style, colours, fonts, labels and any other components that can ensure an optimal UX are specified. The Atomic Design methodology [48], which lies at the interface between design and development, allows complex interfaces to be composed of complex elements (organisms) made up of simpler elements (atoms).

To achieve a successful UX [49], it is necessary to consider facets such as usefulness, usability, findability, credibility, desirability, accessibility and product value [50] throughout all phases of development. Additionally, other facets such as dependability, playability, plasticity and emotionality [51] should be included. It is also important to employ a wide variety of UX research techniques to understand the aspects that can enhance the user's experience [52].

In addition, Accessible User Experience (AUX) [53, 54] aims to integrate accessibility into UX design to create enjoyable digital experiences for all users, regardless of their abilities. Observing the creation of web content following WCAG guidelines, conducting user tests with people with disabilities who are part of the audience [55], and considering it as a requirement from the beginning of the system's development [56] are essential steps. Several research studies have analysed the impact of web accessibility barriers on the emotions of people with disabilities, including those with intellectual [57], blind and low vision [58–60], hearing [61] and motor [62] impairments. These studies demonstrate that users with disabilities have more pleasant and satisfying experiences when developers have considered accessibility in the system, just like any other user.

3 MPIu+aX Methodology

The MPIu+aX methodology represents an improved iteration of the MPIu+a methodology and focuses on using agile methodologies and User Interface design, and UX and AUX techniques. The following section explains the contributions made to the MPIu+a methodology, which will be renamed MPIu+aX methodology (see Fig. 1). It is important to consider that the model proposed by the MPIu+aX methodology can be configured for all types of users with any type of disability. It observes the characteristics of each group, and it is possible to adapt the systems to the specific

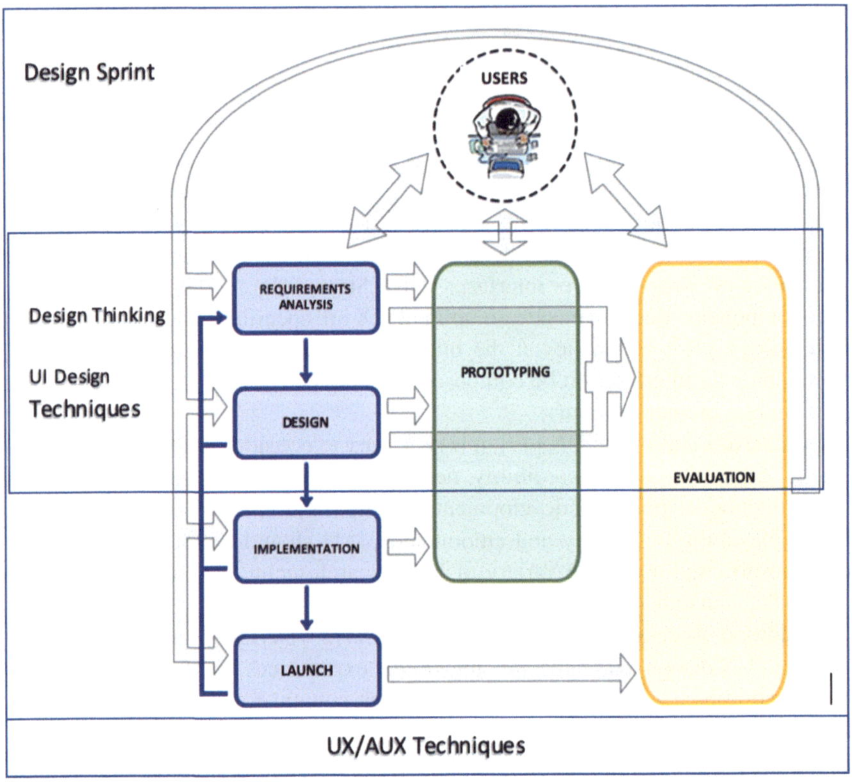

Fig. 1 Outline of the MPIu+aX proposal contributing to the MPIu+a methodology, design sprint techniques, design thinking, user interface design, and UX and AUX techniques

needs of the users through the techniques to be followed in each phase of the methodology. Also, the system to be developed can be designed for a web environment and also for any other environment (mobile app, TV app…).

3.1 Requirements Analysis

The Requirements Analysis,[1] includes finding out, through UX research techniques, the needs and preferences of the user who is the object of the system. This phase is composed of the first three stages of Design Thinking [39]: (1) Empathising with the user by researching their needs; (2) Defining needs and problems; (3) All this analysis helps the development team to deeply understand the user's needs with respect to the system and to discover the important elements that can empathise with what the

[1] Techniques of the requirements analysis phase of MPIu+a: https://mpiua.invid.udl.cat/fases-mpiua/analisis-de-requisitos/.

Table 1 List of original MPIu+a techniques from the requirements analysis phase, together with the techniques considered for the proposed MPIu+aX methodology

MPIu+a	Extending techniques for MPIu + aX
Ethnographic Analysis	**Journey customer map,**[2] defines the customer experience in the use of a product or service **Empathy map,**[3] identifies what the user does, thinks, feels, says, hears, etc. in a given situation
Stakeholders	**Map of actors,**[4] which graphically reflects the connections between the different social actors that make up a service
User classification technique	**Personas**[5] are fictional characters created to represent different types of users who might use the system

user really needs when interacting with the system. The MPIu+ax employs Design Thinking techniques to enhance understanding of user needs, as presented in Table 1, which displays various techniques from the MPIu+a methodology phases alongside Design Thinking techniques deemed important for each case.

The Ethnographic Analysis incorporates Design Thinking techniques to gain a comprehensive understanding of the users' needs and their environment. The stakeholder analysis and user classification employ similar techniques to the MPIu+a methodology, but with a different approach. For instance, the Persona technique provides more detailed user information than the user classification technique.

3.2 Design

The Design Phase[6] involves analysing how to present the information in the interface so that the user can navigate and interact with it: defining an appropriate information architecture helps to present an organisation of the content that best fits the user's mental model; creating an interaction map helps to define what the user can do in the system; devising a design system with principles, patterns and rules for the design of the user interface facilitates the work of the developers [63]. Table 2 shows the techniques included in the MPIu+aX model. Techniques from the Atomic Design methodology and Design Thinking have been included to speed up the design and make partial deliveries of early results and thus evaluate significant progress in the different iterations of the project.

The techniques for defining the information architecture do not contribute anything new with respect to the MPIu+a methodology, but the user interaction

[2] Customer Journey Map: https://www.interaction-design.org/literature/topics/customer-journey-map.

[3] Empathy map: https://www.nngroup.com/articles/empathy-mapping/.

[4] Map of actors: https://servicedesigntools.org/tools/ecosystem-map.

[5] Personas: https://www.interaction-design.org/literature/topics/personas.

[6] MPIu+a design phase: https://mpiua.invid.udl.cat/fases-mpiua/diseno/.

Table 2 List of original MPIu+a techniques from the design phase, together with the techniques considered for the proposed MPIu+aX methodology

MPIu+a	Extending techniques for MPIu+aX
Navigation models	Definition of the **navigation architecture**,[7] is about the website navigation that impacts the User Experience (UX)
Activity design	**User interaction map**,[8] reflects the different tasks that all end-users of a possible solution perform throughout the different stages of use, defining the interactions between them
Interface design	**Design system** is a robust, consistent and centralised set of hierarchical and reusable elements that allow UX design and development teams to work faster and more efficiently. Using the atomic design technique[9] **Benchmarking**,[10] to learn about the characteristics of our product's competitors and/or to find out how other products—not necessarily competitors—solve certain problems

map, which comes from the Design Thinking methodology, does. Regarding the design system, the use of the Atomic Design methodology facilitates the subsequent development of the interface and avoids future design errors related with accessibility elements. The atomic design methodology allows elements of the system to be designed in an accessible way. First, the atoms are designed with labels and contrast (for example: icons, labels, text boxes); second, the molecules are designed to be interactive and accessible at the same time (a "search engine component" is built with the elements of the atoms mentioned above); third, the organisms to develop the header as a part of the screen (it could contain a "menu component" and a "search engine component") and finally a template that composes a makeup of web page (containing several organisms menu, footer, body, search page, …).

3.3 Prototyping

The prototyping phase,[11] is the stage where teams create a tangible representation of an idea or solution that they can test. In this case, no significant improvements have been included in the MPIu+aX methodology because sufficient techniques are already available. However, new tools have been added to speed up the production of prototypes.

Paper sketches can help to clarify ideas about user needs and system objectives discussed in the initial stages of the methodology. Low-fidelity prototypes are useful for initial system evaluations, while high-fidelity prototypes or wireframes can be

[7] Information Architecture: Study Guide. https://www.nngroup.com/articles/ia-study-guide/.

[8] User interaction map: https://www.designthinking.es/inicio/herramienta.php?id=9&fase=define.

[9] Atomic Design: https://bradfrost.com/blog/post/atomic-web-design/.

[10] Benchmarking: http://design-toolkit.recursos.uoc.edu/es/guia/benchmarking/.

[11] MPIu+a prototyping phase: https://mpiua.invid.udl.cat/fases-mpiua/prototipado/.

Table 3 List of original MPIu+a techniques from the prototyping phase, together with the techniques considered for the proposed MPIu+aX methodology

MPIu+a	Extending techniques for MPIu+aX
Sketches	**Paper sketch**[13] to organise the first ideas of the system
Low- and high-fidelity prototype (wireframes)	Use of collaborative **prototyping applications**. For example: marvel,[14] Figma[15] or Adobe XD[16]
Software prototype	**Creation of pages** on the implementation platform (unpublished)

used to evaluate functionalities or designs with the user at an early stage and obtain feedback to improve the design before moving on to software prototyping. Collaborative digital prototyping tools are proposed for creating various wireframe types.[12] Design Thinking methodology already considers these techniques [64]. Table 3 shows these techniques.

3.4 Evaluation

The evaluation phase,[17] activity that comprises a set of methodologies and techniques that analyse the usability and/or accessibility of an interactive system at different stages of the software life cycle. The MPIu+a methodology already has many techniques available to inspect, probe and test the system, so this contribution is limited to indicating digital tools to facilitate the evaluation. Table 4 shows the techniques included in the MPIu+aX model. The Design Thinking methodology already considers these techniques.

Regarding inspection techniques, the use of a new heuristic evaluation approach has been considered, mixing J. Nielsen's Heuristic Usability Principles for User Interface Design and B. Tognazzini's Interface Design Principles [65, 66]. Regarding accessibility, we have validated the evaluation of WCAG guidelines based on the Accessibility Review Report from the Accessibility Observatory [67].

To Conduct expert evaluations, RetLab [68] is used. RetLab is an online tool that enables heuristic evaluations to be conducted among multiple users and displays graphs indicating the percentage of system usability. The inquiry techniques used

[12] Prototyping: http://design-toolkit.recursos.uoc.edu/es/guia/prototipado/.

[13] How to Sketch a UI for Non-Designers: https://www.nngroup.com/videos/sketch-ui-non-designers/.

[14] Marvel: https://marvelapp.com/.

[15] Figma: https://www.figma.com/.

[16] Adobe XD: https://helpx.adobe.com/es/support/xd.html.

[17] MPIu+a fase de evaluación: https://mpiua.invid.udl.cat/fases-mpiua/evaluacion/.

Table 4 List of original MPIu+a techniques from the assessment phase, together with the techniques considered for the proposed MPIu+aX methodology

MPIu+a	Extending techniques for MPIu+aX
Inspection • Heuristic evaluation • Cognitive walkthrough • Inspection of standards	**Heuristic evaluation and WCAG guidelines**. Use of the RetLab[18] system to carry out the evaluation of a new heuristic evaluation[19] and WCAG evaluation proposal based on the accessibility review report (IRA)[20] report criteria
Inquiry • Field observation • Focus groups • Interviews • Questionnaires • Log analysis	**Mass survey**[21] of target users of the system using online forms **Informal guerrilla interviews**[22] are used to gain an understanding of the preferences, habits or desires of a target group and are useful for gaining information about the real needs of the user
Test • Performance measurement • Thinking aloud • Constructive interaction • Card sorting	**Simulation techniques**,[23] in which a system is configured with assistive tools or simulations in order to consult the system as a user with a disability would **Guerrilla test**[24] where the user is given tasks and is expected to show their opinions of the system (Thinking Aloud) **Asynchronous user test**,[25] a form is sent to the user with pre-test, task, post-task and post-test questionnaires that the user can complete at any time. In addition, the user makes a recording of the test and sends it to the evaluator **Remote user test**, a user test is carried out with a videoconferencing platform and data is collected with an online form

are the same as those employed in the MPIu+a methodology, but are conducted using online forms such as Google Forms[26] or other similar tools.

In terms of testing techniques, guerrilla user testing [69] is proposed as it allows for the collection of user feedback on a design or prototype. This technique is more effective than a user test as it enables testing of intermediate prototypes, without all their functionalities, and facilitates evaluations on the published website, collecting data to improve the next iteration. User comments are collected using the Thinking

[18] RetLab: https://retlab.web.app/.

[19] Heuristic evaluation template: https://mpiua.invid.udl.cat/evaluacion-heuristica-una-nueva-propuesta/.

[20] Web Accessibility Observatory https://administracionelectronica.gob.es/pae_Home/pae_Estrategias/pae_Accesibilidad/implantacion-rd-1112-2018/revisiones_accesibilidad.html#INFORMESREVISION.

[21] Questionnaires: http://design-toolkit.recursos.uoc.edu/es/guia/cuestionarios/.

[22] Informal guerrilla interview: https://ictresearchmethods.nl/Survey.

[23] Simulation tools. https://userway.org/blog/disability-simulators-you-should-try/.

[24] HCI Guerrilla: Using Discount https://www.nngroup.com/articles/guerrilla-hci/.

[25] Unmoderated User Tests: How and Why to Do Them. https://www.nngroup.com/articles/unmoderated-usability-testing/.

[26] Google Forms: https://docs.google.com/forms/u/0/.

Aloud,[27] technique to obtain the user's perception of task difficulty and emotional impact caused to the user by the execution of the task, through a framework of emotions [70]. Online forms are used to efficiently collect this data during testing. It is important to maintain objectivity and avoid subjective evaluations.

Moreover, to evaluate the Accessible User Experience, it is proposed to conduct user tests at two levels. Firstly, early evaluations should be carried out during the design and prototyping phase to assess aspects that can be evaluated through disability simulations. However, these types of evaluations only provide partial results as they are limited to the design layer level, such as contrasts and element size. Furthermore, the system cannot be evaluated with an assistive tool as it has not yet been developed. A more comprehensive evaluation can be achieved using a software prototype, which allows for evaluation with assistive tools. At this stage, an expert evaluator can conduct a disability simulation [71] using plugins such as Funkify[28] or Web Disability Simulator,[29] or by using assistive tools such as voice readers, zoom tools, or voice navigation [72]. Performing evaluations with users who have disabilities, including those with visual, hearing, motor and cognitive impairments, can greatly enrich the evaluation process and bring valuable insights to the system. This input can be used to improve the system in future iterations.

3.5 Implementation

The implementation phase[30] involves coding and developing the system using a platform framework (front-end or back-end). This phase can be completed in different stages: initial publication with minimum content and basic functionality, publication of an intermediate system with more content and developed functionality, and publication of the final system with all functionalities and content implemented. During this phase, it is crucial to select the appropriate development platform, whether it is a front-end or back-end framework, depending on the complexity of the system being developed. The MPIu+a methodology does not delve deeply into this phase, but the MPIu+aX methodology lists techniques and best practices for implementation. Table 5 shows these techniques.

Section 4, Case Study, describes the development of the Interaction 2023 website. The development process combined various phases of the MPIu+a methodology, Design Thinking, and Design Sprint strategies to ensure a quick and efficient process. Additionally, the development process considered aspects of UX and AUX as the backbone, applying the MPIu+aX methodology. All of this is done to create a website

[27] Thinking Aloud (2012). https://www.nngroup.com/articles/thinking-aloud-the-1-usability-tool/.

[28] Funkify: https://www.funkify.org/.

[29] Web Disability Simulator: https://chrome.google.com/webstore/detail/web-disability-simulator/olioanlbgbpmdlgjnnampnnlohigkjla.

[30] Fase de Implementación: https://mpiua.invid.udl.cat/fases-mpiua/implementacion/.

Table 5 List of original MPIu+a techniques from the implementation phase, along with the techniques considered for the proposed MPIu+aX methodology

MPIu+a	Extending techniques for MPIu+aX
Coding	The development process can be facilitated by using templates and web elements, depending on the chosen framework Additionally, content creation can be streamlined by utilising a web editor
Accessibility	Selection of accessible templates and elements following WCAG guidelines

with high interactivity and, above all, to empathise with the real needs of the user accessing the website, generating satisfactory user experiences for all.

4 Case Study

Next, the background of the Interaction Conference website is presented, outlining the objectives to be considered in the system and the execution of the phases proposed in the MPIu+aX methodology.

4.1 Background

The International Human–Computer Interaction Conference[31] has been held annually since 2000. Its purpose is to bring together researchers, students and practitioners of Human–Computer Interaction (HCI) from both academia and industry. The conference aims to promote the presentation of innovative proposals, exchange of ideas, and discussion. In 2003, a website was created to provide the conference schedule. Prior to this, the conference did not have an online presence. The website design was developed in collaboration with the organising committee during the 2005, 2010 and 2013 editions of the conference, which were held within the Congreso Español de Informática (CEDI).[32] The website was required to adopt the visual design proposed by the organisation. From 2018 onwards, the conference website has followed the same WordPress template (Zerif Lite[33] developed by ThemeIsle[34]). However, it had some accessibility problems that were directly related to the template and the content [72].

[31] List of interacción conferences: https://aipo.es/investigacion/congresos/.

[32] Congreso Español de Informática (CEDI): https://www.scie.es/actividades/cedi/.

[33] Zelle Lite. https://themeisle.com/themes/zelle-lite/.

[34] Themeisle: https://themeisle.com/.

4.2 Goals

The approach to the new Interaction 2023 conference website was based on several premises designed to meet the specific needs of a conference website development. These include:

- Inspiration from the aesthetics of the interaction conference website held in Lleida in 2004, taking into account the colour scheme of the University of Lleida for the interface design.
- Additionally, the website allows users to customise the interface, including the option of a dark or light mode.
- The content is also adapted to the device through responsive design.
- The development of a content management system (CMS) will allow any member of the conference committee to create content.
- Information will be presented in a clear and concise manner, taking into consideration the mental model and needs of the conference attendees.
- The website will be designed with usability and accessibility features to ensure a good Accessible User Experience for all users.
- To obtain user feedback, a form will be provided on the website to analyse the usefulness of the information displayed and receive proposals for improvement.
- Members attending the conference will have the opportunity to create a network of IPO experts through the creation of a LinkedIn group.
- Additionally, a web interface for the conference interaction will be available to identify it in future editions.

4.3 Follow-Up on the MPIu+aX Methodology

The MPIu+aX methodology underwent several iterations to systematically advance the creation of the system. Each sprint lasted one week, and significant progress was presented at the fortnightly conference committee meetings. The following is a summary of the project's different phases. However, due to space limitations of this document, all the information generated for the development of the website can be found in more detail on the project summary website: https://interaccion2023.udl.cat/desarrollo-del-proyecto-web-interaccion2023.

4.3.1 Requirements Analysis

A survey[35] was conducted among AIPO members to understand their conference attendance needs. Additionally, university professors with conference experience and PhD students were informally interviewed (e.g. in elevators, while walking to

[35] Survey launched to members of the Human–Computer Interaction Association: https://docs.google.com/forms/d/1vyRS9QRM1_R3541hHgPgSW3HGrlxn9bcbk27zJ-J3Ac/edit.

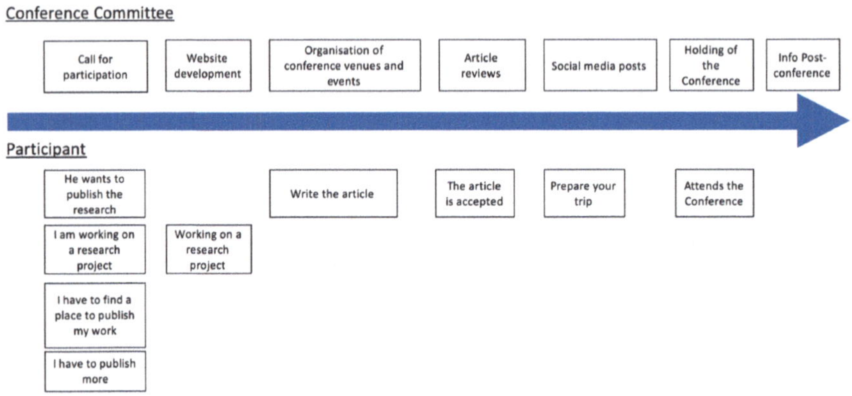

Fig. 2 Journey customer map schema developed for the conference website

their office, or in the cafeteria). The objective was to gain insight into and comprehend the genuine requirements of attendees regarding the life cycle of a conference.

The feedback from participants mainly focused on the need for clear information regarding the conference dates and the submission guidelines. Upon receiving acceptance notifications, attendees prioritised registration and sought information about the venue, such as its location in relation to hotels, public transportation options and tourist information. Transportation to and from the city was also a key concern. The participants found the option to contact other attendees interesting. Additionally, they considered accessibility and usability in a comprehensive manner, including the ability to personalise the interface for the user. The Empathy Map (see Fig. 2), Journey Customer Map (see Fig. 3), Map of Actors (see Fig. 4), and 2 user Personas were developed based on these inputs. The system design was focused on senior conference attendees with vision problems and junior conference attendees. We focused on covering only these two profiles, even though we were aware that we might not cover other permanent or temporary disabilities.

4.3.2 Design

To approach this phase, we conducted an evaluation of the information presented in the various editions of the conference interaction (benchmarking) to determine the main menu items and common content across all websites. This allowed us to create an information architecture (see Fig. 5) and an initial interaction map (see Fig. 6), and to start developing the design system using Atomic Design. At this point, we also worked on the conference logo, which determined the main colours of the website. The idea for incorporating dark mode into the interface came from the Interaction 2004[36] edition [73]. This feature was added to improve contrast and visualisation of

[36] Interaction Conference 2004 website: https://web.archive.org/web/20151122024337/http://grho2.udl.es/i2004/index.htm.

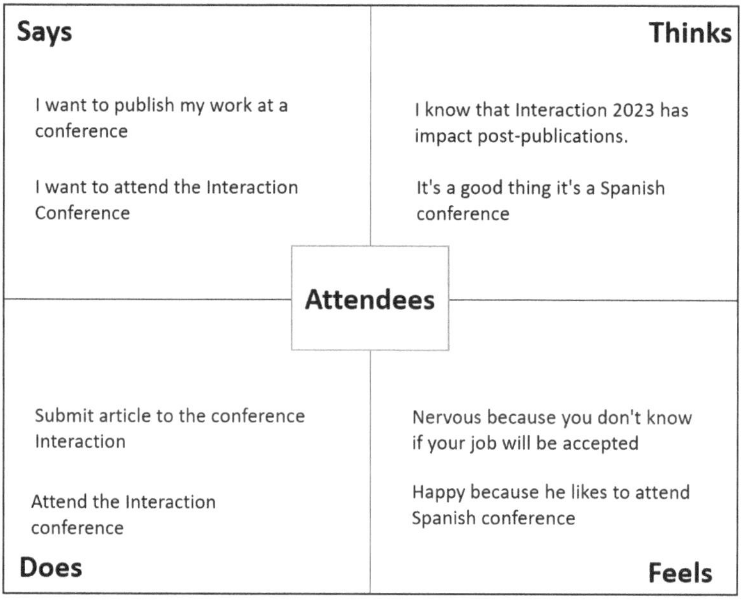

Fig. 3 Empathy map schema developed for the conference website

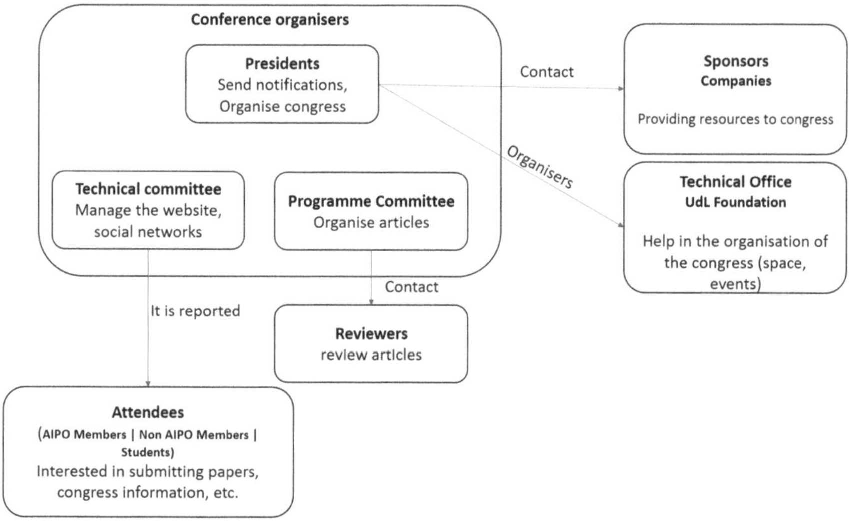

Fig. 4 Schematic of the stakeholder map worked on for the conference website

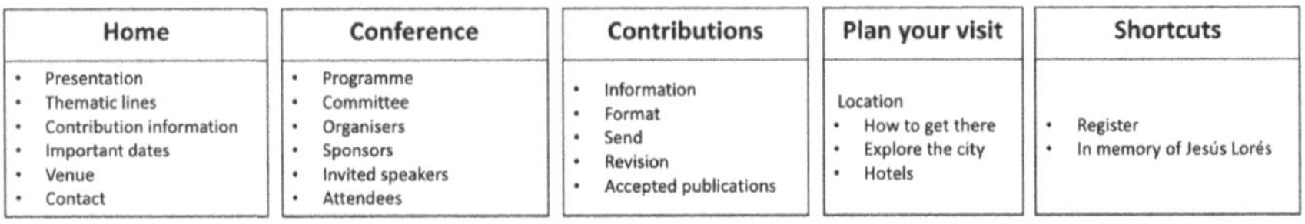

Fig. 5 Information architecture from the benchmarking analysis

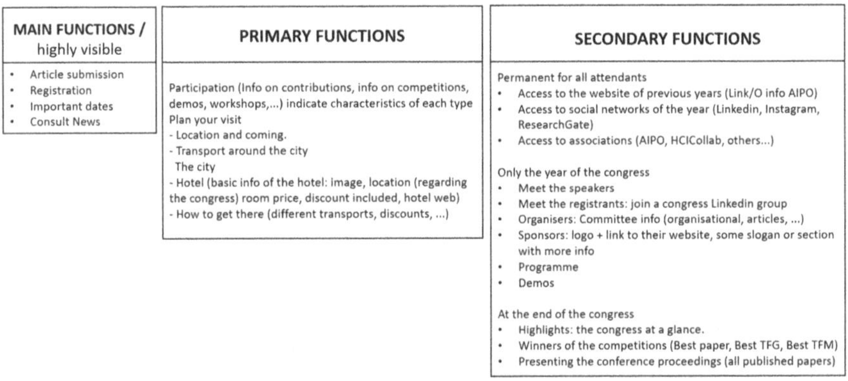

Fig. 6 Sketch of an initial interaction map showing only the main, primary or secondary functionality of the conference website that directly impacts the user "participants"

the content [74], making it more comfortable for users to consult the content on their mobile phones in bright environments [75].

4.3.3 Prototyping

Two versions of the website were produced. The first version was only a landing page[37] to show the most important information from the Call For Papers (CFP). A few weeks later we worked on the final design implementing more functionalities and content. The first prototypes were made with a digital prototyping tool (see Fig. 7), and after evaluations with experts and users, the results were implemented and published directly in the prototype software.[38]

4.3.4 Evaluation

Three prototype versions were made (low-level prototype, software prototype/ landing page and software prototype/published page). They were evaluated by

[37] Landing Page of the conference (First version): http://congresoipo-old.accesibilidad.digital/.

[38] Final Interaction2023 conference website: https://interaccion2023.udl.cat/.

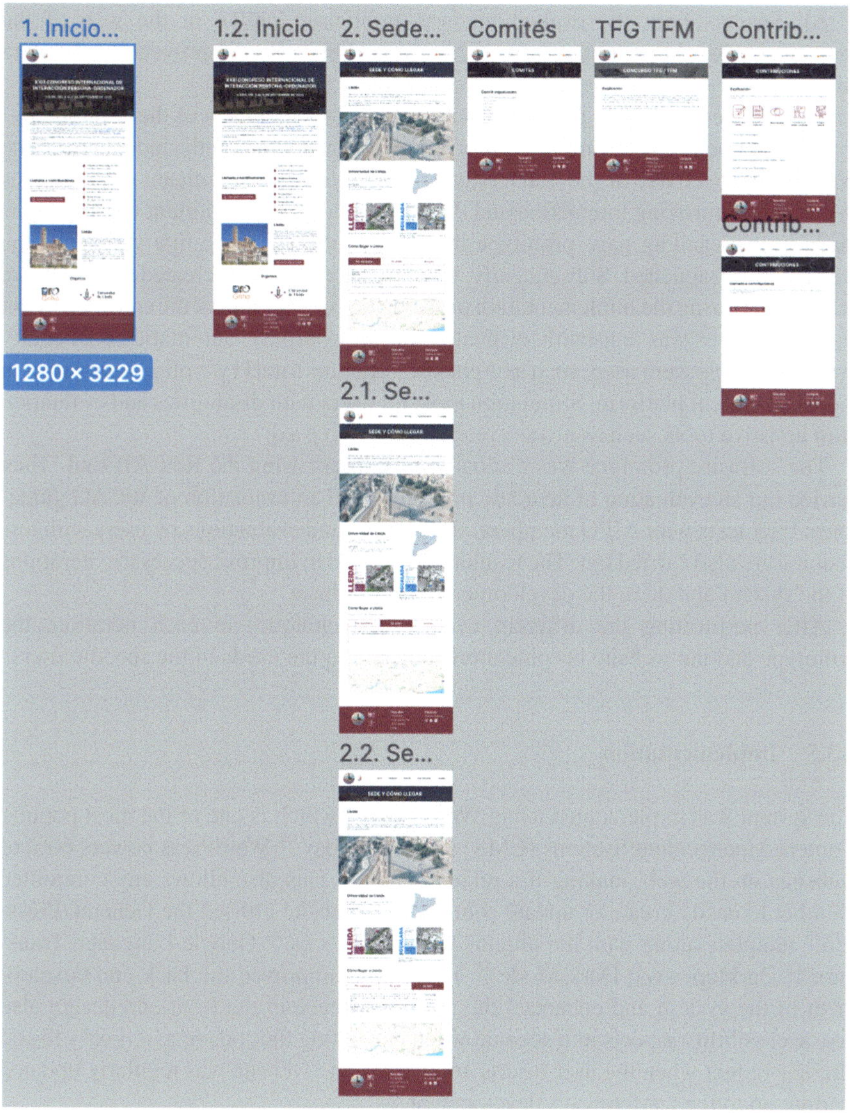

Fig. 7 A sketch made in Figma[39] (first iteration)

user testing, to get feedback and improve the accessible user experience in further developments.

[39] First iteration of web page: https://www.figma.com/file/eKWZlWs9J9aHqJI99qRfGA/1a-iteraci%C3%B3n---correcciones?type=design&node-id=1-72&mode=design.

All results about the evaluations was publicised online in the web of the project results: https://interaccion2023.udl.cat/desarrollo-del-proyecto-web-interaccion2023/.

The first version of the prototype was evaluated by members of the committee.

After, a Focus Group and User Test were also carried out with students from the Web Design[40] course at the University of Lleida to offer significant contributions in terms of improving interaction and design. This allowed important changes to be made to the Landing page prototype that was published as the first version of the website to be launched. Subsequently, the third prototype was created as a software prototype. During the implementation process, the accessibility of the created content and interactions was constantly evaluated. For this purpose, automatic accessibility evaluation tools were used, such as Acheker[41] and the Total11y[42] plug-in included in the development platform. Simulation tools for users with disabilities and evaluation with assistive tools such as a voice reader were also used.

The software prototype was evaluated by experts using the RetLAB tool. They carried out an evaluation of heuristic principles and an evaluation of WCAG guidelines. User tests with AIPO members, simulations and evaluations by users with low vision were also carried out. The results will be used to improve successive iterations of the system and drive the development of the website.

After performing the different evaluation techniques in each iteration, the prototype and the website become more concrete to the needs of the specific users.

4.3.5 Implementation

The system was implemented using WordPress,[43] which is one of the most popular Content Management Systems (CMS) available today.[44] WordPress powers 60% of websites on the web, making it a reliable choice. This also allows any committee member to easily create or update content. The website utilised the GeneratePress-Pro[45] template along with the plugins GenerateBlocks,[46] Google Language Translator,[47] Darklup—WP Dark Mode.[48] These tools improved the back-end development of the system and enhanced the user experience in the front-end design also take accessibility aspects into account when generating the code (e.g. it is easy to add alternative text when the user inserts an image). The website was regularly updated leading up to the conference's development.

---

[40] Asignatura de Diseño Web (UdL): https://guiadocent.udl.cat/pdf/es/102184.

[41] Acheker: https://achecker.achecks.ca/checker/index.php.

[42] Total11y para WordPress: https://es.wordpress.org/plugins/wp-total1y/.

[43] WordPress: https://es.wordpress.org/.

[44] W3Techs—World Wide Web Technology Surveys. https://w3techs.com/.

[45] GeneratePress de WordPress: https://es.wordpress.org/themes/generatepress/.

[46] GenerateBlocks: https://generateblocks.com/.

[47] Google Language Translator. https://gtranslate.io/.

[48] Darklup—WP Dark Mode: https://darklup.com/.

The result is available at the Conference url: https://interaccion2023.udl.cat/.

5 Advancements and New Challenges in UCD Methodologies

The disciplines associated with User-Centred Design (UCD) are continuously evolving and will encounter new challenges in the future. These challenges will be in three significant areas: (1) New challenges with users: adapting to and understanding people's characteristics, lifestyles and needs; (2) New challenges with devices: considering the new wearable devices and the Internet of Things (IoT) that are emerging with the advancement of technology; and (3) New challenges with end-to-end interactive systems: analyse trends in new, more end-to-end interactive systems such as Artificial Intelligence (AI). The following subsections will introduce each challenger area.

5.1 Users: New Challenges

It is crucial that interactive systems are accessible to all individuals, regardless of their sensory, physical, or cognitive characteristics [75]. Recent global standards, such as those in Europe and America [11], emphasise the importance of providing an appropriate accessible user experience (AUX) [60]. In this context, it is important to consider the sensory, physical and cognitive characteristics of users when creating systems to promote inclusion for all.

Users use technology in many different contexts, such as at home, at work, in their leisure time, while exercising, eating, travelling, etc. Technology is woven into the fabric of users' daily lives, creating new habits, needs and lifestyles. However, technology must adapt to the characteristics and needs of users, not the other way around [77]. This means that good design must consider what the user wants but it must ultimately frame those desires within the limits of the technology.

In addition, the planet's ecological crisis is encouraging users to be more aware and look for more sustainable products, just as companies are trying to minimise the environmental impact of their products and services [78]. The hyper-connectivity of people makes it possible to obtain very precise data on users' preferences and tastes, but it is important to consider the ethical and respectful limits of this, avoiding manipulation and protecting the privacy and security of the data [79].

5.2 Devices: New Challenges

The last decade has seen tremendous growth in the development of wearable technologies ("wearables") and the Internet of Things (IoT). Wearables refer to electrical or mechanical systems that are worn on the human body, either as part of clothing or as an additional device attached by straps or belts [80].

For example: smartwatches, fitness bands, smart glasses, smart clothing and health monitoring devices. The Internet of Things (IoT) refers to the interconnection of physical devices over the Internet, allowing them to communicate with each other and with external systems [81, 82]. They can be any object equipped with sensors, software and connectivity to collect and share data. Examples include devices that enable health monitoring at home, smart energy management in buildings, precision agriculture and intelligent transport systems. The huge impact of these emerging technologies is mainly due to the consideration of UCD in the design of these products and it is a challenge to create devices that are as adapted to the users as possible [83, 84]. Designers address user needs with an approach that focuses not only on technology, but above all on analysing the needs and characteristics of people, and it has been found that the use of UCD methods improves the use of these devices because they are better adapted to the people who will use them [85]. In this case, the human being is the main protagonist of social life, surrounded by technological devices that allow him/her to connect, discover and learn in any condition and place.

The combination between the needs expressed by users and the possibilities offered by these new innovative technologies related to the Internet of Things and Wearables, makes it possible to target and design new solutions for elderly users, ensuring their well-being, health and care, and improving their quality of life [86].

In this sense, there is a trend of research and new challenges that uses UCD methods to adapt the device to the needs of the user profile. For example, to improve the lives of elderly or disabled people [87], or to improve the medical care and well-being of people in general [88]. However, there are currently unresolved technological limitations which, as technology advances, could lead to more accurate measurements [89–92] to produce more reliable products for users, and the UCD methods can help.

5.3 Artificial Intelligence: New Challenges

The age of Artificial Intelligence (AI) is already impacting humanity in ways that are substantial not well understood yet [93]. In recent years, AI has undergone exponential growth and has revolutionised many aspects of daily life [94]. One such area is usability/UX evaluation, where AI is introducing new tools and techniques that are likely to significantly improve the process. The evaluation of usability/UX using techniques such as computer vision and natural language processing can be challenging. For example, it can be difficult to recognise gestures, facial expressions and other non-verbal cues to determine user satisfaction. Additionally, analysing the content of messages to identify specific problems or needs can also be challenging. All these new techniques help to overcome new challenges that may exist in the future related to further UCD design methodologies.

Despite the advantages that AI can offer to usability evaluation, it is important to be aware of its limitations and challenges. AI cannot fully replace evaluation by human experts as subjective and contextual aspects require human understanding and interpretation. Improving evaluation through AI clearly can offer significant benefits in terms of reducing errors, increasing accuracy and improving efficiency in evaluation processes. AI's capacity to identify patterns that affect usability makes it easier to minimise errors, while its ability to learn from historical data results in more accurate and personalised information. Additionally, AI streamlines and refines the evaluation process, reducing both time and associated costs. In the field of enhanced assessment, AI has the potential to make several contributions. These include Mood Analysis, which enables the measurement of users' satisfaction with a product, often through online surveys. Additionally, Conversational AI tools can collect feedback data from users, thereby promoting more effective results. Machine learning and physical interaction analysis can also be effectively applied. Cameras can be used to examine human–computer interaction and facial gestures to assess user satisfaction [95].

All this technological approach can provide several challengers related with UCD methodologies, such as the ability to analyse users' behaviour on a website and generate personalised recommendations to base on their preferences and needs. AI can also optimise the design and structure of a website by testing different versions and assessing their impact on usability. Similarly, AI can improve the generation of high-quality content, including text, images, video and audio, by producing relevant, informative and engaging material for users [96]. However, it is important to acknowledge that the implementation of AI has certain drawbacks. One of the main concerns is the potential loss of human control, as AI may make decisions about website design and content without sufficient oversight or consent. This raises ethical, legal and security issues that must be addressed. Furthermore, dependence on algorithms may lead to a dearth of creativity and diversity, resulting in the production of comparable or repetitive content, which can have an adverse effect on originality and innovation. Lastly, the requirement for a substantial amount of high-quality data for optimal AI performance may raise concerns regarding data privacy and security, as the data may be vulnerable to cyberattacks or privacy breaches. These are all aspects to be taken into account in order to have more optimal UCD methodologies.

6 Conclusions

The chapter focuses on the main advances in the field of UCD. Initially, the efforts were concentrated on the development of technology, but later shifted towards considering people's characteristics as crucial for the understanding and satisfactory use of systems. Additionally, the MPIu+a, a specific UCD methodology, has undergone a significant update and is analysed in this review. Methodological techniques have been incorporated to expedite the development of systems that follow the Accessible User Experience (AUX) methodology. And the methodology has been renamed MPIu+aX.

To validate MPIu+aX methodology, we present a case study that observes the process used to create a professional conference website (Interacción 2023). We provide evidence of its successful implementation in a real-world context. It is worth noting that incorporating new techniques from other disciplines, such as: Design Thinking and Design Sprint, can generate greater empathy with the user and aid in the progress of the project. User Interface (UI) development techniques not only organise visual information but also contribute to graphic aspects. Additionally, techniques related to User Experience (UX) and Accessible User Experience (AUX) can improve user satisfaction when interacting with the system. The work has progressed rapidly, following the phases or sprints outlined by the Design Sprint methodology.

In the future, UCD methodologies should focus on understanding more deeply the needs, motivations and behaviour of users to create interactive systems that are better adapted to their specific characteristics and preferences. As previously mentioned, future challenges include changes in the preferences and characteristics of traditional users. Their function is no longer solely focused on work or organisational contexts, but also includes numerous and varied functions such as leisure, socialisation, sport, perception and expression of emotions, and cultural areas. Additionally, the use of new devices such as wearables and the IoT involve new habits, needs and lifestyles of people. Finally, current interactive systems have evolved from being an application aimed at an end-user to an integral service where understanding the needs of the different agents involved is fundamental.

In this context, it is essential to have a comprehensive understanding of all the actors involved, including users, devices and interactive systems. This will enable the development of new methodologies that meet all needs.

These challenges demonstrate that there is still work to be done to improve the discipline of User-Centred Design (UCD). However, AI is significantly impacting usability/UX evaluation, providing advanced tools and techniques to better understand user needs and preferences. It is important to maintain a balance between the use of AI and human expertise to ensure a complete and accurate evaluation.

Acknowledgements We would like to express our gratitude to all members of the Interaccion2023 conference committee and other users who participated in the tests for their valuable contributions to the project.

References

1. ISO 9241-210:2019 (2018) Ergonomics of human-system interaction part 210: human-centred design for interactive systems. https://www.iso.org/standard/77520.html

2. Interaction Design Foundation (2023). https://www.interaction-design.org/literature/topics/user-centered-design
3. Muñoz J, Hernández Bieliukas Y, Amador V, Chavarría A, Calderón M, Collazos C, Méndez Y, Solano A, Mendoza J, Rodriguez F, Mendoza-Gonzalez R, Gonzalez Calleros J, Callero J, Rodríguez-Vizzuett L, Granollers T, Gil Ro, Céspedes-Hernández D (2014) Temas de diseño en Interacción Humano-Computadora
4. ISO/CD 9241-11 (1998) Ergonomics of human-system interact-n-part11: guidance on usability. http://www.iso.org/iso/catalogue_detail.htm?csnumber=63500
5. Introduction to web accessibility (2021). https://www.w3.org/standards/webdesign/accessibility
6. ISO 9241-210:2008. Ergonomics of human system interacti-n-part 210: human centred design for interactive systems. ISO, Geneva
7. Horton S, Sloan D, Swan H (2015) Manifesto for accessible user experience. Consultar. https://accessibleux.wordpress.com/manifesto/
8. World Health Organization (2023) Ageing and health. https://www.who.int/news-room/fact-sheets/detail/ageing-and-health
9. Abou-Zahra S, Brewer J (2003) Diverse abilities and barriers. https://www.w3.org/WAI/people-use-web/abilities-barriers/
10. World Health Organization (2021). Developed by the education and outreach working group (EOWG). Disabilities. https://www.who.int/topics/disabilities/
11. Web Accessibility Laws & Policies (2023). https://www.w3.org/WAI/policies/
12. WCAG (2018) Web content accessibility guidelines (WCAG) 2.1. https://www.w3.org/TR/WCAG21/
13. Pascual Almenara A, Humanes Elich J, Granollers Saltiveri T (2023) Wiki colaborativa con ejemplos accesibles y no accesibles de pautas WCAG. In: 5th workshop on accessibility in educational resources. En prensa
14. Ballesteros E, Ribera M, Pascual A, Granollers T (2015) Reflections and proposals to improve the efficiency of accessibility efforts. Univ Access Inf Soc 14:583–586. https://doi.org/10.1007/s10209-014-0356-1
15. Pascual A, Ribera M, Granollers T (2012) Perception of accessibility errors to raise awareness among web 2.0 users. In: Proceedings of the 13th international conference on Interacción Persona-Ordenador. https://doi.org/10.1145/2379636.2379652
16. Pascual A, Ribera M, Granollers T (2015) Comunicability of two web 2.0 accessibility evaluation tools. In: 2015 10th computing Colombian conference (10CCC), pp 269–272. https://doi.org/10.1109/ColumbianCC.2015.7333425
17. Watanabe T (2017) Communication model of web accessibility. In: International conference on human–computer interaction, pp 80–87. https://doi.org/10.1007/978-3-319-58750-9_11
18. The WebAIM Million (2023). https://webaim.org/projects/million/
19. EU10. European Commission (2021) Accessibility: essential for some, useful for all. https://digitalstrategy.ec.europa.eu/en/library/accessibility-essential-some-useful-all
20. Granollers T (2004) Mpiu+a. Una metodología que integra la ingeniería del software, la interacción persona-ordenador y la accesibilidad en el contexto de equipos de desarrollo multidisciplinares. Tesis Doctoral. Departament de Llenguatges i Sistemes Informàtics, Universitat de Lleida, Lleida, España. https://mpiua.invid.udl.cat/
21. Pascual Almenara A (2015) Accesibilidad en entornos web interactivos: superación de las barreras digitales. https://www.tdx.cat/handle/10803/314581
22. Araújo CMM, Santos IM, Canedo ED, Araújo APF (2019) Design thinking vs. design sprint: a comparative study. In: Marcus A, Wang W (eds) Design, user experience, and usability. Design philosophy and theory. HCII 2019, lecture notes in computer science, vol 11583. Springer, Cham, pp 291–306
23. Turner JA, Karasek Jr RA (1984) Software ergonomics: effects of computer application design parameters on operator task performance and health. Ergonomics 27(6):663–690.https://doi.org/10.1080/00140138408963539

24. Bjørn-Andersen N (1988) Are 'human factors' human? Comput J 31(5):386–390. https://doi.org/10.1093/comjnl/31.5.386
25. Norman DA (1988) The psychology of everyday things. Basic Books
26. Bevan N, Kirakowski J, Maissel J (1991) What is usability?
27. Nielsen J, Molich R (1990) Heuristic evaluation of user interfaces. In: Proceedings of the SIGCHI conference on human factors in computing systems (C'I'90). Association for Computing Machinery, New York, NY, USA, 249–256. https://doi.org/10.1145/97243.97281
28. Dumas JF, Redish JC. A practical guide to usability testing. Greenwood Publishing Group Inc. Box 5007 88 Post Road W. Westport, CT, United States. ISBN: 978-0-89391-991-7
29. Junior PTA, Filgueiras LVL (2005) User modeling with personas. In: Proceedings of the 2005 Latin American conference on human–computer interaction (CLI'C'05). Association for Computing Machinery, New York, NY, USA, 277–282. https://doi.org/10.1145/1111360.1111388
30. Rebaque-Rivas P, Gil-Rodríguez EP, Manresa-Mallol I (2010) Mobile learning scenarios from a UCD perspective. In: Proceedings of the 12th international conference on Human computer interaction with mobile devices and services, pp 389–390
31. Spencer D, Warfel T (2004) Card sorting: a definitive guide. Boxes Arrows 2(2004):1–23
32. Beck K, Beedle M, Van Bennekum A, Cockburn A, Cunningham W, Fowler M, Thomas D (2001) The agianifestósto
33. Da Silva T, Martin A, Maurer F, Silveira M (2011) User-centered design and agile methods: a systematic review. In: Proceedings—2011 agile conference, agile 2011, 7–86. https://doi.org/10.1109/AGILE.2011.24
34. Moré Martín A, Granollers Saltiveri T, Oliva Solé M (2010) MPIu+a Ágil: El modelo de proceso centradoen el usuario como metodología ágil. Consultar. https://repositori.udl.cat/server/api/core/bitstreams/a9752d53-805c-4e44-a8c6-b8b7bd4f319e/content
35. Nielsen Norman Group (2023) Effective agile UX product development. https://www.nngroup.com/reports/agile-development-user-experience/
36. Silva da Silva T, Selbach Silveira M, Maurer F, Hellmann (2012) User experience design and agile development: from theory to practice. J Softw Eng Appl 5(10):743–751. https://doi.org/10.4236/jsea.2012.510087
37. Fox D, Sillito J, Maurer F (2008) Agile methods and user-centered design: how these two methodologies are being successfully integrated in industry. Proc Agile 4–8:63–72
38. Hartson R, Pyla PS (2018) The UX book: agile UX design for a quality user experience. Morgan Kaufmann. ISBN: 9780128010624
39. Serrat O (2017) Design thinking. In: Knowledge solutions. Springer, Singapore. https://doi.org/10.1007/978-981-10-0983-9_18
40. Design Thinking (2023) Interaction design foundation, 2nd edn. In: The Encyclopedia of human–computer interaction. https://www.interaction-design.org/literature/topics/design-thinking
41. Villegas Portero E. Capítulo design thinking. Libro AIPO. https://hci-collab.com/libro/design_thinking/
42. Tillberg-Webb H, Collier N (2018) Using the design thinking cycle to tell the story of innovative learning spaces. In: Hokanson B, Clinton G, Kaminski K (eds) Educational technology and narrative. Springer, Cham, Switzerland, pp 141–153
43. Dam RF, Siang TY (2021) 5 stages in the design thinking process, interaction design foundation (IxDF). Available at https://www.interaction-design.org/literature/article/5-stagesin-the-design-thinking-process
44. Knapp J, Zeratsky J, Kowitz B (2016) Sprint: how to solve big problems and test new ideas in just five days. Simon & Schuster, New York
45. Wangsa K, Chugh R, Karim S, Sandu R (2022) A comparative study between design thinking, agile, and design sprint methodologies. Int J Agile Syst Manage 15:2022. https://doi.org/10.1504/IJASM.2022.10049716
46. Tidwell J, Brewer C, Valencia A (2019) Designing interfaces. Patterns for effective interaction design. Estados Unidos'. O'Reilly Media. ISBN: 9781492051930

47. MacDonald D (2019) Practical UI patterns for design systems. Fast-track interaction design for a seamless user experience. Apress, Alemania. ISBN: 9781484249383
48. Frost B (2016) Atomic design. Estados Unidos: Brad Frost. ISBN: 9780998296609. https://bradfrost.com/blog/post/atomic-web-design/
49. Garrett JJ (2003) The elements of user experience: user-centered design for the web. New Riders, Reino Unido
50. Morville P (2005) Experience design unplugged. In: ACM SIGGRAPH 2005 web program (SIGGRA'H'05). Association for Computing Machinery, New York, NY, USA, p 10. https://doi.org/10.1145/1187335.1187347
51. Masip L, Oliva M, Granollers T (2011) User experience specification through quality attributes, 656–660. https://doi.org/10.1007/978-3-642-23768-3_106
52. Nunnally B, Farkas D (2016) UX research: practical techniques for designing better products. Estados Unidos'. O'Reilly Media
53. Oswal SK (2019) Breaking the exclusionary boundary between user experience and access: steps toward making UX inclusive of users with disabilities. In: Proceedings of the 37th ACM international conference on the design of communication (SIGDOC'19), Portland, Oregon, USA, Article 12, 1–8. https://doi.org/10.1145/3328020.3353957
54. Graham G, Chandrashekar S (2016) Inclusive process and tool for evaluation of accessible user experience (AUX). In: Antona M, Stephanidis C (eds) Universal access in human–computer interaction. Methods, techniques, and best practices. UAHCI 2016. Lecture notes in computer science, vol 9737. Springer, Cham. https://doi.org/10.1007/978-3-319-40250-5_6
55. Henry SL (2007) Just ask: integrating accessibility throughout design. Estados Unidos: Lulu.com. http://www.uiaccess.com/justask/
56. Watson L (2014) Global accessibility awareness day. GAAD. https://web.archive.org/web/20180221061545/https://storify.com/UXPAUK/global-accessibility-awareness-day-2014
57. Pascual A, Ribera M, Granollers T (2013) Grado de afectación de las barreras de accesibilidad web en usuarios con discapacidad intelectual. Interacción
58. Pascual A, Ribera M, Granollers T, Coiduras (2014) Impact of accessibility barriers on the mood of blind, low-vision and sighted users. Procedia Comput Sci 27:431–440. https://doi.org/10.1016/j.procs.2014.02.047
59. Aizpurua A, Harper S, Vigo M (2016) Exploring the relationship between web accessibility and user experience. Int J Hum Comput Stud 91:13–23
60. Graham G, Chandrashekar S (2016) Inclusive process and tool for evaluation of accessible user experience (AUX). Universal access in human–computer interaction. Methods, techniques, and best practices. UAHCI 2016. Lecture notes in computer science, 9737. https://doi.org/10.1007/978-3-319-40250-5_6
61. Pascual A, Ribera M, Granollers T (2014) Impact of web accessibility barriers on users with hearing impairment. Interacción'14: XV international conference on human computer interaction, pp 1–2. https://doi.org/10.1145/2662253.2662261
62. Pascual A, Ribera M, Granollers T (2015) Impact of accessibility barriers on the mood of users with motor and dexterity impairments. J Accessibility Design All 5(1):1–26. https://doi.org/10.17411/jacces.v5i1.93
63. Allen JJ, Chudley JJ (2012) Smashing UX design: foundations for designing online user experiences. Smashing Magazine Book
64. Iu Siang T (2021) The ultimate guide to understanding UX roles and which one you should go for. Interaction Design Foundation. https://www.interaction-design.org/literature/article/the-ultimate-guide-to-understanding-ux-roles-and-which-one-you-should-go-for
65. Granollers T (2018) Usability evaluation with heuristics. New proposal from integrating two trusted sources. In Marcus A, Wang W (eds) Design, user experience, and usability: theory and practice. Springer International Publishing, Cham, pp 396–405. https://doi.org/10.1007/978-3-319-91797-9_28
66. Granollers T (2018) Usability evaluation with heuristics, beyond Nielsen's list. http://personales.upv.es/thinkmind/dl/conferences/achi/achi_2018/achi_2018_4_10_20055.pdf

67. Pascual-Almenara A, Granollers-Saltiveri T (2021) Combining two inspection methods: usability heuristic evaluation and WCAG guidelines to assess e-commerce websites. In: Ruiz PH, Agredo-Delgado V, Kawamoto ALS (eds) Human–computer interaction. HCI-COLLAB 2021. Communications in computer and information science, vol 1478. Springer, Cham. https://doi.org/10.1007/978-3-030-92325-9_1
68. Capdevila M, Rodrigues K, Pascual A, Granollers T, Monné E (2024) Whitepaper: remote usability laboratory to perform user and expert evaluations. In: Proceedings of the XXIII international conference on human computer interaction (Interaccion'23). Association for Computing Machinery, New York, NY, USA, Article 20, 1–9. https://doi.org/10.1145/3612783.3612804
69. Hampshire N, Califano G, Spinks D (2022) Guerrilla testing. In: Mastering collaboration in a product team. Apress, Berkeley, CA. https://doi.org/10.1007/978-1-4842-8254-0_35
70. Desmet PMA, Vastenburg MH, Van Bel D, Romero, NA (2012) Pick-Amood; development and application of a pictorial mood-reporting instrument. In: Brassett J, Hekkert P, Ludden G, Malpass M, McDonnell J (eds) Proceedings of the 8th international design and emotion conference. Central Saint Martin College of Art & Design, London (UK), 11–14
71. Tigwell G (2021) Nuanced perspectives toward disability simulations from digital designers, blind, low vision, and color blind people.https://doi.org/10.1145/3411764.3445620
72. Abou-Zahra S, Brewer J (2017) Tools and techniques. https://www.w3.org/WAI/people-use-web/tools-techniques/
73. Pascual A, Granollers T (2023) Empathetic communication of accessibility barriers on the dynamic web to understand the accessible user experience (AUX). https://doi.org/10.21203/rs.3.rs-3397192/v1
74. Maixner G, Smith A (2020) Keeping users in the dark: the design and implementation of a dark mode for a university library website. https://hdl.handle.net/1805/29068
75. Eisfeld H, Kristallovich F (2020) The rise of dark mode: a qualitative study of an emerging user interface design trend. http://www.diva-portal.org/smash/record.jsf?pid=diva2%3A1464394&dswid=7570
76. ONU (2022) Universal declaration of human rights. https://www.un.org/en/about-us/universal-declaration-of-human-rights
77. Rolston M (2018) The myth of human-centered design. FastCompany. https://www.fastcompany.com/90208681/the-myth-of-human-centered-design
78. Rossi E, Attaianese E (2023) Research synergies between sustainability and human-centered design: a systematic literature review. Sustainability 15(17):12884. https://doi.org/10.3390/su151712884
79. Moallem A. Chapter 43. Cybersecurity, privacy, and trust. In: Salvendy G, Karwowski W (eds). https://doi.org/10.1002/9781119636113.ch43
80. Chan M, Estève D, Fourniols JY, Escriba C, Campo E (2012) Smart wearable systems: current status and future challenges. Artif Intell Med 56:137–156
81. Martinho Guimaraes Pires Pereira A, Benessia A, Curvelo Da Silva Campos Alves P (2013) Agency in the internet of things. EUR 26459. Publications Office of the European Union, Luxembourg. JRC87270
82. Gupta R, Gupta R (2016) ABC of internet of things: advancements, benefits, challenges, enablers and facilities of IoT. In: 2016 symposium on colossal data analysis and networking (CDAN). IEEE, pp 1–5
83. Ferraro V, Ugur S (2011) Designing wearable technologies through a user centered approach. In: Proceedings of the 2011 conference on designing pleasurable products and interfaces (DPPI'11). Association for Computing Machinery, New York, NY, USA, Article 5, 1–8. https://doi.org/10.1145/2347504.2347510
84. Ystgaard KF, Atzori L, Palma D et al (2023) Review of the theory, principles, and design requirements of human-centric internet of things (IoT). J Ambient Intell Human Comput 14:2827–2859. https://doi.org/10.1007/s12652-023-04539-3
85. Salisbury LJ, McGinley C, Yenigun EO (2023) Applying people-centred design methods to enhance the development of wearable technology for everyday use. Woodhead Publishing, pp 447–483. ISBN 9780128195260. https://doi.org/10.1016/B978-0-12-819526-0.00018-7

86. Scataglini S, Imbesi S, Marques G (2022) Internet of things for human-centered design. Springer Nature, Singapore. https://doi.org/10.1007/978-981-16-8488-3. ISBN: 978-981-16-8487-6
87. Perez AJ, Siddiqui F, Zeadally S, Lane D (2023) A review of IoT systems to enable independence for the elderly and disabled individuals. Internet Things 21:100653. ISSN 2542-6605.https://doi.org/10.1016/j.iot.2022.100653
88. Scataglini S, Imbesi S, Marques G (2022) Internet of things for human-centered design. Springer Nature, Singapore. https://doi.org/10.1007/978-981-16-8488-3
89. Kim KB, Baek HJ (2023) Photoplethysmography in wearable devices: a comprehensive review of technological advances, current challenges, and future directions. Electronics 12(13):2923. https://doi.org/10.3390/electronics12132923
90. Kaongoen N, Choi J, Choi JW, Kwon H, Hwang C, Hwang G, Jo S (2023) The future of wearable EEG: a review of ear-EEG technology and its applications. J Neural Eng
91. Devi DH, Duraisamy K, Armghan A, Alsharari M, Aliqab K, Sorathiya V, Das S, Rashid N (2023) 5G technology in healthcare and wearable devices: a review. Sensors 23(5):2519. https://doi.org/10.3390/s23052519
92. Moshawrab M, Adda M, Bouzouane A, Ibrahim H, Raad A (2023) Smart wearables for the detection of cardiovascular diseases: a systematic literature review. Sensors 23(2):828. https://doi.org/10.3390/s23020828
93. Ozmen Garibay O, Winslow B, Andolina S, Antona M, Bodenschatz A, Coursaris C, Xu W (2023) Six human-centered artificial intelligence grand challenges. Int J Human–Comput Interaction 39(3):391–437
94. Margetis G, Ntoa S, Antona M, Stephanidis C (2021) Human-centered design of artificial intelligence. Handbook of human factors and ergonomics, 1085–1106
95. Hartikainen M, Väänänen K, Olsson T (2023) Towards a human-centred artificial intelligence maturity model. In: Extended abstracts of the 2023 CHI conference on human factors in computing systems (CHI EA'23). Association for Computing Machinery, New York, NY, USA, Article 285, 1–7. https://doi.org/10.1145/3544549.3585752
96. Weller AJ (2019) Design thinking for a user-centered approach to artificial intelligence. She Ji J Des Econ Innov 5(4):394–396. ISSN 2405-8726. https://doi.org/10.1016/j.sheji.2019.11.015

An Analysis of Videogames to Compose an Adapted Heuristic Evaluation

Roger Larriba Baudilio, Toni Granollers Saltiveri, and Juan Enrique Garrido Navarro

Abstract This chapter presents the results of a basic research carried out on the user experience applied to the videogames. It is key to identify parameters of videogames that allow us to know the general needs of users. In the same way, it is necessary to know the elements used to cover the needs detected. That is why an analysis has been carried out to obtain certain parameters that must be considered as fundamental in videogames in terms of user experience: usability, engage-ability, motivation, emotion, immersion, and commitment to the game. With them, we have worked on a specific heuristic evaluation, with a contrasted basis and foundation. The result has been to obtain a new version of it, adding to the principles on which it is based, questions to improve the evaluation of videogames. This extension becomes optional, as it can only be considered when the software to be analyzed is a videogame.

1 Introduction

Videogames are essential software in today's world. In this sense, this work aims to respond to the need to know formally how the usability of a videogame is and consequently, to know what can be improved and why. To this end, the work has focused on discovering the needs to be taken into consideration that are presented/ generated in the interaction between a videogame and its users. Subsequently, it has been explored how certain principles of the discipline of Human–Computer Interaction (HCI) are applied to videogames.

R. Larriba Baudilio · T. Granollers Saltiveri (✉)
Department of Computer Engineering and Digital Design, University of Lleida, Higher Polytechnic School. Jaume II, 69, 25001 Lleida, Spain
e-mail: toni.granollers@udl.cat

R. Larriba Baudilio
e-mail: roglarbau@gmail.com

J. E. Garrido Navarro
Department of Computing Systems, Faculty of Computer Science Engineering, University of Castilla-La Mancha, 02071 Albacete, Spain
e-mail: juanenrique.garrido@uclm.es

S. Sayago et al. (eds.), *Future Perspectives on Human-Computer Interaction Research*,
https://doi.org/10.1007/978-3-031-71697-3_3

Being aware that each videogame contains needs depending on certain variables such as its genre and the audience it is aimed at, it is necessary to define what differentiates a videogame from other types of software [1, 2]. A videogame is a piece of software that is used by the user for the purpose of having fun/enjoying. To develop a consistent user experience, you need to make your user experience as engaging as possible. Consequently, the two components that have been identified as playing a major role in this are usability and engage-ability, which will be discussed in detail in the chapter along with other parameters considered relevant such as motivation, emotion, immersion, and commitment to the game.

These parameters allow the present work to know what need to be considered in a videogame, from the point of view of usability. Their knowledge enables, in this case, how to incorporate the acquired knowledge into a tool with an adequate theoretical basis to evaluate usability in videogames.

Because the objective is to work on the evaluation of the quality of use in videogames interfaces, it is considered essential to know the evaluation activities on videogames that are carried out and under what conditions. This is an important knowledge to be able to place the tool finally obtained within the real context of videogames, from the point of view of its evaluation, and, in this way, to have the knowledge of what the scope of said tool may be. To this end, the framework offered by Rohrer (Fig. 1) has been analyzed based on the following three axes [3]:

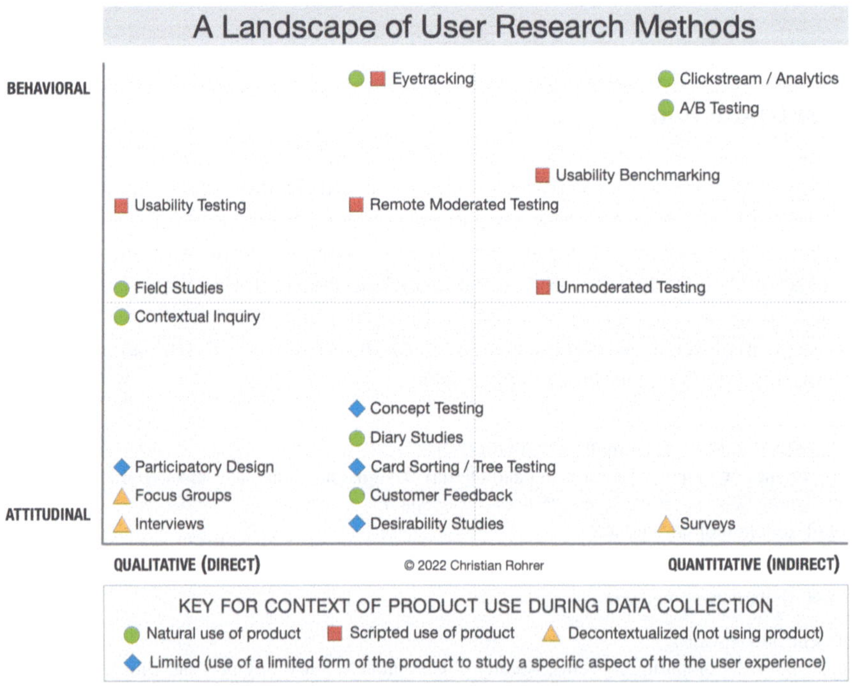

Fig. 1 Classification of video game evaluation and analysis methodologies [3]

- **Attitude and Behavior**: Synthesized as "what people say about what people do". The first is used to find out what users are thinking, what information they are aware of, and what information they are willing to share. On the other hand, behavior is used to find out how they respond to actions and situations that the product or its changes present to users.
- **Qualitative and Quantitative**: The two extremes of this axis differ in the level of personalization that users have and the extent to which responses are modeled to obtain data with or without a researcher. Qualitative methodologies offer a more individual approach since they focus on discovering the why of the answers and the process in which users have arrived at them. Quantitative ones don't require as much on-site presence, as their questions are measurable so that numerical patterns/data can be extracted from the answers to facilitate analysis in a greater number of users.
- **Context of Use**: Delimited by the conditions in which the user is at the time of the test and with which part of the product they interact.

Along with the methodologies and techniques for evaluating videogames offered by the aforementioned framework, there are also heuristic evaluations [4, 5]. These can be used when looking for simple answers to more complex situations without the need for direct user intervention, involving expert evaluators. Generically, they consist of a set of principles (guidelines, guides, or approaches to a problem), called heuristic principles, which are used to obtain an answer in terms of usability of the user interface of the system analyzed. In user experience, they are used to find out what state a product is in regarding certain aspects (the aspects of the selected heuristic principles themselves). The way in which the principles are addressed and evaluated is by means of expert evaluators who analyze each principle by beginning through posed questions that must be answered based on what the evaluated software offers. It is possible that heuristic principles are in turn divided into sub-principles, allowing an internal classification of the questions asked (in our case, as we will see, more than sub-principles, they will be questions associated with each particular principle).

The heuristic evaluation technique will be the focus of this work. By analyzing the parameters that are studied as fundamental elements in videogames, a heuristic evaluation (with a contrasted basis, foundation, and validity) will be updated including new questions for use in this context. This evaluation corresponds to the one prepared by the GRIHO research group of the University of Lleida as part of the MPIu+a Software Engineering methodology [6, 7] focused on User-Centered Design [7].

1.1 Heuristic Evaluation

As the Heuristic Evaluation (HE) technique is relevant for this work, the most important aspects will be explained in this section.

HE is a usability inspection method that was first introduced by Nielsen and Molich [5]. They describe a usability evaluation method where expert evaluators assess the quality of use of an interactive system based on inspecting its User Interface (UI) by checking the degree of compliance of a set of a predefined usability guidelines or heuristics (hence the name). This technique is based on a chosen list of guidelines and, by the experts' knowledge, where their experience may help to understand and identify in an effective way usability problems or enhancements. Their method provided a set of 10 heuristics to be used on the evaluations [8]. First the experts answer the questionnaires by themselves, preparing an individual list of the problems encountered and possible improvements, then they gather with other evaluators to have a discussion and aggregate their answers, to find out a more cohesive final list. By the end of the discussions, evaluators rank the problems taking into account the scales of severity, frequency, and critical aspects of the items found. Performing heuristics evaluations have various advantages (1) it is cost-effective as it requires neither much time nor a lot of users compared to traditional user testing; (2) it does not require a demanding planning, less people involved and smaller procedure of analysis; (3) it is applicable in multiple phases of software, being able to be applied on planning, development and on ready-to-use products as well [5, 9]. Nevertheless, there are also disadvantages, such as: (1) it is hard to encounter evaluators that are experts, and will be able to give good quality feedback; (2) depending on project stage, evaluators might have a hard time to understand what are the possible tasks they can perform on the software; (3) the results may not have suggestions on how to resolve the usability problems found, which could require an extra data collecting [10, 11] and, finally, (4) original punctuation from Nielsen and Molich [10] has traditionally been confusing for the evaluators by scoring the three different attributes [10] (severity, frequency and criticality), causing that most of the experts end up using only one attribute (usually criticality) being and important argument why many of the subsequent proposals have focused on improving this part.

The initial set of heuristics created by Nielsen and Molich were considered too general [12], opening up new studies to improve the initial set to be more specific to the desired object of study and also the proposal of new sets, such as the well-known Shneiderman's eight golden rules [13], Norman's seven principles [14] or Tognazzini's first principles of interaction design [15].

In order to explain the work done, this chapter is structured as follows: Sect. 2 will show the fundamental parameters in videogames that have been selected and studied for consideration in the adaptation of an existing heuristic evaluation. The process for obtaining the new version of the heuristic evaluation tool, adapted to videogames, is explained in Sect. 3. Finally, Sect. 4 will show the conclusions obtained, as well as the future work that the research carried out raises.

2 User Experience in Videogames

It is necessary to have an adequate knowledge of certain aspects related to the user experience within videogames, to obtain the necessary knowledge to objectively analyze the heuristic evaluation method that is intended to be extended to be applicable to said software.

Usability, engage-ability, motivation, emotion, and game flow are considered key, which represent characteristics or attributes of a videogame. Next, each of these aspects will be analyzed, trying to highlight those components or considerations that should be treated within the heuristic principles that may make up a future usability evaluation.

2.1 Usability

Usability [16] in general terms focuses on the ease of use achieved, taking into account the requirements and limitations presented by users and the environment. This can be expressed as follows: "*usability serves the purpose of reducing as much as possible the difficulties that the user may encounter in the use of a product*".

From the point of view of a videogame, the following points must be taken into account when trying to know the level of usability of the game:

- **Signals and Feedback**. Similar to the "system state visibility" principle, the main difference is the general use of vocabulary within the videogame industry.
- **Clarity**. We understand clarity as a player's ability to understand all signals from their perception and perspective. Considering the subjectivity that this implies being aware that different ways of differentiating elements can be contemplated. To help in this, one can follow guidelines such as font guidelines (for the fonts chosen in the texts shown to have notions of how to choose a font for better readability), or the *Gestalt Principles of Perception* [17], to know how to present elements in a way that is comfortable according to the patterns by which we order them in an environment.
- **Form Follows Function**. In industrial design, there is a term for a similar concept called "Affordance" [18]. The difference lies between whether or not there is an external agent to judge whether the form of the element contains/suggests its function or purpose. In a videogame this is vitally important for the player's fluency through it. Quickly understanding what it is for, what it indicates or how an interactive element can act is essential for the player to feel that they can concentrate on the experience and not struggle to understand what is presented to them.
- **Consistency**. Similar items should behave similarly. The same goes for stocks. All this at all times and in all interactions.
- **Minimal Workload**. Our bodies have both physical and cognitive limitations. As long as it's not a load level that the game requires, either due to hardware

limitations or the game's intentionality with its challenge and/or experience, it should be reduced.

- **Error Prevention and Recovery**. It is important to pay attention to where you think users may have difficulties with the environment. Adapting mechanics, collision zone/hitbox, or being able to undo actions in certain systems, even if it is in a real-time online game, are options that give flexibility so that players do not feel too punished by failures that do not have to be essential parts of the challenge/experience offered.

2.2 Engage-Ability

The concept of engage-ability refers to everything we do to make the experience of interacting with the videogame more immersive and interesting. To achieve this experience, it is necessary to generate situations in which the player must make decisions, since what a videogame offers is a marked interaction on the part of the user. Designing for this objective is not always easy since you must take into account the state of the player with respect to the system and what you are trying to generate in the player in each of the situations. With this in mind, it can be considered what elements should be used to provide the motivations, emotions, and game flow users want.

2.2.1 Motivation

Thanks to the work carried out in [19], it is interesting to know the different motivations that a user can find in a videogame:

- **Intrinsic Motivation**. It refers to performing a task for the sake of it as well as for the enjoyment of completing it. An approach for when seeking to generate this type of motivation is that our game has to satisfy those needs related on a personal level to competence (feeling of control, mastery, and progression), autonomy (feeling of being able to make important decisions, control of their actions and meaning about what they do), relationships (weighty social interactions, meaning), and meaning (sense of purpose, value, and impact).
- **Extrinsic Motivation**. Motivations generated by the needs acquired/generated by the environment. They are learned through what is received as a result of the user's attitude toward the environment, where the user tends to repeat those with which he receives positive feedback as a reward and, in principle, will avoid those for which he is punished.
- **Individual Needs and Implicit Motives**. We must be aware that, although we work in a very similar way, there are different types of people and, therefore, different types of players. That is why it is important to know which audience a videogame will focus on in order to design an activity according to them. By this we mean both what genres our player is looking for, the level of challenge they

expect and how they plan to interact with the rest of the elements of their environment [20]. It is worth mentioning the study mentioned by [2] in which a survey of more than 100,000 players was carried out from which the following classification was obtained: action-social (related to destruction, excitement, competition, and community), mastery-achievement (related to mastery, strategy, completion and power), and immersion-creativity (related to fantasy, History, Design, and Discovery).

2.2.2 Emotion

According to Hodent [2] there are five experiences for the player: aesthetic sense of control, pleasure of learning a skill, extension of the senses, extension of identity, and interaction with a physical reality unique to the game.

To create these emotions, we must think about the elements that have to be added, what role they will play in the reality to be simulated and how they will be perceived by the player. It should not be misunderstood that these elements are only those with which the player actively interacts, the music itself has a great capacity to evoke emotions.

The sum of all the elements to be added, if they have been placed correctly, will contribute positive aspects together to the immersion that the player can feel through reinforcing/building the experiences. That's where emotion comes in as a key part of the user experience.

2.2.3 Game Flow

Flow, according to Isbister [1] can be defined as "*a state in which the player is completely immersed and engaged in an activity that has an intrinsic motivation associated with* it". This concept is the subject of debate since it is not possible to fully define the components that are required to achieve it, even so, Isbister observed that in most of the proposals the following aspects are found: concentration, challenge, skills developed by the player, sense of control, clear objectives, direct feedback, and immersion / loss of the notion of time.

The game flow is a point that is reached after going through different phases of the game experience, since the player will have required to develop mastery/control of certain skills and with a challenge appropriate to the situation. Too hard will frustrate the player and too easy will lead to boredom.

2.3 Other Aspects

When evaluating or developing a product, or in this case a videogame, during development different situations present in the sector may arise that can greatly affect both the quality of the experience for players and the amount they will have the ability to enjoy the product. There are points that directly address the interests of the players, placing them in second place to those of the company. For this reason, it is recalled that user experience is not only about usability, but another layer also to add is which emotions the systems evoke in their users, looking for the desired emotions to create a stronger bond between the parties involved. But what happens when they are used against users?

Much of the software seeks greater retention, user participation and/or monetization of users, but we enter the realm of the unethical when techniques are used that make it easier for users to spend more time than they want, to lose track of the value of things, to generate feelings of dependency, etc. By extension, dark patterns are those patterns used to consciously create negative experiences for their users, which are then exploited in favor of the application/company [21]. These patterns can be categorized according to the type of capital they affect (time, monetary or social):

- **Temporal Dark Patterns**: have the players the feel that they lost their time, restricted when to expend it, used it more than wanted or had a different expectation of how much of it would take make anything in the system? Examples of this could be having to play by appointment, grinding and the use of daily rewards. This could generate sensations in the player like fear of missing out (FOMO) or that since they have invested so much time in something, now it is hard to throw it away, related to the loss aversion bias.
- **Monetary Dark Patterns**: If one resource to be spent by the player was time, now comes the other side of the coin, money. To identify whether the use of these is involved through a dark pattern, answers must be sought to the questions of how informed the user is about the use he is going to make, how aware he is of the amounts involved in the actions he performs, what amounts the game requires of him and what is the value of what he will obtain within the game. Scarcity or paying to skip, that in certain context might be acceptable, if meet certain intentions are absolutely registered as ones. For example, paying to skip might be exploited by the developers designing a certain level that will be impossible to achieve or overcome without aid (monetary in this case). It is remarkable to point out that gambling or betting is not marked as a monetary dark pattern as long as the player is complicit with the interaction and knows enough to answer the previous questions. That does not exempt it to also say that it might abuse mechanisms like the intermittent reinforcement, but it is not the point here.
- **Social Capital-Based Dark Patterns: using players' social relationships as a** resource can affect players in a very negative way, beyond placing a value on them, thought should be given to how such relationships may be affected by the way they are linked to the systems that use them or whether the player may feel a sense of obligation to play under pressure in relation to them. Examples such as social pyramid schemes or impersonations, are present and not only in small games, for example in Farmville, when the game requires you to have other people join and schedule your activities around it in order to progress in it or to pay for

it, the game dynamic becomes a clear manifestation of the dark pattern behind to everyone.

Over the years there have been times when public opinion has had some concern about how video games could affect different sectors of the population, sometimes more accurately than others. What is noteworthy for this paper is that recently several political bodies have decided, or are in the process of, regulating the practices mentioned here. The most notorious case would be the Chinese government,[1,2,3] who talks about restrictions or prohibitions on actions that encourage a player to connect regularly due to FOMO, limitations on how much each user can spend, or variable rewards or rewards with probability involved, among others. It is important to mention that although the debate today is not global in institutions that can regulate it, in other regions it is also present, an example is the European Parliament.[4]

3 Adapting a Heuristic Assessment to Videogames

Considering the aspects previously highlighted within videogames and associated with the user experience, it is possible to carry out the objective set out in this research work. Specifically, it is intended to incorporate in a complete heuristic evaluation, aspects obtained from the studied parameters being reflected in the different heuristic principles. Using an existing, well-founded, and validated assessment represents an advantage because the work starts on a solid foundation. In particular, the evaluation that has been regarded and used as the basis of this work has been the one carried out by the GRIHO research group of the University of Lleida [22, 23].

The following subsections describe, firstly, the existing evaluation serving as a starting point, and secondly, the process undertaken to modify the base heuristic evaluation with the analyzed aspects of video games in order to obtain a new version of this evaluation applicable in gaming environments.

3.1 Existing Heuristic Evaluation as the Basis for the Proposal

The starting point of the presented work in this paper is an existing technique for usability evaluation created at the University of Lleida. This technique is focused on

[1] https://www.reuters.com/world/china/why-how-china-is-drastically-limiting-online-gaming-under-18s-2021-08-31/.

[2] https://www.weforum.org/agenda/2021/09/what-S-behind-china-S-video-game-restrictions/.

[3] https://www.reuters.com/world/china/china-issues-draft-rules-online-game-management-2023-12-22/.

[4] https://www.europarl.europa.eu/news/de/press-room/20231208IPR15767/new-eu-rules-needed-to-address-digital-addiction.

combining two remarkable sets of heuristic principles: Nielsen's and Tognazzini's lists. These are remarkable references and do not need so much effort to be refined but present aspects which confirm the need to complete a new proposal resulting from combining both. On the one hand, Nielsen's list needed something more to be useful at all. Our experience reveals that often (not to say almost always) when someone uses Nielsen's list [8] it is due to a lack of (deep) knowledge about it and, most worryingly, about the technique itself. This assertion is based on Nielsen's statement: "these principles are broad rules of thumb and not specific usability guidelines" [8], making the list itself impossible to be used to evaluate. On the other hand, Tognazzini's is too big and detailed to be widely used.

The evaluation was done by a process inspired by the recommendations found in [24] and [25] works:

1. Revision of the two chosen lists. The first step is to read carefully all the principles of Nielsen's and Tognazzini's lists. The revision has been done in terms of understanding the deep meaning of each principle.
2. Compare similarities. As the intention is to get a compact and complete solution for evaluating all kinds of user interfaces, we compared all the similarities in order to merge principles as much as possible.
3. Integrate these similarities.

As a result, a final list with 15 general principles (or heuristics) resulting from mixing Nielsen's and Tognazzini's lists was created (see Table 1). However, to effectively use the principles we need "something more specific". This is also what every experienced usability/UX evaluator agrees upon. This "something more specific" are precise questions to be answered by the evaluators to assess every principle. Then, beyond the list of principles, a set of questions to evaluate every heuristic was created. In this case, 60 questions cover all the principles.

Beyond the list of 15 principles (or heuristics), a set of questions to evaluate every heuristic was created. In this case, 60 questions cover all the principles [22]. It is important to know that each question should be able to be answered with a

Table 1 Principles defined by the existing heuristic evaluation used as basis for the proposal

1. Visibility and system state	9. Aesthetic and minimalist design
2. Connection between the system and the real world, metaphor usage and human object	10. Help and documentation
3. User control and freedom	11. Save the state and protect the work
4. Consistency and standards	12. Color and readability
5. Recognition rather than memory, learning and anticipation	13. Autonomy
6. Flexibility and efficiency of use	14. Defaults
7. Help users recognize, diagnose, and recover from errors	15. Latency reduction
8. Preventing errors	

simple "Yes" or "No", and if the answer is "Yes", it will mean good usability for this characteristic and "No" means bad usability.

Once the principles were defined, formally, the heuristic evaluation method where evaluators rate every question to deliver a final report is considered.

The intention was to combine the qualitative and quantitative findings, but usually, the reports are mainly qualitative. So, some efforts were made to improve the qualitative answer to the client. Concretely, the method considers a simple but effective rating procedure with three main characteristics:

1. 7-option rating scale: "Yes, in all cases"; "Yes, but some cases missing"; "Not always"; "No, in no case"; "Not applicable"; "It is not a problem"; and "Impossible to check".
2. Questions for the principles are interrogative questions written in a way that the positive answer always means good usability level.
3. A final usability value, called "Usability percentage" (UP), provides the quantitative rationale. It is calculated with values assigned to each of the 7 options from the rating scale: "Yes, in all cases" is weighted with 1 point; "Yes, but some cases missing" with 0,66; "Not always" with 0,33; "No, in no case" with 0; and "Not applicable", "It is not a problem" or "Impossible to check" will not be taken into consideration, as if they do not exist. As a result, the method adds up all the values to obtain the final number. Within this, the maximum value is 60, corresponding with the case that all the questions have been answered with a "Yes, in all cases". Nevertheless, as the "Not applicable", "It is not a problem" or "Impossible to check" answers make it impossible to know the maximum number for every evaluation, we translate this value to a percentage value, taking into consideration only the valued response. It provides a number (a percentage) that enables the comparison among the assessments done by the other evaluators.

3.2 Adding Gaming Features to the Existing Heuristic

The evaluation explained in the previous subsection assumes the basis to start from. Its utility is to assess usability as a key element of the user experience, for applications or websites in general. However, from the perspective of video games, it does not consider aspects specific to them. As the base heuristic evaluation stands, a video game can be evaluated in the same way as other types of software, such as a customer management application or a web browser. Considering the particularity of video games, as described in Sect. 2, they contain specific attributes and characteristics that are not found together in other types of software but are crucial in shaping the user experience in them. Because of all this, it is necessary to update the heuristic evaluation proposed by the GRIHO group to take into account aspects specific to video games and, therefore, allow for a correct and above all precise evaluation of their usability.

The first step toward the stated goal is to analyze heuristics based on video games and, therefore, take into consideration in some way the characteristics described in

Sect. 2. Their content and study allow us to reason and list heuristics already used in video games and thus be able to compile a list that can be used to achieve the stated goal. After conducting a search, the analyzed heuristics are as follows:

- **Heuristics and Usability Guidelines for the Creation and Evaluation of Fun in Videogames** [26]. The first set of game specific UX heuristics. In his work he reflects a set of heuristics based on literature where he works with a team of videogame developers.
- **Using Heuristics to Evaluate the Playability of Games** [27]. They provide heuristic evaluation for gameplay (HEP), aimed at evaluating games of all kinds in their earliest stages (prototypes and mock-ups).
- **Game Usability Heuristics (PLAY) for Evaluating and Designing Better Games: The Next Iteration** [28]. They present a more refined version of HEP, where apart from the early phases it is indicated that it can also be used throughout the development cycle of a videogame.
- **User Experience Design for Inexperienced Gamers: GAP—Game Approachability Principles** [29]. Heuristics designed to give you a better first contact with the game.
- **Using Heuristics to Evaluate the Overall User Experience of Videogames and Advanced Interaction Games** [30]. They present a set of heuristics formed from the literature on heuristics in videogames, not focused solely on usability, trying to cover all the concepts of user experience related to gameplay, story, and interface.

The analysis conducted led to identify coincidences since they had similar or the same questions, not by chance but because it is mentioned that several of them are already based on each other and other usability heuristics for general software (the latter especially in those works done before 2010, since there were not many references related to videogames).

Knowing their content, the logical next step to define heuristics to incorporate in the base evaluation was to generate an initial list obtained from the existing ones which are shown in the left column of Table 2. Giving an initial compilation of 9 principles to be added, generating a total of 33 questions associated with their set and that allow them to be evaluated.

Based on the list obtained from the analysis, a distribution of Jakob Nielsen's usability heuristic principles for user interface design was made [31]. These provide a standard classification, in addition to being compatible and reference of the heuristic evaluation of [22, 23] (basis of this work), in which the new questions will be added and, in case of having questions that do not fit into any of the existing principles, they will be defined more specific to videogames. Thus, the obtained result is shown in Table 2 in its entirety by indicating, for each heuristic obtained in the previous step (left column), which Jakob Nielsen principle it can be included in (middle column). On the other hand, the right column shows the new principle that the heuristic generates and that is related to video games. It is worth mentioning that in this step there were heuristics from the first step that do not fall under any Jakob Nielsen principle or under a new principle related to video games. Therefore, they were marked as "stand by" awaiting a decision in the next step about them.

Table 2 Analysis obtained from the heuristic principles obtained as first step related to Jakob Nielsen's proposal

Heuristics obtained from existing sources	Relation with principles of Jakob Nielsen	
	Associated to an existing principle	New principle
A. *Heuristic: documentation/tutorial*		
A1. The player does not need to read the manual or documentation to play	Help and Documentation	
A2. The player does not need to access the tutorial in order to play		
B. *Heuristic: status and score*		
B1. The controls in the game remain consistent within the game and follow standard conventions	Consistency and standards	
B2. Status indicators are fluid, obvious, available, and don't interfere with gameplay	System visibility and health	
B3. The controls are intuitive, configured/distributed in a natural way; they are customizable and default to industry-standard settings	Flexibility	
B4. Consistency reduces the learning curve by following trends in the videogame industry to achieve user expectations. If there is no standard in the industry, conduct usability/gameplay research to figure out the best layout for the most target players	Consistency and Standards	
C. *Heuristic: game provides feedback*		
C1. The game provides feedback and reacts consistently, immediately, defiantly, and excitingly to the player's actions		Feedback
C2. Provides appropriate auditory/visual/visceral feedback (music, sound effects, vibration in the controller)		
D. *Heuristic: terminology*		
D1 The objectives of the game are clear. The game provides clear objectives or supports the player's creation of these, presenting overarching objectives at the start, as well as short-term objectives throughout the game		Terminology
D2. The skills needed to achieve goals are taught early enough to play or use later, or just before they are needed		

(continued)

Table 2 (continued)

Heuristics obtained from existing sources	Relation with principles of Jakob Nielsen	
	Associated to an existing principle	New principle
D3. The game gives rewards that immerse the player more in the experience by increasing their capabilities, skill, or expanding their customization capacity, for example		
E. *Heuristic: burden on player*		
E1. The game doesn't put unnecessary burdens on the player		Stand by
E2. The player gets controls that are basic enough to be learned quickly, but expandable with advanced options for advanced players		Player load
E3. The game provides enough practice opportunities for the new skills/tools		
E4. The player is proficient with the skills and tools gained after an initial training		
E5. The game should give hints, but not too many		
E6. The mechanics of the game should feel natural and have the right weight and momentum/momentum. In addition, they must be appropriate for the situation the player is facing		Player charge
F. *Heuristic: screen layout*		
F1. The screen design is efficient, visually appealing, and integrated	Aesthetic design	
F2. The player experiences the UI as consistent (in controller, color, typography, dialogue, and UI design)		
F3. Players experience the UI/HUD as part of the game		
F4. The art is recognizable to the player and speaks to its function		
F5. The interface should be as non-intrusive as possible		In doubt

(continued)

Table 2 (continued)

Heuristics obtained from existing sources	Relation with principles of Jakob Nielsen	
	Associated to an existing principle	New principle
F6. The player must be able to identify elements of the game such as avatars, enemies, obstacles, power ups, threats or opportunities. Objects should stand out, even for players with vision impairments or color blindness, and should not be easily misinterpreted	Color and readability	
F7. Objects "must resemble what they are"		
F8. The camera behaves correctly		Stand by
G. *Heuristic: navigation*		
G1. The navigation is consistent, logical, and minimalist		Stand by
H. *Heuristic: error prevention*		
H1. Player error is avoided		Stand by
H2. Player interruption is supported, so that players can easily turn the game on and off and can save games in different states	Save status	
H3. By turning on the game, the player has enough information to start playing	Error prevention	
H4. Sensitive contextual help should be provided during gameplay so that players don't get stuck and need to turn to a help manual		
H5. All levels of players can play and participate quickly and easily with progressive or adjustable tutorials and/or difficulty levels	Flexibility	
H6. The player cannot make irreversible mistakes	Error prevention	
I. *Heuristic: game story immersion*		
I1. The game's story encourages immersion (if the game has a story component)		Stand by

Based on the previous definition of the heuristic principles obtained in the previously defined combination, an evolution of the resulting list was made:

- First, the principle of Terminology in Motivation/Emotion was renamed, as the original name did not illustrate the purpose of the principles clearly enough. Subsequently, the questions from the Feedback principle to the Motivation/Emotion principle (C1 and C2) were transferred. This was due to the fact that they try to generate sensations and emotions according to the situation and the actions that the user is performing or has carried out. D2 is moved from Terminology to Flexibility. The question deals with the prior learning of a skill to be used.

- The questions assigned at the beginning to the player are redistributed between the principles of Recognition (E5 and E6) and Flexibility (E2 and E3). Similarly, changes were made to improve their comprehension in questions B1 and B2.
- Finally, certain questions have been removed for the following reasons:
  - E4 because players were required to evaluate them.
  - H5 because the aspect dealt with has more weight in accessibility than in usability.

Once the previous modifications were made, a second phase of modifications was carried out. In this case, the aim was to identify the existence of specific videogame terms that can be extrapolated to user experience terms in order to generalize them. In this sense, it was observed that feedback is one more type of signal offered by the system, being a group of signals that are shown as a reaction to the actions and situations in which the player finds himself. In addition, the questions in Motivation/ Emotion gave rise to a question: "What is the difference between the satisfaction generated in usability and that which is related to the engage-ability aspect?" To do this, we contacted a researcher with a remarkable track record in the field, Celia Hodent, author of The Gamer's Brain [2], to clarify whether engage-ability principles could also be interpreted in some way as usability principles. To which she replied[5]:

> Usability is about making a product efficient, effective, and safe to perform a task. The goal is to eliminate all frustrations. In a game, we add frustrations: players are challenged, fail, have to try again, etc. What makes a game fun isn't just about usability.
>
> Games are not tools: we don't use them to achieve goals. We interact with games for the sake of it. Therefore, fun, emotional design, engage-ability, or whatever we want to call it, is fundamental, not just usability (ability of the game to be used). Hope this helps!.

Having considered the answer, several questions from *Motivation/Emotion* were transferred to the principles of *Consistency and* Standards (*C*1) *and* Visibility and System Health (*C*2 and D1). In addition, certain questions were clarified by adding examples for better understanding (H3 and F1) and several questions were eliminated for the following reasons:

- Redundant targets, other questions also cover them (G1, E1 and H1).
- Assessment complexity (E1 and H1).
- Not applicable to all videogame genres (I1).
- Terms with vague definitions (F5).
- A proper purpose has not been found for it (F8).
- Both the Motivation/Emotion principle and the remaining question in this one (D3) were removed, both of which did not deal with usability aspects.

[5] Hodent, C. [@CeliaHodent]. (2022, May 3). Usability is about making a product efficient, effective, and safe to accomplish a task. The goal is to remove all [Tweet]. Twitter. https://twitter.com/CeliaHodent/status/1532642547532763143.

3.2.1 Results Generated

The result generated consists of the heuristic evaluation given by the University of Lleida with the addition of 28 questions obtained through the process described and examples for better understanding by external evaluators. The new questions could be broadly categorized into these three concepts:

- To provide information about the user's situation, as this changes a lot during the course of a gaming session.
- To deal with user learning, the recognition of what has been learned.
- To prevent the user from feeling lost or blocked by the system.

It is important to note that there are heuristic principles that do not have added questions. The main reason is that we simply didn't find questions that can be generalized to all types of games. An easily remarkable example: in competitive online multiplayer games, having feedback and responses in the shortest possible time means that latency and connection have a greater weight in their usability on average compared to any other genre. Thus, it has been considered important to highlight that these questions are general knowing that each product has its own needs to which its quality control and user experience processes will have to adapt. It seems logical that those principles that have been ended up with the most added questions are visibility, consistency, readability, and aesthetic design.

Finally, it is considered interesting to locate the tool obtained within the classification shown in Fig. 1 based on the axes marked in the Rohrer analysis [3] and summarized in Fig. 2. Based on these axes, it can be considered that the proposed heuristic evaluation can be located in an intermediate zone close to the question of why and how to solve each point detected. This is due to the fact that, when experts participate in the evaluation, it must be centered according to the y-axis, as it does not directly apply the opinion of the users. Likewise, it would be located to the left on the x-axis since the experts would offer a why and an idea close to a possible solution to problems or recommendations found in each heuristic principle analyzed.

4 Integration of the Videogames Heuristics into Our Methodology

Once all this analysis has been carried out, the next and final step is to integrate the videogames heuristics into the heuristic evaluation methodology from which we start. Remember, we begin with a list of 15 heuristic principles that evaluators evaluate by answering 60 questions distributed in a non-uniform way.

After this analysis, we have a new heuristic that can be used to evaluate video game user interfaces. This proposal follows the same methodology as the previous one and, as we have seen, it has not been necessary to add any new heuristics, as happened in the proposal to evaluate collaborative interfaces [32]. The modification

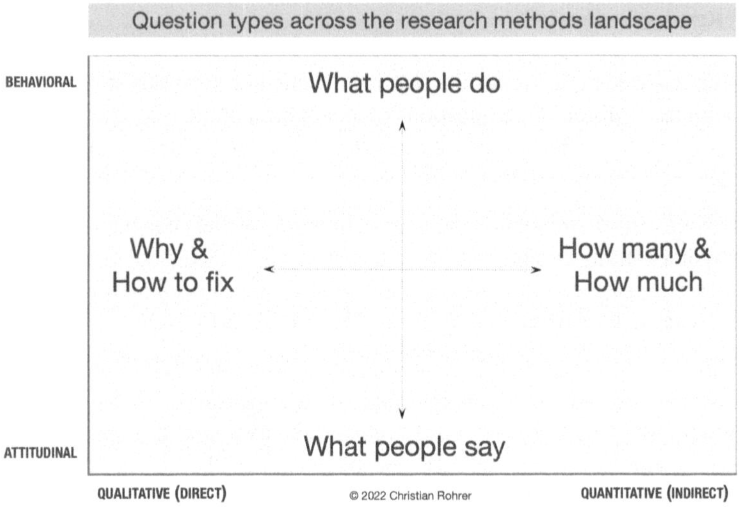

Fig. 2 Fundamentals for the definition of the axes that allow classifying methodologies for the evaluation and analysis of videogames [3]

has been manifested by the inclusion of the 28 questions indicated in the previous section, leaving a total of 15 heuristic principles that are evaluated by means of 88 questions.

In the following list we will see how the questions are integrated considering only the new questions corresponding to the video game part are shown, the others can be found in the previous works [22, 23]:

1. Visibility and system state: 8 questions (5 pre-existing + 3 new), these being the new ones:
   - Are status score indicators seamless, obvious, available and do not interfere with game play?
   - Do the game provides clear goals or supports the creation of them by the player?
   - Does the game provide appropriate audio/visual/visceral feedback? (music, sound effects, controller vibration)
2. Connection between the system and the real world, metaphor usage and human objects: 4 questions (none added).
3. User control and freedom: 3 questions (none added).
4. Consistency and standards: 10 questions (6 pre-existing + 4 new), these being the new ones:
   - Do the controls follow industry-standard settings? Example: The video game, compared to other titles of the same genre, has its actions assigned/mapped in the same way. In first person shooter/action games for PC the space is

usually assigned as the key to execute a jump, if the game allows this action (as in titles like Counter-Strike: Global Offensive, Valorant, Fortnite, etc.).
- Are the controls consistent?
- Does the game provide feedback and reacts in a consistent, immediate, challenging and exciting way to the players' actions?
- Does the consistency shorten the learning curve (usually by following the trends set by the gaming industry to meet users' expectations)?

5. Recognition rather than memory, learning and anticipation: 7 questions (5 pre-existing + 2 new), these being the new:

   - Does the game provide clues but not too many?
   - Do the game mechanics feel natural and feel like they have corrected weight and momentum? Furthermore, are the game mechanics appropriate for the situations the user is facing?

6. Flexibility and efficiency of use: 12 questions (6 pre-existing + 6 new), these being the new ones:

   - All levels of players can play and get involved quickly and easily with tutorials, and/or progressive or adjustable difficulty levels?
   - Are the controls intuitive?
   - Are the controls customizable? (These being on default to industry standard settings)
   - Are the skills needed to attain goals addressed early enough to play or use later, or right before the new skill is needed?
   - Does the game provide controls that are basic enough to learn quickly, yet expandable for advanced options for advanced players?
   - Does the game allow opportunities for sufficient practice of new skills/tools?

7. Help users recognize, diagnose and recover from errors: 4 questions (none added).
8. Preventing errors: 6 questions (3 pre-existing + 3 new) which are listed below:

   - Upon turning on the game, does the player have enough information to begin playing? Example: When starting the system, the first time the player is aware/recognizes what is required in order to play. For example, the player is in the initial menu and the player can intuitively reach the screen or button that allows him to start the game.
   - Does the system give context sensitive help to the player while playing so that they are not stuck and need to rely on a manual for help?
   - Does the system prevent the player on making irreversible errors?

9. Aesthetic and minimalist design: 8 questions (4 pre-existing + 4 new) which are listed below:

   - Is the screen layout efficient, integrated, and visually pleasing? Example: The interface elements during the game are integrated in a way that they follow the rest of the art, are pleasant and make sense. For example, we can

take the interface elements in Halo gameplay. Since the game is first-person, they've treated the interface elements to look as if they're part of what's displayed on the helmet worn by the player-controlled character, following the art of the rest of the game.
- Does the player experience the user interface as consistent? (in controller, color, typographic, dialogue and user interface design)
- Does the player experience the user interface/HUD as a part of the game?
- Is art recognizable to the player and speaks to its function?

10. Help and documentation: 7 questions (5 pre-existing + 2 new), these being the new ones:
    - Is the player able to play without needing to read the manual or documentation?
    - Does the player not need to access the tutorial to play?
11. Save the state and protect the work: 4 questions (3 pre-existing + 1 new), this being the new ones:
    - Is player interruption supported, so that players can easily turn the game on and off and be able to save the games in different states?
12. Color and readability: 7 questions (4 pre-existing + 3 new), these being the new ones:
    - Is the player able to identify game elements such as avatars, enemies, obstacles, power ups, threats or opportunities?
    - Do the objects stand out, even for players with bad eyesight or color blindness and are not easily be misinterpreted?
    - Do the objects "look like what they are for"?
13. Autonomy: 3 questions (none added).
14. Defaults: 3 questions (none added).
15. Latency reduction: 2 questions (none added).

5 Discussion

We have talked about practices that intentionally seek to negatively affect the player's experience. However, as is has been deal with those elements that are in a greyer spectrum, they are not perfect, but they fulfill their function, they are not the most elaborate or ingeniously designed elements, but they use a common language that facilitates the understanding of their audience or at least part of it. We can argue the importance of immersion in an interactive experience whose purpose is to enjoy what video games present to you, but how do we analyze the elements that come into play to evaluate it? The first question to be answered is whether the elements are integrated within the global of the game, for which we subdivide the question into two others:

Table 3 Classification of elements integrated into the videogame

		Present in the game space	
		No	Yes
Present in the game story	No	Non-diegetic	Spatial
	Yes	Meta	Diegetic

- Are the elements within the game space?
- Are the elements present in the story of the game?

Depending on the result we can classify them according to Table 3.

Elements in all categories have their functions and do not have to be disruptive per se [33], but those that come close to answering yes to both or either of the questions are more likely to keep the player focused on the world itself. However, the above immersion is that the player knows what to do, and that the player plays the product is even more necessary. Hints, mechanisms to facilitate readability or resources to convey information in a way that requires less from the player have always existed.

There is debate around this, not so much around that we have them, they are necessary, the question is how far they have or should go, as one of the many debates that return cyclically in gaming communities. For example, the one related to the accessibility with easy mode vs base difficulty of an experience, with immersion appears related to the use of yellow paint in various titles that at first you do not expect by the world in which you are presented. Developers and publishers,[6,7] comment that this is due to new standards presented by younger audiences, due to those games that they have as a reference at a generational level, therefore those products that want to appeal to various audiences or include the one that is coming up must keep in mind their language and how much they are willing to invest to understand what is presented to them. It is always easier for companies to adapt to the lowest common denominator visual language of who they want to target (i.e., the elements that require the least to be consumed), than to try to trend-set or educate according to their style. Can you blame them for that? It depends, are they able to include in more clever ways elements that are more immersive that in turn retain players and communicate their function just as effectively? The answer can be fairly aligned.

6 Conclusions

User experience is a differentiating factor when it comes to gaining or losing users, therefore, obtaining a tool to evaluate it is considered essential. In this sense, this chapter has described how, by detecting important parameters in videogames, it has been possible to obtain a heuristic evaluation resulting from the incorporation of new assessable questions to an already developed and validated heuristic evaluation. The

---

[6] https://www.youtube.com/watch?v=vLZ6eHVshXw.

[7] https://twitter.com/nao_chan_91/status/1756633893573185824.

result obtained is not intended to be a perfect tool in its current state, but it certainly adds value, as it provides the opportunity to give a more personalized or concrete diagnosis if it is a question of evaluating the usability of a videogame. This is so considering the previous state and that obtained from the evaluation tool worked on, since it did not previously consider the specific aspects studied for videogames. In this work, we have extended a pre-existing heuristic evaluation to adapt it to evaluate video game interfaces. With this, we took advantage of the best of what we already had, the methodology and its particular way of evaluating and calculating a quantitative value to offer HCI practitioners an effective tool to evaluate video games.

As a future work, it is intended to make intensive use of the evaluation obtained, improving it together with evaluation methods that complement it in order to generate a study that allows expert evaluators, as well as in videogames, to continue with the expansion of the proposal presented.

References

1. Isbister K (2017) How games move us. The MIT Press. ISBN: 9780262534451
2. Hodent C (2017) The gamer's brain. Taylor & Francis. ISBN: 9781315154725. https://doi.org/10.1201/9781315154725
3. Rohrer C (2022) When to use which user-experience research methods. Nielsen Norman Group. https://www.nngroup.com/articles/which-ux-research-methods
4. Nielsen J (1993) Chapter 5: usability heuristics. In: Usability engineering. Academic Press, Inc., pp 115–164. ISBN: 0125184050
5. Nielsen J, Molich R (1990) Heuristic evaluation of user interfaces. In: Proceedings of the SIGCHI conference on human factors in computing systems, pp 249–256. https://doi.org/10.1145/97243.97281
6. Granollers T, Lores J, Perdrix F (2003a) Usability engineering process model. Integration with software engineering. In: Proceedings of the HCI international. ISBN: 978-0805849349
7. Granollers T (2003) User centred design process model integration of usability engineering and software engineering. In: Interact 2003. ISBN: 978-1-58603-363-7
8. Nielsen J (1995) 10 usability heuristics for user interface design. https://www.nngroup.com/articles/ten-usability-heuristics
9. Scholtz J (2004) Usability evaluation. National Institute of Standards and Technology 1
10. Paz F, Paz FA, Pow-Sang JA, Collantes L (2014) Usability heuristics for transactional web sites. In: Proceedings of the 2014 11th international conference on information technology: new generations. IEEE, pp 627–628
11. Jaspers MW (2009) A comparison of usability methods for testing interactive health technologies: methodological aspects and empirical evidence. Int J Med Inform 78:340–353
12. Shneiderman B (1987) Designing the user interface: strategies for effective human-computer interaction. Addison-Wesley Longman Publishing Co. Inc.
13. Norman D (1988) The design of everyday things. Basic Books
14. Inostroza R, Rusu C, Roncagliolo S, Rusu V, Collazos CA (2016) Developing SMASH: a set of SMArtphone's uSability Heuristics. Comput Stand Interfaces 43:40–52
15. Tognazzini B (2014) First principles, HCI design, human computer interaction (HCI), principles of HCI design, usability testing
16. Bevan N, Kirakowskib J, Maissel J (1991) What is usability. In: Proceedings of the 4th international conference on HCI, pp 1–6
17. Verstegen I (2010) Gestalt psychology. The Corsini Encyclopedia of psychology, pp 1–3. ISBN: 9780470479216. https://doi.org/10.1002/9780470479216.corpsy0386

18. Heras-Escribano M (2019) The philosophy of affordances. Springer series new directions in philosophy and cognitive science. ISBN: 978-3-319-98829-0
19. Manzano JA, Vela FL, Rodríguez PP (2022) Objetivos de juego y motivadores en sistemas basados en juego. Interacción Revista digital de AIPO 3(2):78–89
20. Valera-Aranguren R, Paderewski-Rodriguez P, Gutierrez-Vela F, Arango-López J (2022) Un Catálogo de Patrones de Mecánicas y Elementos de Juego para Experiencias de Juego Sociales Pervasivas. Interacción Revista digital de AIPO 3(2):149–160
21. Zagal JP, Staffan B, Lewis C (2013) Dark patterns in the design of games. In: Proceedings of the 8th international conference on the foundations of digital games (FDG 2013), pp 39.46. ISBN: 978-0-9913982-0-1
22. Granollers T (2018a) Usability evaluation with heuristics. new proposal from integrating two trusted sources. In: Marcus A, Wang W (eds) Design, user experience, and usability: theory and practice. Lecture notes in computer science, vol 10918. Springer, Cham
23. Granollers T (2018b) Usability evaluation with heuristics, beyond Nielsen's list. In: Proceedings of the eleventh international conference on advances in computer–human interactions (ACHI 2018). Rome, Italy. ISBN: 978-1-61208-616-3, pp 60–65
24. Quiñones D, Rusu C (2017a) How to develop usability heuristics: a systematic literature review. Comput Stand Interfaces 53:89–122. ISSN 0920-5489,.https://doi.org/10.1016/j.csi.2017.03.009
25. Quiñones D (2017b) A methodology to develop usability/user experience heuristics. In: Proceedings of the XVIII international conference on human computer interaction (Interacción'17). ACM, New York, NY, USA, Article 57, 2 p. https://doi.org/10.1145/3123818.3133832
26. Federoff MA (2002) Heuristics and usability guidelines for the creation and evaluation of fun in videogames. Indiana University. https://citeseerx.ist.psu.edu/viewdoc/summary?doi=10.1.1.89.8294
27. Desurvire H, Caplan M, Toth JA (2004) Using heuristics to evaluate the playability of games. Association for Computing Machinery. https://doi.org/10.1145/985921.986102
28. Desurvire H, Wiberg C (2009) Game usability heuristics (PLAY) for evaluating and designing better games: the next iteration. https://www.researchgate.net/publication/221099657_Game_Usability_Heuristics_PLAY_for_Evaluating_and_Designing_Better_Games_The_Next_Iteration
29. Desurvire H, Wiberg C (2010) Chapter 8, user experience design for inexperienced gamers: GAP—game approachability principles. Isbister, K. Enabling social play: a framework for design and evaluation. In: Bernhaupt R (ed) Evaluating user experience in games. Human–computer interaction series. Springer, London. https://doi.org/10.1007/978-1-84882-963-3_2
30. Koeffel C, Hochleitner W, Leitner J, Haller M, Geven A, Tscheligi M (2010) Using heuristics to evaluate the overall user experience of videogames and advanced interaction games. https://doi.org/10.1007/978-1-84882-963-3_13
31. Nielsen J (2020) 10 usability heuristics for user interface design. Norman Group, Nielsen. https://www.nngroup.com/articles/ten-usability-heuristics/
32. Costaguta R, García G, Granollers T (2024) Proposal for a heuristic principle to evaluate interfaces of collaborative systems. In: XXIII international conference on human computer interaction (Interaccion 2023). Association for Computing Machinery, New York, NY, USA, Article 2, 1–2. https://doi.org/10.1145/3612783.3612786
33. Galati E (2020) Understanding UX in video games: the diegesis theory. https://uxdesign.cc/understanding-ux-in-video-games-diegesis-theory-f59d5a94cbcf?gi=d0ce5afb282d

Towards Trustworthy and Human-Centred AI Explanations

Cristina Manresa-Yee, Silvia Ramis, F. Xavier Gaya-Morey, and Jose Maria Buades Rubio

Abstract The need for human-centred Explainable Artificial Intelligence (XAI) arises from the increasing complexity and pervasiveness of AI systems in many aspects of daily life and critical decision-making processes. Mining the literature, research shows a lack of human-centred methods applied to the design and evaluation of XAI. In this work, we compile current works in human-centred XAI and present a case study contributing to user studies to assess explanations. The case study aims at evaluating the impact of local and global explanations on human's trust and understanding of a facial expression recognizer. Results show that explanations are appreciated when present, but when no explanations are given, users apply their own mental model on how the system works and trust it if their experience using it is positive.

Keywords Explainability · Explanations · Transparency · Trust · Intelligent systems · Explainable Artificial Intelligence · Facial expression recognition

1 Introduction

Artificial intelligence (AI) has made remarkable developments in recent years, revolutionizing industries and transforming the way we live, work, and interact with technology. From intelligent virtual assistants to autonomous vehicles, AI is present

C. Manresa-Yee (✉) · S. Ramis · F. X. Gaya-Morey · J. M. Buades Rubio
Department of Mathematics and Computer Science, Universitat de les Illes Balears, Carretera de Valldemossa, km 7.5, 07122 Palma, Illes Balears, Spain
e-mail: cristina.manresa@uib.es

S. Ramis
e-mail: silvia.ramis@uib.es

F. X. Gaya-Morey
e-mail: francesc-xavier.gaya@uib.es

J. M. Buades Rubio
e-mail: josemaria.buades@uib.es

S. Sayago et al. (eds.), *Future Perspectives on Human-Computer Interaction Research*,
https://doi.org/10.1007/978-3-031-71697-3_4

in every facet of our lives, promising to enhance our efficiency, decision-making, and overall wellbeing. However, as AI continues to evolve and integrate into society, the need for trustworthy AI has become increasingly evident, especially in high-stakes domains such as healthcare or finance.

In this new ecosystem, a challenge is building AI technologies that are human-centred, that is, AI that is designed responsibly, respects privacy or follows human-centred design principles [11, 22]. Further, to ensure that AI's economic and social benefits are broadly shared across society, building "trust in tech" and social acceptance around AI is fundamental. In this sense, trust can be defined as "a psychological state comprising the intention to accept vulnerability based upon positive expectations of the intentions or behaviour of another", in this case, the AI [54]. Trust is an essential human mechanism needed to manage factors such as vulnerability, uncertainty, complexity, and ambiguity, which together represent risk [31].

The field of eXplainable Artificial Intelligence (XAI) can help achieve these objectives. XAI can be described as "AI systems that can explain their rationale to a human user, characterize their strengths and weaknesses, and convey a understanding of how they will behave in the future" [24]. Therefore, XAI can make AI systems more transparent, understandable, and trustworthy [1, 9, 59].

Focusing on trustworthiness [3], for AI systems to be trusted and to comply with legal and accountability standards, it is crucial that humans can comprehend the processes through which AI algorithms derive their decisions and predictions.

The social sciences have studied how people define, generate, select, evaluate, and present explanations, but research in XAI frequently uses only the researchers' intuition of what constitutes a "good" explanation [44] without considering how humans explain, the profile of the person receiving the explanation or the context around the explanation. In XAI, explanations are rarely provided by end-user needs [8].

On the one hand, recent studies show that the well-known human-centred methods developed in the Human–Computer Interaction (HCI) discipline are not used in the design of XAI systems [53]. On the other hand, regarding evaluation, the state-of-the-art lacks user studies, methods, and metrics to evaluate whether XAI systems provide adequate explainability to humans [16, 21].

In this research line, the role of explanations is crucial: when AI systems provide clear and meaningful explanations, users are better equipped to understand the rationale behind the system's decisions and actions, and consequently, this knowledge may build trust. How to design and deliver these explanations is still an open issue as there are some key considerations to take into account when designing and delivering effective explanations in XAI such as the explanation goals, the person receiving the explanation, the content to include in an explanation or the type of explanation [8]. Explanation goals involve answering questions such as, *why did the algorithm predict x? why did it predict x rather than y? or why did the algorithm fail?* [35]. The existing literature lists many desirable properties for explanations to be useful [37, 44] and make the model and/or the prediction more human-understandable [23].

In this work, we will explore how human-centred techniques are currently applied to designing and evaluating XAI with end-users and study the field's shortcomings to guide future research. Then, we will focus specifically on the automated Facial Expression Recognition (FER) context as it is an important field for the discipline of HCI. Expressions can be related to emotions, and therefore their recognition can improve the naturalness and personalization aspects of HCI [29, 30, 42, 50], in varied domains such as security, assistance, healthcare or entertainment. Therefore, understanding how the system works, and investigating the best way to deliver explanations in this context can contribute to improve the users' comprehension and trust. The case study analyses the effectiveness of different explanations and explores how different explanations shape user perceptions towards the system.

The remainder of the work is structured as follows. Section 2 outlines related work on human-centred XAI, Sect. 3 presents the case study and Sect. 4 the results of the user study. The last Section concludes the work and presents the future work lines.

2 Human-Centred Explainable Artificial Intelligence: Past, Present, and Future

The concept of explainable AI is not a novel idea in the field [61] but state-of-the-art AI algorithms use more complex representations and algorithms (e.g. deep neural networks (DNNs)), which make them harder to interpret, and therefore pose an increased need for explanations.

The past few years have seen a growth in efforts across the academic, industry, and regulatory landscapes to advance the field of XAI. Research has specially focused on developing XAI techniques [1]; however, there currently is no universal solution to XAI [25]. Speith [59] reviewed recent approaches to constructing taxonomies of XAI methods and explored the overarching challenges associated with these approaches, in addition to their benefits and drawbacks. In general, techniques consider the next dimensions of explainability: data–model, direct–post-hoc, global–local, and static–interactive [5, 59].

First, explanations can focus on understanding the characteristics and features of the data used in the models or how the model behaves. Examples of the former would be understanding important samples or criticisms [26] or higher-level features describing the dataset [34]. When explaining the model, the distinction is between directly interpretable models (e.g. linear regression, tree-based methods) and post-hoc explainability, that is, explaining the model after it was trained (e.g. LIME (Local Interpretable Model-agnostic Explanation) [51], CEM (Contrastive Explanation Method) [15]). The models explained are usually black box models such as DNNs. For post-hoc explainability methods, there is often a further distinction between model-agnostic methods which can be applied to any model and model-specific ones. Another distinction is explaining a single prediction (local) or describing the behaviour of the entire model globally. Finally, explanations can be static or as Miller [44] recommends, they can be designed to enable interactive engagement with the user.

Regarding the design of XAI, to consider the users' explainability needs, numerous efforts [24, 52] aim to categorize the various user groups seeking explainability that can be summarized in [9]:

- Domain experts or users of the model that seek to trust the model and understand it to make informed decisions.
- Users affected by the model's outcomes that seek to understand the decision or verify its fairness.
- Regulatory entities or agencies that seek to certify and verify compliance with legal regulations and ethical issues.
- Developers that seek to improve and debug the model.
- Managers and executive board members that seek to assess regulatory compliance, understand corporate AI applications and determine their adoption and usage.

The emergence of frameworks aiming at considering the users' explainability needs also benefits the design of XAI. Chronologically, Wang et al. [63] proposed a theory-driven conceptual framework linking XAI explanations to user reasoning goals. They considered how people ideally reason, how they actually reason with errors, and why they seek for explanations. This helps informing the design of XAI, linking to specific reasoning approaches and counteracting human decision-making biases. Aiming at designing user-centred displays of explanations for machine learning model predictions, Barda et al. [8] presented a framework that helps identifying specific explanation goals (why), the person receiving the explanation (who), the content to include in an explanation (what), the type of explanation or explanation approach (how), the moment to explain (when) and the environment in which the explanation will be used (where). They applied their framework to the healthcare context. Suresh et al. [60] presented a framework for identifying the stakeholders of XAI and their needs. They depicted the stakeholder expertise as a two-dimensional space that describes the knowledge they possess, and the contexts in which this knowledge manifests. The framework also details the needs as a three-level typology of long-term goals, shorter-term objectives and immediate tasks. Sanneman and Shah [56] introduced the Situation Awareness Framework for Explainable AI, a framework comprised by three levels for the development and evaluation of explanations about AI system behaviour: perception, which includes AI system inputs and outputs; comprehension, which provides information about causality; and projection, which explains what would happen if certain inputs or parameters changed or respond to users' particular actions. Recently, Kaplan et al. [33] introduced a framework designed to enable a comprehensive understanding of every facet of an AI application's lifecycle, from data collection and model development to evaluation protocols and decision analysis. They incorporated user-centric design principles and enabled interaction between users and the decisions made by AI models to support the effective debugging and optimization of AI models. The proposed framework emphasized incorporating transparency from the initial design phase of AI systems.

In addition, other works have contributed to facilitate the development of XAI considering the explanation needs like the XAI Question Bank presented by [35] comprising 50 questions organized in nine categories: how, why, why not, how to be that, how to be this still, what if, performance, data and output. Zhu et al. [67] proposed a human-centred approach for facilitating designers, specifically game designers, to co-create with AI/ML techniques, focusing on a specific user group, their needs and tasks. Their approach is aligned with three axes: the spectra of explainability (explanations to understand the operation of AI techniques to observations that offer insights of the input–output pattern), initiative (degree and type of initiative that it can take in performing its tasks), and domain overlap (amount of overlap between the tasks performed by the designer and the tasks performed by the AI). In this line, Eiband et al. [18] also presented a stage-based participatory process for designing transparent interfaces incorporating perspectives of diverse stakeholders, and focusing on the improvement of users' mental models when working with the system. Their process is based on identifying what can be made transparent and what information is interesting and relevant to users. Consequently, the first three stages of the process focus on what to explain in the system (content of an explanation, understanding the expert, user and target mental model) and the last two on how to explain (presentation format, iterative prototyping and evaluating).

Regarding evaluation, the state-of-the-art shows a lack of frameworks, methods, and metrics to evaluate whether XAI systems provide adequate explainability to humans [21]. Burkart et al. [10] also noted the absence of standard procedures for measuring, quantifying and comparing the explainability of AI systems. In this sense, research identifies two critical challenges that must be addressed to effectively evaluate XAI systems: assessing explainability to determine if similar responses yield comparable levels of explainability [2]; and evaluating the quality of explanations to ascertain whether users comprehend and trust the outcomes produced by AI systems [28, 36].

Related to this, Rong et al. [53] highlight the limited presence of XAI user evaluations, often lacking insights from cognitive or social sciences. Supporting this fact, Wells et al. [65] published a systematic review analysing the works from a user perspective. They evidenced that most works had not been tested with users, or when they did, limited details of the testing were published, failing to describe where the participants were recruited from, how many were recruited, or if the participants were knowledgeable in machine learning.

Despite the advances made in XAI, further research is required to design human-centred XAI [17] and understand user experiences and perceptions when using explanations. Liao et al. [62] outline the upcoming research lines applying human-centred approaches to XAI:

1. Guiding technical decisions based on users' explainability needs which requires understanding the user, their knowledge, their goals and their context. As commented previously, there is no universal solution to XAI [24] and both researchers and practitioners need tools and methods to effectively choose among the XAI techniques.

2. Identifying pitfalls of current XAI methods and inform new methods through empirical research. Empirical studies have already shown the inefficacy of the explanations to improve the users' tasks [7]. Therefore, user studies need to be conducted to understand the impact of the explanations on the users. Further, the inclusion of human-centred perspectives in developing XAI techniques is also needed.
3. Providing conceptual frameworks for human-compatible XAI. Research in theoretical analysis of human explanations, and cognitive and behavioural processes, can inspire new design frameworks to make XAI more human-compatible.

Further, the need to include legal and ethical imperatives for providing explanations, call for an interdisciplinary work [20].

Summarizing, there is still a need for further research to analyse how human-centred approaches can be used in XAI: the design space of XAI, along with other factors such as human-grounded evaluations to analyse how explanations impact on users' tasks and user experience, the adoption of usability principles, and conceptual frameworks that leverage user reasoning processes to inform XAI, also remain largely unexplored in depth.

3 The Case Study: Exploring Explanations' Impact on Users for Facial Expression Recognition

Aiming at exploring through empirical research how explanations impact on users, we present a case study on a facial expression recognition task. We developed a facial expression recognizer based on a Convolutional Neural Network (CNN) [49], which classifies expressions into one of the six basic ones [19]: sadness, happiness, fear, surprise, disgust and anger. We focus on the problem of explaining the behaviour of the facial expression recognizer based on a CNN. In particular, we explore the effects of global (model-level) and local (instance-level) post-hoc explanations on the users' trust and understandability. A local explanation explains why a model made a specific prediction for a particular instance or observation. These explanations are thought to be less overwhelming for novices [45]. A global explanation, on the other hand, explains the overall behaviour of the model by identifying the features or variables that are most important across all the predictions the model makes (e.g. visualizing a model such as decision tree). In this case study, we therefore seek answer to the question: Does a local or global visual explanation invoke a different level of trust and understanding in an automatic facial expression recognition system than no explanation at all? We present the results of a user study analysing the effects of different types of explanations on trust and understandability of a facial expression recognizer.

3.1 Explanations in Facial Expression Recognition

Research has been conducted to improve the techniques to recognize facial expressions, from traditional computer vision to current deep learning techniques [43]. However, there is a scarce number of works including explanations, and this number drops when addressing the evaluation of the explanations on psychological aspects such as trust or mental model.

In the case of visual-based XAI, visualization techniques are used to make more transparent the model by adopting XAI techniques. Alicioglu et al. [4] presented an extensive survey on visual analytics in interpreting deep learning models by adopting XAI methods and considering both the model usage (i.e. feature-based, rule-based or propagation-based) and the visual approaches (i.e. data representation, local and global explanations).

Regarding works applying XAI techniques to facial expression recognition, Schiller et al. [57] presented saliency maps generated by Layer-wise Relevance Propagation (LRP) [6] and eye-tracking to identify the most relevant face regions for facial expressions recognition and transferred that knowledge by hiding non-relevant information to speed up training in a new domain. The aim was not to evaluate the users' perception, but to improve the training of the model. However, they found that although the model was overall considering similar facial features as human annotators (e.g. mouth, eyebrows), it was not using the most characteristic features.

Del Castillo et al. [12] presented a FER system and applied LIME and CEM [15] to explain the images. Their conclusion, based on observation, was that LIME was more intuitive than CEM probably due to the complexity of the images.

Manresa-Yee et al. [40, 41] applied LIME to analyse how gender affected the important regions for the model to classify an image into an expression. Their aim was to improve FER systems by understanding the rationale of the model and identifying the source of any inequality. Their results showed that there exist common regions in some expressions both for females and males with different intensities (e.g. happiness); however, there are other expressions like disgust, where important face regions differ.

Considering the pain emotion, Prajod et al. [48] used LRP saliency maps to visually compare and understand the most influential regions for the classification of emotions and pain, related to Action Units (AUs). They used the saliency maps to investigate concepts that might have been forgotten in their implementations but did not evaluate them with humans. Weitz et al. [64] applied LRP and LIME methods to investigate a CNN trained to distinguish facial expressions of pain, happiness, and disgust. The XAI techniques were used to explain how the model distinguished facial expressions of pain from facial expressions of emotions such as happiness and disgust and found that the CNN considered both the face and background of the image. Sabater-Gárriz [55] also used LIME to understand important regions of people with cerebral palsy, in this case the recognizer selected areas within the face region.

The most similar work to the one presented is the one by Heimerl et al. [27], which included XAI techniques in their emotional behaviour annotation tool to aid non-expert users with automatic annotation of four out of Ekman's six basic emotions, leveraging confidence values and visual explanations generated by LIME. They conducted a study with four conditions (no XAI information, confidence values, LIME visualizations and confidence values and LIME visualization) to analyse the task-performance, computer self-efficacy, cognitive workload, and subjective trust of non-expert users towards the annotation tool. We note that concerning the level of explanation, this work just evaluated local explanations. Regarding these visual explanations, users had to mark the regions which they thought had been important for the system to classify a face into a specific expression. Results showed that: (1) users applied their own mental model on how the system works when no information on the internal working is presented, (2) XAI information was considered comprehensible and helpful, but although the LIME visualizations were helpful to create a correct mental model, they were not sufficient to provide enough transparency about a given system.

3.2 Facial Expression Recognizer

We employed the VGG19 network [58] to identify the six fundamental facial expressions as defined by Ekman [19]: anger, disgust, fear, happiness, sadness, and surprise. To leverage shared visual features across computer vision tasks and expedite training, the model was initialized with pre-trained weights from the ImageNet dataset [14].

The training dataset was built by merging five smaller datasets: Extended Cohn-Kanade (CK+) [38], BU-4DFE [66], JAFFE [39], WSEFEP [47], and FEGA [49]. Although all datasets consist of acted expressions, the inclusion of different sources ensures substantial variability in user characteristics (e.g. age, gender, and ethnicity) and photographic conditions (e.g. lighting, perspective, distance). The CK+ dataset consists of 593 sequences collected from 123 subjects, each sequence annotated with one of the described six basic facial expressions, plus the "contempt" expression, which was left unused. The BU4DFE dataset comprises 606 sequences from 101 subjects, each contributing six sequences one for each basic facial expression. Similarly, the JAFFE and WSEFEP datasets include a neutral class in addition to these six facial expressions. The JAFFE dataset contains 213 images captured from 10 female Japanese actresses, while the WSEFEP dataset consists of 210 images from 30 individuals. Notably, the FEGA dataset features multi-label annotations, encompassing facial expression, gender, and age, with 51 subjects performing the same seven facial expressions as JAFFE and WSEFEP, with eight repetitions for each expression.

Prior to using any images from these datasets, normalization and augmentation procedures were implemented following Ramis et al. approach [49]. Normalization involved face detection, alignment, and cropping, which aimed to zoom, translate, and rotate the face to approximately align the eyes in a consistent location across all images, thereby facilitating the classification task. Augmentation techniques, on the other hand, encompassed variations in lighting and small affine transformations, aimed at enhancing the model's robustness to minor changes in the images.

We employed K-cross validation with $k = 5$ to more accurately estimate the model's performance, independent of the dataset partition used for training and testing. This approach yielded an average accuracy of 83%.

3.3 Explanation Methods

Two types of explanations were provided to users, attending to different levels of generalization: local and global. The primary aim of presenting explanations to end-users was to enhance their comprehension of the system, thereby increasing their trust and confidence.

The research team discussed various types of explanations (e.g. showing the global accuracy of the automated system) and paper prototyped the explanations to explore different designs.

Local Explanations

We employed the Local Interpretable Model-Agnostic Explanations (LIME) technique [51] to compute local explanations. As the name suggests, LIME explanations are model-agnostic, meaning they are independent of the model. They operate by observing how predictions change when modifying the input (in our case, images) and leveraging this information to construct a simpler surrogate model that assigns relevance to each input feature (image region). To enhance the interpretability of the explanations presented to users, negative relevance was discarded, retaining only positive relevance. Additionally, histogram stretching was applied. The explanations were visualized in green, with greener regions indicating higher importance, and superimposed over the original image using alpha compositing. Figure 1 provides two examples of local explanations for each of the six facial expressions.

Global Explanations

A global explanation was generated for each facial expression by extrapolating from the local LIME explanations, following the methodology outlined in [41]. This approach involves translating the local explanations to a normalized space (see Fig. 2) to ensure translation, rotation, and scale invariance in the global explanations. To achieve this, we identified 68 facial landmarks in each image and transformed the local explanations to align these landmarks to a fixed normalized location. This normalization process was repeated for 100 images randomly sampled from the test subset for each cross-validation fold and per expression. Subsequently, the normalized explanations were averaged using the arithmetic mean, producing global explanations represented as heatmaps. Hotter regions (in red) indicate higher relevance to the classification task in these heatmaps, while colder regions (in blue) signify lower relevance. Notably, unlike previous studies [51, 64], our model predominantly

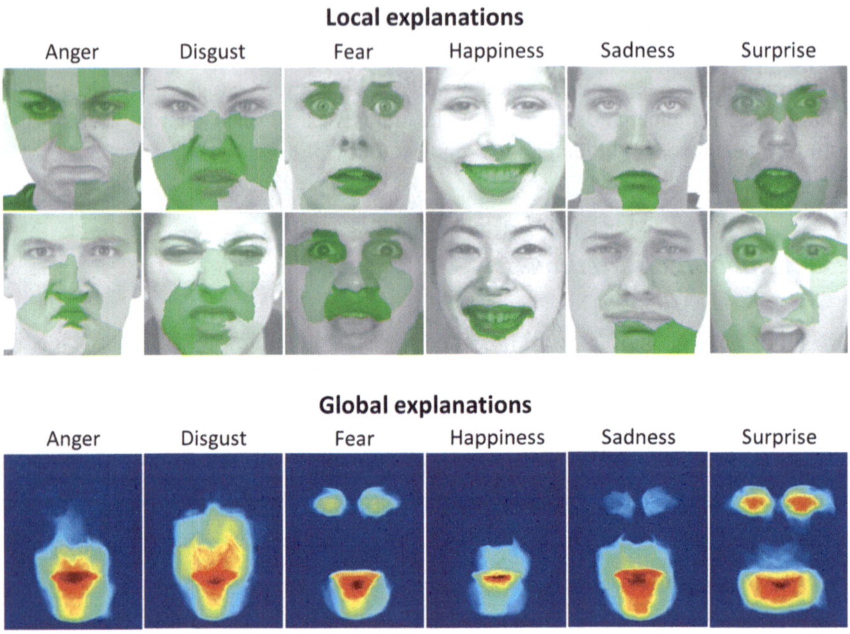

Fig. 1 Two examples of local explanations based on the XAI technique LIME (top), and the computed global explanation for each facial expression (bottom)

focuses on facial regions rather than the image background, enhancing trust in the system. Figure 1 illustrates the resulting heatmaps, explaining each facial expression.

Fig. 2 Normalized location of the facial landmarks

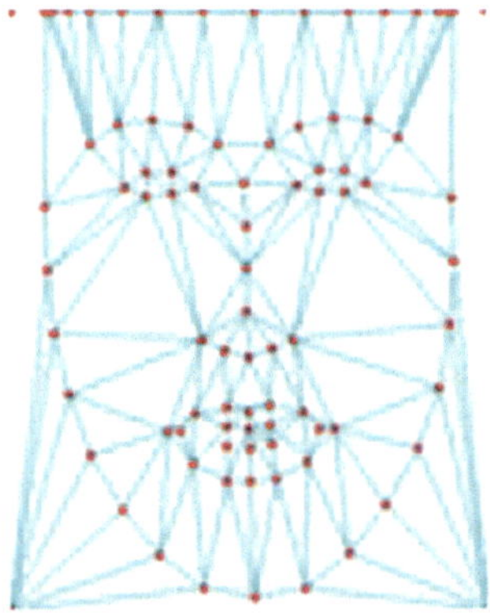

3.4 User Study

To evaluate and understand how people interact with the system, we conduct a user study.

Study design

To investigate the impact of including or excluding local and global explanations on users' trust and understanding of the FER system, we conducted a user study using a between-groups design. Three distinct groups were formed: a baseline condition group, a local explanation group, and a local/global explanation group. Users in the baseline condition group were provided only with the classified image alongside the automatic label (refer to Fig. 3a). In addition to the classified image and automatic label, users in the local explanation group were presented with LIME explanations (refer to Fig. 3b). Lastly, users in the local/global explanation group were provided with both local and global explanations (refer to Fig. 3c). Importantly, we refrained from disclosing the accuracy metric to users across all conditions to prevent potential biases in their responses.

Participants

A total of 109 participants were recruited for the experiment from the university and diverse social networks. On average, the participants were 37.1 years old, with a standard deviation of 13.13. Among them, 43 self-identified as female, 65 as male, and one as another gender. Only 30 participants self-rated themselves with machine learning knowledge, and therefore this data was not treated as an independent variable. Recruitment did not impose any specific requirements related to experience in facial expression annotation, machine learning, or XAI, and participants were not offered compensation for their participation. No special criteria were used in the assignment of users. Table 1 provides an overview of the distribution of participants across different experimental conditions. Although gender and machine learning knowledge was gathered, no statistical analysis with these variables was performed.

A limitation of the study is the assumption that all participants possess the ability to recognize facial expressions. This assumption may not hold for individuals with conditions like autism spectrum disorder, which can impair facial recognition abilities.

Further, none of the participants is associated with the development of the facial expression recognition system.

Apparatus

Utilizing the facial expression recognizer described in Sect. 3.2, we applied automatic annotation to each image in the test set. Subsequently, a subset of ten images per facial expression (60 images in total) was selected, of which 80% received correct automatic labels from the system, corresponding to its accuracy. Table 2 presents the distribution of images across different facial expressions, as per both ground truth and automatic annotation.

(a) Baseline: no explanation.

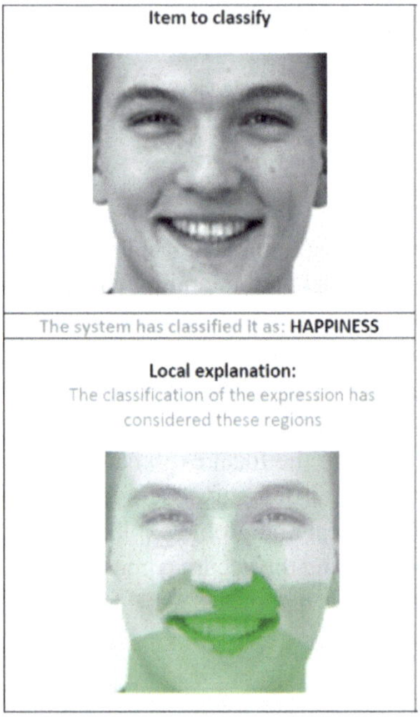

(b) Second condition: local explanation.

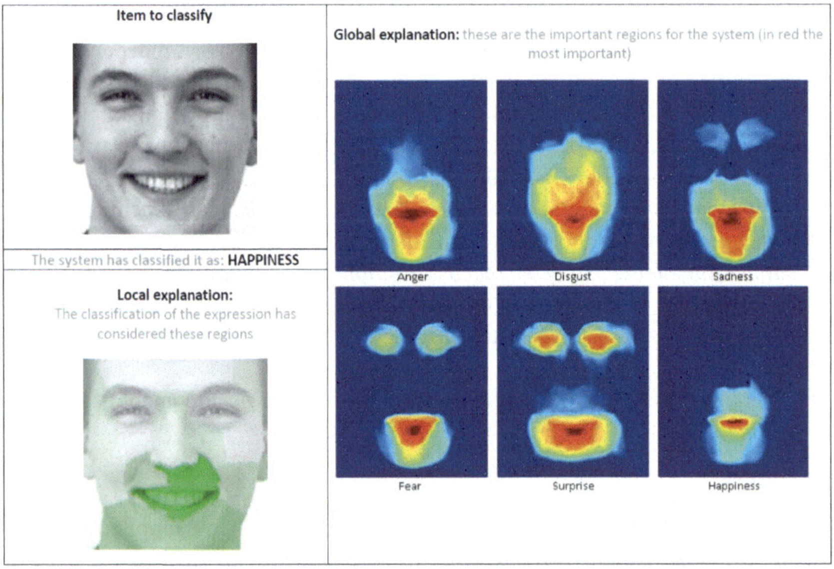

(c) Third condition: local and global explanation.

Fig. 3 Experimental conditions

Table 1 Number of participants and average age per condition

	No explanation	Local explanation	Local and global explanation
Sample	49	30	30
Avg. age	39.8	36	34.3

Table 2 Number of images corresponding to each facial expression based on the ground truth and the automatic labelling by the system. The automatic labelling misclassifies 6 images

Expression	Ground truth	Automatic label
Sadness	12	10
Happiness	8	10
Surprise	9	10
Anger	10	10
Fear	11	10
Disgust	10	10

Subsequently, the local and global explanation techniques outlined in Sect. 3.3 were employed to generate local explanations for the sample of 60 images and to derive global explanations based on the complete set of local explanations, respectively.

Three Google Forms were created, each corresponding to one of the three groups outlined previously: no explanations (baseline), local explanations, and local/global explanations. All three forms adhered to a consistent three-section format: (1) socio-demographic data, (2) facial expression recognition, and (3) final questionnaire. Each form included details about the study's objectives, descriptions of the explanations provided, and a disclaimer that the reasoning of the AI system might not align with human perception (in the local and local/global questionnaires). The questionnaires were self-contained; therefore, all the instructions were included. All questionnaires included the next common information "We have designed an intelligent system that helps us classify images by identifying 6 facial expressions: anger, surprise, fear, disgust, happiness, and sadness. Our objective with this study is to know your perception of the functioning of the system. We are presenting 60 images and the result of the automatic classification. You will also be asked to classify the image. Finally, you will have to answer a questionnaire about your perception of the system".

In the socio-demographic data section, participants were asked to provide information about their gender, age and machine learning knowledge. The facial expression recognition section presented a sample of 60 images (common to all questionnaires), with no explanation, local explanations, or local/global explanations, depending on the user group. The images of facial expressions were presented in a random order to prevent any priming effect, ensuring unbiased responses. Although automatic annotations were provided, users were still asked to classify the images based on their own perception. Participants may be influenced by the information given; however, this approach aimed to gain insights into users' questionnaire responses and to assess human accuracy in the facial expression recognition task, relative to the system.

The questionnaire section (see Table 3) provided users with the opportunity to share their perceptions of the system and their confidence in it. It included questions adapted from the trust and predictability categories outlined in the studies by Eiband et al. [18] and Corritore et al. [13]. Additionally, three questions regarding the utility of the system and the explanations were included, along with a final open-ended question prompting users to suggest improvements for better understanding the system's automatic labels. Questions Q1 to Q10 were rated on a 5-point Likert scale (from 1 = strongly disagree to 5 = strongly agree). To ensure clarity and relevance, questions related to explanations were omitted from the baseline condition form, as it did not include any explanations. Similarly, the last two questions pertaining to global explanations were excluded from the form for the second condition, which only included local explanations.

Data Analysis

We examine the responses from three different groups of individuals to questions Q3 to Q8, each of which can be answered using a numerical scale from 1 to 5. The aim is to determine if there are statistically significant differences in the responses among the three groups. ANOVA, or Analysis of Variance, is a suitable statistical test for this purpose because it is designed to compare the means of three or more independent groups under the assumption of normality and homoscedasticity. In our model we have assumed normality and homoscedasticity due to the discretization of responses.

ANOVA, in this context, allows us to efficiently handle the factorial design of our study, in which responses to several questions across different groups are collected. This method is particularly useful as it can reveal not only the main effects of the group on the response scores but also potential interactions between the groups and the specific questions asked. If significant differences or interactions are found, further post-hoc tests can be conducted to explore these differences in greater detail. Other tests, such as Chi-Square, were consistent with the ANOVA test, with even higher p-values. However, for simplicity, we have only included the ANOVA test results in this document for its high sensitivity.

Procedure

Participants were not subjected to any time limit or location constraints, allowing them to complete the form at their convenience and on their preferred device, such as a mobile phone or computer. They were encouraged to take their time to carefully observe the images and any accompanying explanations before responding to the questions. The form was designed to be self-contained, providing clear instructions and a description of the study's objectives. Additionally, participants had the flexibility to modify their responses before final submission.

Table 3 Questionnaire

ID	Question	Type of answer	Form		
			No	Local	Local/global
Q1	The scope and content of the explanations on the functioning of the system are adequate	Likert		✓	✓
Q2	The operation of the system has become more understandable to me thanks to the explanations offered	Likert		✓	✓
Q3	I have the feeling that I have understood how the system processes the data and returns the result	Likert	✓	✓	✓
Q4	It is easy for me to predict the results of the system, even if they do not match my perception of the expression	Likert	✓	✓	✓
Q5	The results obtained by the system are what I expected	Likert	✓	✓	✓
Q6	I think the system is trustworthy	Likert	✓	✓	✓
Q7	I trust the system and its result	Likert	✓	✓	✓
Q8	I believe the system could help me classify facial expressions automatically	Likert	✓	✓	✓
Q9	The visual explanation of the particular areas of the image important for the system has helped me to better understand how the system works	Likert		✓	✓
Q10	The visual explanation of the areas of the image together with the explanation at a global level important for the system has helped me to better understand the functioning of the system	Likert			✓
Q11	From the visual explanations, which is the most informative option to help you better understand the system functioning? Options: local explanation, global explanation, local + global explanations, the visual explanations were of no use	Closed			✓
Q12	Comment, if there are, which aspects have helped you understand how the system works	Open	✓	✓	✓

4 Results

In this section, we explore in depth the participants' answers to the forms.

4.1 Accuracy of the Participants' Answers

With 109 participants in the experiment, each labelling ten images for each of the six facial expressions, we gathered a total of 6540 responses. These responses were used to compute two accuracies: one using the ground truth labels and another using the automatic labels provided by the facial recognition system as the ground truth. This approach allowed us to compare the participants' performance in facial recognition with that of the system, as well as to examine the similarity between their responses and the system's. Results revealed a coincidence between human and system classifications of over 75% in four out of six facial expressions (refer to Table 4), with happiness and surprise achieving the highest agreement, and disgust and fear exhibiting the lowest. Existing literature has shown that negative emotions, such as anger and disgust, can be easily confused [57].

The third accuracy displayed in Table 4 represents the accuracy of the trained VGG19 model. As observed, the system's performance exceeded that of the participants on average, achieving higher accuracy in all classes except for "happiness", where the participants scored 3% higher. However, for "fear" and "disgust", the participants' scores lagged significantly behind the system's, with a difference of 8.8% and 12.6%, respectively. These results highlight the challenging nature of the task and demonstrate the notable performance of the automatic system.

Table 4 Per-class accuracy (different expressions by rows) of the participants on the facial expression recognition task (2nd column), their accuracy when using system's labels as ground truth (3rd column), and accuracy of the system on the same task (4th column)

Expression	Participants (GT, %)	Participants (system, %)	System (GT, %)
Sadness	75.5	76.0	77.9
Happiness	96.6	82.5	93.6
Surprise	88.6	86.9	91.6
Anger	78.4	78.3	80.3
Fear	59.5	60.9	68.3
Disgust	63.4	69.9	76.0

Ground truth are the human annotated labels. System's labels are the response of the system to the recognition task

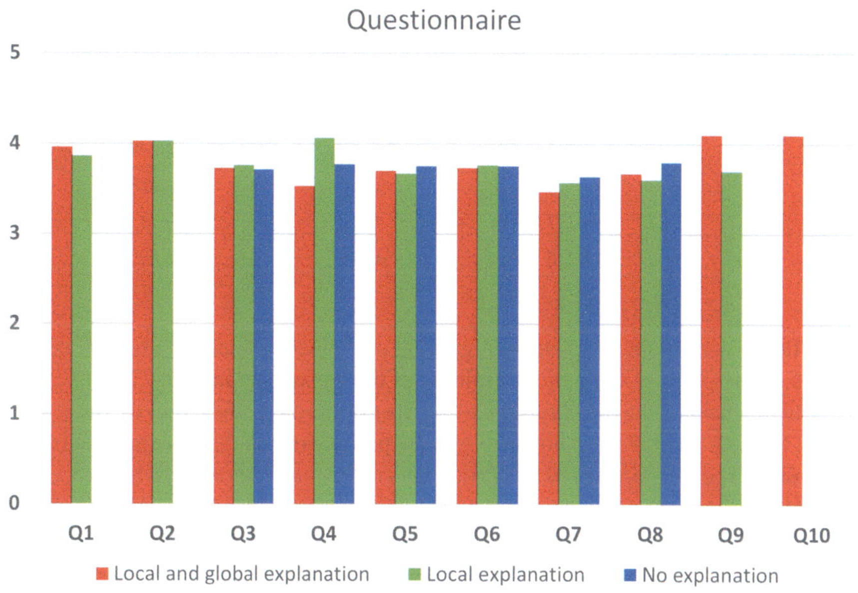

Fig. 4 Mean of the answers to the questionnaire for the three conditions

4.2 *Trust and Understanding by User Groups*

Figure 4 shows the average values of the participants' responses to the questionnaire. The questions can be categorized into three groups: understanding the rationale behind the automatic facial expression recognizer (first three questions) [18], trust in the system and predictability [13] (questions four to seven), and participants' perception of the usefulness of the system and its explanations (last three questions).

We conducted a hypothesis test to examine significant differences between groups of participants. Specifically, we applied an ANOVA test on questions answered by all participants (i.e. questions three to eight), assuming the normal distribution of the groups and homoscedasticity. Results indicate no significant differences between groups of participants, suggesting that the presence or absence of explanations (local or global) does not impact participants' opinions of the system. Table 5 shows p-value for each test. The question with the highest likelihood of rejection is the fourth one ($F2,108 = 2.583$, $p > 0.05$).

Despite this, the results indicate that participants value the visual explanations when presented, even though the absence of explanations does not significantly impact their perceptions of predictability and understanding of the system. Surprisingly, participants demonstrated similar levels of trust towards the system (Q7), expectations regarding the facial expression recognizer's results (Q5), and perception of the system's usefulness in automatically classifying facial expressions (Q8), independently of the presence and type of explanations. However, overall, the results

Table 5 Statistical analyses for questions Q3 to Q8

Question	Statistic *F*	*p*-value
Q3	0.0213	0.9790
Q4	2.583	0.0803
Q5	0.129	0.8793
Q6	0.015	0.9853
Q7	0.339	0.7134
Q8	0.383	0.6826

for all three user groups are positive regarding participants' understanding and trust, predictability of the system, and usefulness of the visual explanations.

Participants rated the questions on a scale from 1 (strongly disagree) to 5 (strongly agree). Q1, Q2, and Q9 were not answered by participants in the baseline condition. Question 10 was only answered by participants in the third condition, which received both local and global explanations detailed explanations. One participant from the baseline condition noted that "analysing 60 images and observing a similar result of the system with [her] perception was an aspect that helped building trust". Additionally, participants' lack of understanding of the inner workings of AI [46], combined with the common belief that machines are more accurate and reliable decision-makers than humans [32], may partially account for the results, particularly when no explanations are provided. However, this behaviour can be risky, as the system might be placing undue emphasis on non-facial regions, which should not be relied upon, as observed in previous studies [51, 64]. Fortunately, this was not the case with the trained VGG19 network, which primarily focused on facial regions such as the mouth and the eyes, demonstrating consistent and reasonable local and global explanations. This reinforces the trust in its correct functioning.

Among participants in the baseline condition, 44.9% did not reflect on the behaviour of the system, while the remainder elaborated various mental models to explain its rationale. Some speculated: "I think the system looks at patterns of the mouth or eyes expressions", "The system responds according to the contracted facial features", "I think the system analyses a set of features, such as visible teeth".

Participants in the second group, who were provided with local explanations, remarked on the usefulness of highlighting significant facial regions. Some expressed curiosity about the regions deemed important by the system: "I found it curious to notice that the system seems to give a lot of weight to the position of the mouth, ignoring some specific eye-mouth combinations specifically associated with disgust or fear, expressions that are many times more subtle than the others". Another noted, "The system mainly uses the mouth as a reference and then the eyes and eyebrows, it seems that the rest of the face does not have much importance".

Finally, participants in the third group, who were presented with both local and global explanations, valued the inclusion of both types, particularly the global ones.

One participant stated, "The heatmaps have been the most useful part of the explanation". They also highlighted the additional insights provided by the global explanations: "The global explanation allows me to better understand the expressions annotated by the system based on the areas marked on the image. In the case of the local explanation, although it helps, it is easy for the overlapping of the important regions to confuse the understanding of the information provided.", "After seeing the analysis that the system has made of the 60 images, and with the help of the explanations, especially the local ones, it is easy to see which areas are analysed most frequently. Based on that, it is possible to see when we will not have the same result according to the face areas that have been analysed in greater depth, being able to predict errors in cases of negative emotions in which the eyes and eyebrows are not too analysed". Among these participants, 83.3% agreed that the combination of local and global explanations was the most informative. A minority, comprising 10%, considered local explanations to be the most informative, while 3.3% expressed a preference for global explanations. Finally, 3.3% of participants stated that visual explanations did not aid in understanding the functioning of the facial expression recognizer at all.

5 Conclusions

Human-centred explainable artificial intelligence is gaining importance in developing and deploying AI systems, particularly as state-of-the-art algorithms become increasingly complex. By placing humans at the core of XAI design, it highlights the necessity of creating AI systems that are not only transparent but also answer to explanation needs and are aligned with human cognitive processes. Benefits such as transferability, causality understanding, or trustworthiness will directly impact on all stakeholders.

Open research questions still remain comprising the integration of a human perspective in new XAI developments, in the selection of XAI techniques and assessing empirically the effectiveness, benefits and pitfalls of the existent ones. Addressing these queries is vital for advancing the field and ensuring that XAI solutions are practical and beneficial to users.

To contribute to this domain, particularly to the lack of user studies aimed at assessing XAI, we present a case study focused on the automated facial expression recognition task and the evaluation of characteristics such as trustworthiness and understandability based on the local–global dimension.

The case study analyses if diverse visual explanations invoked a different level of trust and understanding applied to a facial expression recognition system. We conducted a between-groups user study evaluating a local explanation, a local explanation combined with a global one and a no explanation. Results showed similar results regarding understandability, predictability, trust and perceived usefulness, probably due to the high coincidence of the humans' annotations with the systems annotations. Consequently, although explanations were appreciated to observe a reasonable functioning of the AI, explanations were not so important when humans perceived a high performance of the facial expression recognizer and had a good experience with it. However, we stress the need of offering explanations to increase transparency and make AI systems more accountable to users and stakeholders, to build proper mental models on how the system works, and to achieve more trustworthy and effective AI systems.

Future work includes assessing other explanation dimensions in the FER task to deliver the best explanations to the user.

Acknowledgements This work has been supported by Project PID2023-149079OB-I00 (EXPLAINME) funded by MICIU/AEI/10.13039/501100011033/ and FEDER, EU; Project PID2019-104829RA-I00 (EXPLAINING) funded by MCIN/AEI/10.13039/501100011033 and Project PID2022-136779OB-C32 (PLEISAR) funded by MICIU/AEI/10.13039/501100011033/ and FEDER, EU.

In addition, F.X. Gaya-Morey also acknowledges the importance of the FPU scholarship from the Ministry of European Funds, University and Culture of the Government of the Balearic Islands.

This work is an extension of the conference work C. Manresa-Yee, S. Ramis, F. X. Gaya-Morey, and J.M. Buades. 2024. Impact of Explanations for Trustworthy and Transparent Artificial Intelligence. In Proc. of the XXIII International Conference on Human Computer Interaction (Interaccion'23). ACM, New York, NY, USA, Article 14, 1–8. https://doi.org/10.1145/3612783.3612798.

References

1. Adadi A, Berrada M (2018) Peeking inside the black-box: a survey on Explainable Artificial Intelligence (XAI). IEEE Access 6:52138–52160
2. Adebayo J, Gilmer J, Muelly M, Goodfellow I, Hardt M, Kim B (2018) Sanity checks for saliency maps. In: Proceedings of the 32nd international conference on neural information processing systems. Curran Associates Inc., Red Hook, NY, USA, pp 9525–9536
3. Ali S, Abuhmed T, El-Sappagh S, Muhammad K, Alonso-Moral JM, Confalonieri R, Guidotti R, Del Ser J, Díaz-Rodríguez N, Herrera F (2023) Explainable Artificial Intelligence (XAI): what we know and what is left to attain Trustworthy Artificial Intelligence. Inf Fusion 99:101805. https://doi.org/10.1016/j.inffus.2023.101805
4. Alicioglu G, Sun B (2022) A survey of visual analytics for Explainable Artificial Intelligence methods. Comput Graph 102:502–520. https://doi.org/10.1016/j.cag.2021.09.002
5. Arya V, Bellamy RKE, Chen P-Y, Dhurandhar A, Hind M, Hoffman SC, Houde S, Liao QV, Luss R, Mojsilović A, Mourad S, Pedemonte P, Raghavendra R, Richards JT, Sattigeri P, Shanmugam K, Singh M, Varshney KR, Wei D, Zhang Y (2020) AI Explainability 360: an extensible toolkit for understanding data and machine learning models. J Mach Learn Res 21:1–6
6. Bach S, Binder A, Montavon G, Klauschen F, Müller K-R, Samek W (2015) On pixel-wise explanations for non-linear classifier decisions by layer-wise relevance propagation. PLoS ONE 10:1–46. https://doi.org/10.1371/journal.pone.0130140
7. Bansal G, Wu T, Zhou J, Fok R, Nushi B, Kamar E, Ribeiro MT, Weld D (2021) Does the whole exceed its parts? The effect of AI explanations on complementary team performance. In: Proceedings of the 2021 CHI conference on human factors in computing systems. Association for Computing Machinery, New York, NY, USA

8. Barda AJ, Horvat CM, Hochheiser H (2020) A qualitative research framework for the design of user-centered displays of explanations for machine learning model predictions in healthcare. BMC Med Inform Decision Mak 20. https://doi.org/10.1186/s12911-020-01276-x
9. Barredo Arrieta A, Díaz-Rodríguez N, Del Ser J, Bennetot A, Tabik S, Barbado A, Garcia S, Gil-Lopez S, Molina D, Benjamins R, Chatila R, Herrera F (2020) Explainable Explainable Artificial Intelligence (XAI): concepts, taxonomies, opportunities and challenges toward responsible AI. Inf Fusion 58:82–115. https://doi.org/10.1016/j.inffus.2019.12.012
10. Burkart N, Huber MF (2021) A survey on the explainability of supervised machine learning. J Artif Int Res 70:245–317. https://doi.org/10.1613/jair.1.12228
11. Cañas JJ (2022) De la interacción con máquinas a la colaboración con agentes inteligentes. Interacción Revista digital de AIPO 3:8–20
12. Del Castillo Torres G, Roig-Maimó MF, Mascaró-Oliver M, Amengual-Alcover E, Mas-Sansó R (2022) Understanding how CNNs recognize facial expressions: a case study with LIME and CEM. Sensors (Basel, Switzerland) 23. https://doi.org/10.3390/s23010131
13. Corritore CL, Marble RP, Wiedenbeck S, Kracher B, Chandran A (2005) Measuring online trust of websites: credibility, perceived ease of use, and risk. In: Americas conference on information systems
14. Deng J, Dong W, Socher R, Li L-J, Li K, Fei-Fei L (2009) Imagenet: a large-scale hierarchical image database. In: 2009 IEEE conference on computer vision and pattern recognition. pp 248–255
15. Dhurandhar A, Chen P-Y, Luss R, Tu C-C, Ting P, Shanmugam K, Das P (2018) Explanations based on the missing: towards contrastive explanations with pertinent negatives. In: Proceedings of the 32nd international conference on neural information processing systems. Curran Associates Inc., Red Hook, NY, USA, pp 590–601
16. Díaz-Rodríguez N, Pisoni G (2020) Accessible cultural heritage through explainable artificial intelligence. In: UMAP 2020 adjunct—adjunct publication of the 28th ACM conference on user modeling, adaptation and personalization. Association for Computing Machinery, Inc, pp 317–324
17. Ehsan U, Wintersberger P, Watkins EA, Manger C, Ramos G, Weisz JD, Daumé Iii H, Riener A, Riedl MO (2023) Human-centered explainable AI (HCXAI): coming of age. In: Extended abstracts of the 2023 CHI conference on human factors in computing systems. Association for Computing Machinery, New York, NY, USA
18. Eiband M, Buschek D, Kremer A, Hussmann H (2019) The impact of placebic explanations on trust in intelligent systems. In: Conference on human factors in computing systems—proceedings. Association for Computing Machinery
19. Ekman P (1992) An argument for basic emotions. Cogn Emot 6:169–200. https://doi.org/10.1080/02699939208411068
20. European Commission (2019) High-level expert group on AI. Ethics guidelines for trustworthy AI
21. Floridi L, Cowls J, Beltrametti M, Chatila R, Chazerand P, Dignum V, Luetge C, Madelin R, Pagallo U, Rossi F, Schafer B, Valcke P, Vayena E (2018) AI4People—an ethical framework for a good AI society: opportunities, risks, principles, and recommendations. Mind Mach 28:689–707. https://doi.org/10.1007/s11023-018-9482-5
22. Garibay OO, Winslow B, Andolina S, Antona M, Bodenschatz A, Coursaris C, Falco G, Fiore SM, Garibay I, Grieman K, Havens JC, Jirotka M, Kacorri H, Karwowski W, Kider J, Konstan J, Koon S, Lopez-Gonzalez M, Maifeld-Carucci I, McGregor S, Salvendy G, Shneiderman B, Stephanidis C, Strobel C, Ten HC, Xu W (2023) Six human-centered artificial intelligence grand challenges. Int J Hum-Comput Interact 39:391–437. https://doi.org/10.1080/10447318.2022.2153320
23. Guidotti R, Monreale A, Ruggieri S, Turini F, Giannotti F, Pedreschi D (2018) A survey of methods for explaining black box models. ACM Comput Surv 51. https://doi.org/10.1145/3236009
24. Gunning D, Aha DW (2019) DARPA's explainable artificial intelligence (XAI) program. AI Mag 40:44–58. https://doi.org/10.1609/aimag.v40i2.2850

25. Gunning D, Vorm E, Wang JY, Turek M (2021) DARPA's explainable AI (XAI) program: a retrospective. Appl AI Lett 2:e61. https://doi.org/10.1002/ail2.61
26. Gurumoorthy K, Dhurandhar A, Cecchi G, Aggarwal C (2019) Efficient data representation by selecting prototypes with importance weights, pp 260–269
27. Heimerl A, Weitz K, Baur T, Andre E (2020) Unraveling ML models of emotion with NOVA: multi-level explainable AI for non-experts. IEEE Trans Affect Comput 1:1–13. https://doi.org/10.1109/TAFFC.2020.3043603
28. Hoffman RR, Mueller ST, Klein G, Litman J (2018) Metrics for explainable AI: challenges and prospects. arXiv:1812.0
29. Hudlicka E (2003) To feel or not to feel: the role of affect in human–computer interaction. Int J Hum Comput Stud 59:1–32. https://doi.org/10.1016/S1071-5819(03)00047-8
30. Hupont I, Tolan S, Gunes H, Gómez E (2022) The landscape of facial processing applications in the context of the European AI Act and the development of trustworthy systems. Sci Rep 12:10688. https://doi.org/10.1038/s41598-022-14981-6
31. Hyesun Choung PD, Ross A (2023) Trust in AI and its role in the acceptance of AI technologies. Int J Hum-Comput Interact 39:1727–1739. https://doi.org/10.1080/10447318.2022.2050543
32. Kapania S, Siy O, Clapper G, SP AM, Sambasivan N (2022) "Because AI is 100% Right and Safe": user attitudes and sources of AI authority in India. In: Proceedings of the 2022 CHI conference on human factors in computing systems. Association for Computing Machinery, New York, NY, USA
33. Kaplan S, Uusitalo H, Lensu L (2024) A unified and practical user-centric framework for explainable artificial intelligence. Knowl-Based Syst 283:111107. https://doi.org/10.1016/j.knosys.2023.111107
34. Kumar A, Sattigeri P, Balakrishnan A (2017) Variational inference of disentangled latent concepts from unlabeled observations. arXiv:1711.0
35. Liao Q V, Gruen D, Miller S (2020) Questioning the AI: informing design practices for explainable AI user experiences. In: Conference on human factors in computing systems—proceedings. Association for Computing Machinery
36. Liao QV, Research M, Kush C, Varshney R, Varshney KR (2021) Human-centered explainable AI (XAI): from algorithms to user experiences. arXiv:2110.1
37. Lim BY, Yang Q, Abdul A, Wang D (2019) Why these explanations? Selecting intelligibility types for explanation goals. In: Trattner C. Parra D. RN (ed) CEUR workshop proceedings. CEUR-WS
38. Lucey P, Cohn JF, Kanade T, Saragih J, Ambadar Z, Matthews I (2010) The Extended Cohn-Kanade Dataset (CK+): a complete dataset for action unit and emotion-specified expression. In: 2010 IEEE Computer Society conference on computer vision and pattern recognition—workshops, pp 94–101
39. Lyons M, Kamachi M, Gyoba J (1998) The Japanese Female Facial Expression (JAFFE) Dataset
40. Manresa-Yee C, Ramis S (2021) Assessing gender bias in predictive algorithms using explainable AI. In: Proceedings of the XXI international conference on human computer interaction. Association for Computing Machinery, New York, NY, USA
41. Manresa-Yee C, Ramis S, Buades JM (in press) Analysis of gender differences in facial expression recognition based on deep learning using explainable artificial intelligence. Int J Interact Multimed Artif Intell. https://doi.org/10.9781/ijimai.2023.04.003
42. Mavromoustakos-Blom P, Bakkes S, Tan CT, Whiteson S, Roijers D, Valenti R, Gevers T (2014) Towards personalised gaming via facial expression recognition. In: Proceedings of the 10th AAAI conference on artificial intelligence and interactive digital entertainment, AIIDE 2014
43. Mellouk W, Handouzi W (2020) Facial emotion recognition using deep learning: review and insights. Procedia Comput Sci 175:689–694. https://doi.org/10.1016/j.procs.2020.07.101
44. Miller T (2019) Explanation in artificial intelligence: insights from the social sciences. Artif Intell 267:1–38. https://doi.org/10.1016/j.artint.2018.07.007
45. Mohseni S, Zarei N, Ragan ED (2021) A multidisciplinary survey and framework for design and evaluation of explainable AI systems. ACM Trans Interact Intell Syst 11. https://doi.org/10.1145/3387166

46. Mori I (2017) Public views of machine learning. The Royal Society
47. Olszanowski M, Pochwatko G, Kuklinski K, Scibor-Rylski M, Lewinski P, Ohme RK (2015) Warsaw set of emotional facial expression pictures: a validation study of facial display photographs. Front Psychol 5
48. Prajod P, Schiller D, Huber T, Andr'e E (2021) Do deep neural networks forget facial action units? Exploring the effects of transfer learning in health related facial expression recognition. arXiv:2104.0
49. Ramis S, Buades J, Perales FJ, Manresa-Yee C (2022) A novel approach to cross dataset studies in facial expression recognition. Multimed Tools Appl 81:39507–39544. https://doi.org/10.1007/s11042-022-13117-2
50. Rawal N, Stock-Homburg RM (2022) Facial emotion expressions in human-robot interaction: a survey. Int J Soc Robot 14:1583–1604. https://doi.org/10.1007/s12369-022-00867-0
51. Ribeiro MT, Singh S, Guestrin C (2016) "Why should I trust you?": explaining the predictions of any classifier. In: Proceedings of the 22nd ACM SIGKDD international conference on knowledge discovery and data mining. Association for Computing Machinery, New York, NY, USA, pp 1135–1144
52. Ribera M, Lapedriza A (2019) Can we do better explanations? A proposal of user-centered explainable AI. In: Trattner C. Riche N. PD (eds) CEUR workshop proceedings. CEUR-WS
53. Rong Y, Leemann T, Nguyen T, Fiedler L, Qian P, Unhelkar V, Seidel T, Kasneci G, Kasneci E (2024) Towards human-centered explainable AI: a survey of user studies for model explanations. IEEE Trans Pattern Anal Mach Intell 46:2104–2122. https://doi.org/10.1109/TPAMI.2023.3331846
54. Rousseau DM, Sitkin SB, Burt RS, Camerer C (1998) Not so different after all: a cross-discipline view of trust. Acad Manag Rev 23:393–404. https://doi.org/10.5465/amr.1998.926617
55. Sabater-Gárriz A, Gaya-Morey FX, Buades JM, Manresa-Yee C, Montoya P, Riquelme I (2024) Automated facial recognition system using deep learning for pain assessment in adults with cerebral palsy. Digit Health 10. https://doi.org/10.1177/20552076241259664
56. Sanneman L, Shah JA (2022) The situation awareness framework for explainable AI (SAFE-AI) and human factors considerations for XAI systems. Int J Hum-Comput Interact 38:1772–1788. https://doi.org/10.1080/10447318.2022.2081282
57. Schiller D, Huber T, Dietz M, André E (2020) Relevance-based data masking: a model-agnostic transfer learning approach for facial expression recognition. Front Comput Sci 2:6. https://doi.org/10.3389/fcomp.2020.00006
58. Simonyan K, Vedaldi A, Zisserman A (2014) Deep inside convolutional networks: visualising image classification models and saliency maps
59. Speith T (2022) A review of taxonomies of explainable artificial intelligence (XAI) methods. In: Proceedings of the 2022 ACM conference on fairness, accountability, and transparency. Association for Computing Machinery, New York, NY, USA, pp 2239–2250
60. Suresh H, Gomez SR, Nam KK, Satyanarayan A (2021) Beyond expertise and roles: a framework to characterize the stakeholders of interpretable machine learning and their needs. In: Proceedings of the 2021 CHI conference on human factors in computing systems. Association for Computing Machinery, New York, NY, USA
61. Swartout WR (1985) Rule-based expert systems: the mycin experiments of the stanford heuristic programming project: B.G. Buchanan and E.H. Shortliffe, (Addison-Wesley, Reading, MA, 1984); 702 pages, $40.50. Artif Intell 26:364–366. https://doi.org/10.1016/0004-3702(85)90067-0
62. Vera Liao Q, Varshney KR (2022) Human-Centered Explainable AI (XAI): From Algorithms to User Experiences. arXiv
63. Wang D, Yang Q, Abdul A, Lim BY (2019) Designing theory-driven user-centric explainable AI. In: Conference on human factors in computing systems—proceedings. Association for Computing Machinery
64. Weitz K, Hassan T, Schmid U, Garbas J-U (2019) Deep-learned faces of pain and emotions: elucidating the differences of facial expressions with the help of explainable AI methods. Tech Mess 86:404–412. https://doi.org/10.1515/teme-2019-0024

65. Wells L, Bednarz T (2021) Explainable AI and reinforcement learning—a systematic review of current approaches and trends. Front Artif Intell 4. https://doi.org/10.3389/frai.2021.550030
66. Yin L, Wei X, Sun Y, Wang J, Rosato MJ (2006) A 3D facial expression database for facial behavior research. In: 7th international conference on automatic face and gesture recognition (FGR06), pp 211–216
67. Zhu J, Liapis A, Risi S, Bidarra R, Youngblood GM (2018) Explainable AI for designers: a human-centered perspective on mixed-initiative co-creation. In: IEEE conference on computatonal intelligence and games, CIG. IEEE Computer Society

Interactive Human-in-the-Loop Topic Modeling

Laura Ham and Luis A. Leiva

Abstract Broadcasting companies produce large amounts of text and audiovisual content. Extracting meaningful insights from these sources requires efficient analysis methods, which are often only palatable to data scientists. Even in large organizations, there is a critical knowledge gap: media experts manually curate work to derive insights, which is very time consuming, while engineers can use advanced data science methods but lack the domain expertise to derive key insights from the data. We propose to bridge this knowledge gap with INTEX, a human-in-the-loop interactive topic modeling application. We designed INTEX considering non-technical media experts as the main stakeholders of the application. A user evaluation shows that INTEX enables domain experts to extract and explore topics in an intuitive and efficient manner. Our work illustrates how complex applications can be made more accessible by hiding low-level details and linking these to high-level interpretations. INTEX overcomes past challenges in topic modeling, representing the future of interactive applications in this domain.

Keywords Interactive machine learning · Human-in-the-loop · Topic modelling · Human–computer interaction · Exploratory data analysis

1 Introduction

We are entering a new era where Artificial Intelligence (AI) is incorporated to every computerized system. It is, therefore, more important than ever to understand the interplay of AI systems and humans, such that they can cooperate toward a common goal, acknowledging their weaknesses and leveraging their strengths. This can be framed as a Human–Computer Interaction (HCI) problem, i.e., instead of focusing on

L. Ham
Independent Researcher, Espoo, Finland

L. A. Leiva (✉)
Department of Computer Science, University of Luxembourg, 6, Avenue de La Fonte, 4364 Esch-Sur-Alzette, Luxembourg
e-mail: luis.leiva@uni.lu

S. Sayago et al. (eds.), *Future Perspectives on Human-Computer Interaction Research*,
https://doi.org/10.1007/978-3-031-71697-3_5

maximizing a target metric, such as classification accuracy, we should think instead about how to best support the users of the AI systems. In this regard, a human-in-the-loop approach seems one of the most promising and effective solutions, since HCI has been (and still is) an enabler of human-in-the-loop AI systems. In a nutshell, human-in-the-loop approaches put humans at the center of the AI systems, aiming at handling this aforementioned interplay between humans and systems as optimally as possible.

This book chapter discusses a real-world use case of human-in-the-loop AI, to support broadcasting companies in the production of audiovisual contents. Broadcasting media companies produce large amounts of text and audiovisual content worth of analysis. For example, the Washington Post produces about 500 stories per day [29] and Netflix has 2.2 million minutes of content, or over 50,000 titles, only in the US [31]. Tapping these sources helps to uncover hidden patterns and gain insights to support data-driven business decisions. This requires efficient analysis methods and modeling techniques for automatic theme discovery, among which topic modeling is the most popular one. In a nutshell, topic modeling infers latent structures of large document collections by automatically coding them into a smaller number of semantically meaningful categories.

A shortcoming of classic topic models is that the discovered topics can be hard to interpret [10, 17, 23]. Likewise, extracting too many or too few topics leads to either too general or too specific results [17, 33]. Interactive Topic Modeling (ITM) was introduced to solve these issues, incorporating human expertise in the modeling process [20]. ITM applications allow users to refine extracted topics by, e.g., keyword and document source. These applications are typically used by data scientists, who are experienced in Natural Language Processing (NLP). However, these NLP experts often lack domain knowledge about the data and its high-level interpretation in a business context. At the same time, domain experts in the broadcasting media, like journalists and data analysts, have this broader knowledge about the produced and consumed media content, but usually lack data science skills to develop and use complex topic models.

This knowledge gap between data scientists and domain experts is excruciating, because strategies for thinking and problem solving differ significantly [39] and also because domain experts find it hard to articulate their problems [37]. We propose to fill this knowledge gap with INTEX (INteractive Topic EXplorer), a human-in-the-loop ITM application designed according to Human-Centered Design (HCD) principles [16] in collaboration with non-technical end-users. This is a unique approach; no previous work has considered the stakeholders in designing such an interactive application for the broadcasting media. Our work illustrates how complex applications can be made more accessible by hiding low-level details and linking these to high-level interpretations.

INTEX's user interface follows five steps covering the users' mental model, which we identified in formative user studies: (1) data selection, (2) model configuration, (3) model output evaluation, (4) model refinement, and (5) exploratory data analysis. The user interface makes high-level model interactions accessible to non-technical domain experts by means of an intuitive design and exploratory visualizations, while low-level complex model details are hidden in the background. Latent theme discovery and further exploratory data analysis of media content are finally accessible to broadcasting end-users like journalists and media planners.

2 Related Work

Topic models aim to reduce the dimensionality of a set of words in a set of documents into a smaller set of interpretable and meaningful themes (most commonly known as topics). As shown in Fig. 1, documents may cover different topics whereas words can be associated with many of those topics.

Classic approaches to topic modeling include Latent Semantic Analysis (LSA) [14] and variations thereof, such as pLSA [18]. While these approaches may create compact semantic representations [45], they are not attractive for real-world use cases because the discovered topics and keywords are hard to interpret. More recently, Latent Dirichlet Allocation (LDA) was shown to discover more descriptive topics [7], however. However, LDA is suboptimal in terms of consistency and convergence [11]. Both model consistency and convergence are important from the user's point of view, as low consistency and slow model convergence lead to bad user experience. Non-negative Matrix Factorization (NMF) overcomes these aforementioned problems [11], leading to outcomes that are naturally interpretable [3, 34] in a computationally efficient way [45], so it is preferred over other topic models in practice.

NMF decomposes the document-term matrix into two matrices: one consisting of n words by k topics and other consisting of k topics by m documents. NMF is often applied in topic modeling applications not only because it leads to the naturally interpretable topics, but also because it is computationally efficient way [45]. Interestingly, NMF is deterministic so user interactions beyond changing static parameters can be easily incorporated via forms or as part of semi-supervised methods.

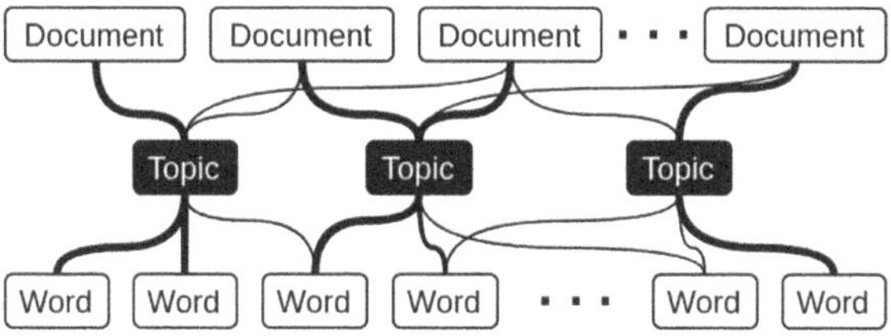

Fig. 1 Topic modeling overview. Documents are associated with one or more topics represented by multiple words. Line thickness indicates the degree to which a topic is represented in each document and word in each topic

2.1 Visualization Techniques

An intuitive representation of the extracted topics, as well as the underlying model, is desired to promote understanding, since in ITM applications the user can control modeling results by direct manipulation. Previous work presented results as word lists [9, 46], word clouds [15], bubble charts [12, 32, 38], and Sankey diagrams [40, 43]. Simple visualizations like word lists and word clouds support a quick initial understanding of topics, while more complex visualizations like Sankey diagrams take longer to understand but reveal better relationships between topics. Smith et al. [42] concluded that there is no 'best' visualization technique for every use case, although, for efficiency and simplicity, simple word lists are the best choice. Lee et al. [25] concluded that topics may be misinterpreted because of the words representing them, and recommended that topic refinement should be focused on topics with low coherence [8].

iVisClustering [24] uses LDA for clustering large document corpora. User revisions include deleting, merging, sub-clustering, and word refinements. It also includes extensive visualizations that allow the user to explore topic modeling results, but requires high cognitive effort and prior knowledge in natural language processing, which makes it less applicable to the broadcasting media.

UTOPIAN [11] uses semi-supervised NMF as topic modeling method, to incorporate user feedback in the matrix factorization process. Quantitative experiments showed that this method outperformed LDA regarding consistency and convergence time. A deterministic (high consistency) and low running time (empirical convergence) of this model are important factors in achieving high user experience. Topic clusters and their relations are visualized using node-link graphs and the t-distributed Stochastic Neighbor Embedding (t-SNE) [27] algorithm. This framework also overshoots the goal of our use case because of the complex visualizations and model refinement possibilities.

ConVisIT [19] allows users to interactively extract topics from asynchronous online conversations. Although the use case (focused on topic modeling of small texts) is different from our current setting, the rich and interactive visualization platform, which allows the user to explore and revise topics on a high level, can be considered as another key prior work in the context of our research.

Finally, ITMViz [36] allows users to incorporate revisions to the LDA model via must-link and cannot-link constraints, a unique revision system not seen in other frameworks. Although these revision possibilities are limited, they showed that constraining topic models by domain knowledge contributes to extracting more meaningful topics.

2.2 *Progress Beyond State-of-the-Art ITM*

Effective collaboration in ITM requires transparency and predictability [1, 22]. However, there is often a trade-off between the two since high transparency, where model outcomes are easy to validate, expects predictable outcomes and makes it difficult to provide users with suitable controls [44]. Therefore, ITM applications must balance user controls and truly model the data to promote trust in the application [4].

To the best of our knowledge, there is no ITM application for broadcasting media companies. Further, since domain and user expertise largely impact how a topic model is perceived and used, they should be considered in the design of any ITM application. On the one hand, machine learning experts or advanced data scientists most likely have a rough understanding of how a model works, so they can assert its flaws, like unexpected results or instability. On the other hand, domain experts without this background, who have less technical understanding and thus a different perception of the model, are more likely to become frustrated if the model is not adherent, stable, or fast.

Smith et al. [41] noted that future ITM applications should provide a history of actions and model results, support 'undo' actions, have a saving option with reminders to save, allow topic freezing, and support multi-word refinements. In a follow-up user study, Smith et al. [44] found that users dislike latency the most. A lack of adherence, whether the user's input is applied as expected, came out as the second most prevalent dislike. They conclude with four recommendations: users want to be in control, users want speed, (unexpected) model output changes should be explained, and parts of the model should be lockable. With these ideas in mind, we elaborate on the design, implementation, and subsequent evaluation of INTEX.

3 System

Following previous work and the HCD principles, a formative user study with stakeholders was conducted to gather business requirements. Primary, secondary, and tertiary stakeholders were identified; see Appendix 1. Primary users are the potential end-users of the application, in our case domain experts in the broadcasting media. Secondary users are journalists, content producers, and media planners interested in using topic modeling in their decision making processes. Finally, tertiary users are managers, system administrators, and product owners, who are not considered in our research.

Later on, participatory design methods were applied, where the users interacted with a product prototype for evaluation purposes. See Appendix 2 for more details. We performed a 'Wants and Needs' analysis: a fast brainstorming method to gather requirements from multiple users simultaneously [6]. Then, recurring one-hour sessions with focus groups were organized, using three user study techniques: Concept testing, Desirability studies, and Participatory design. The three techniques are attitudinal, mostly qualitative, and all incorporate hybrid prototype usage during data collection [35].

3.1 *Design Choices and Interactions*

INTEX's interface is designed according to the mental model of a non-technical end-user. Some screenshots are presented later in Figs. 2, 3, 4, 5, 6 and 7. The workflow of the application is summarized as follows.

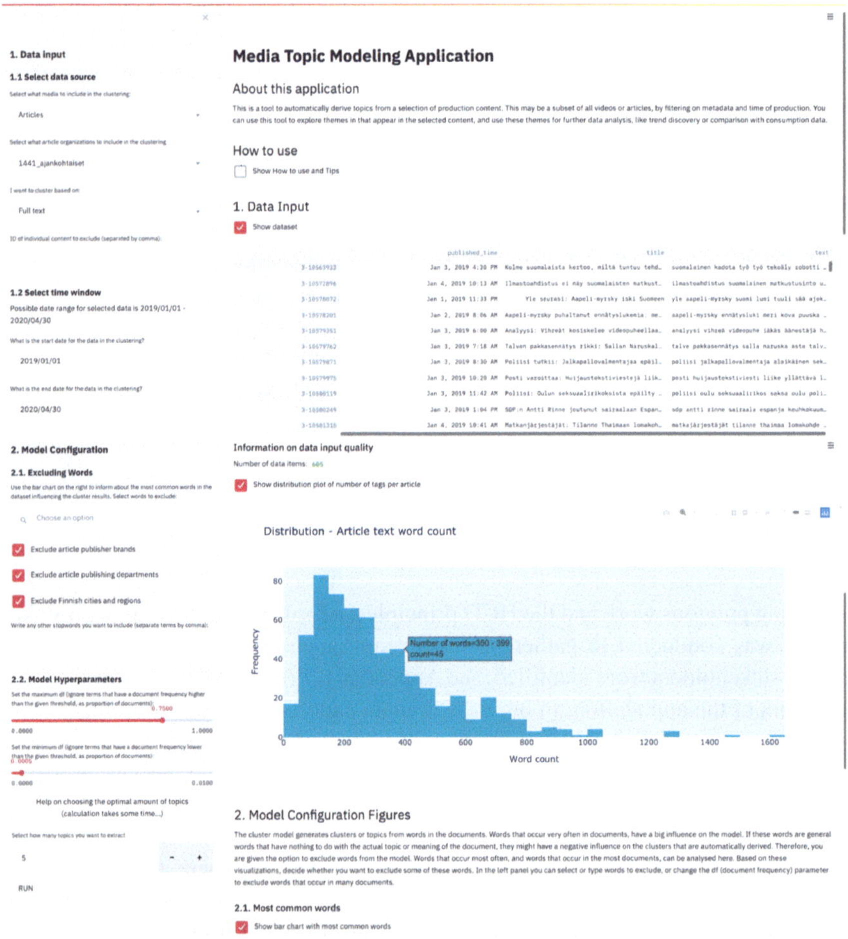

Fig. 2 Screenshot of INTEX's data input and filtering screen

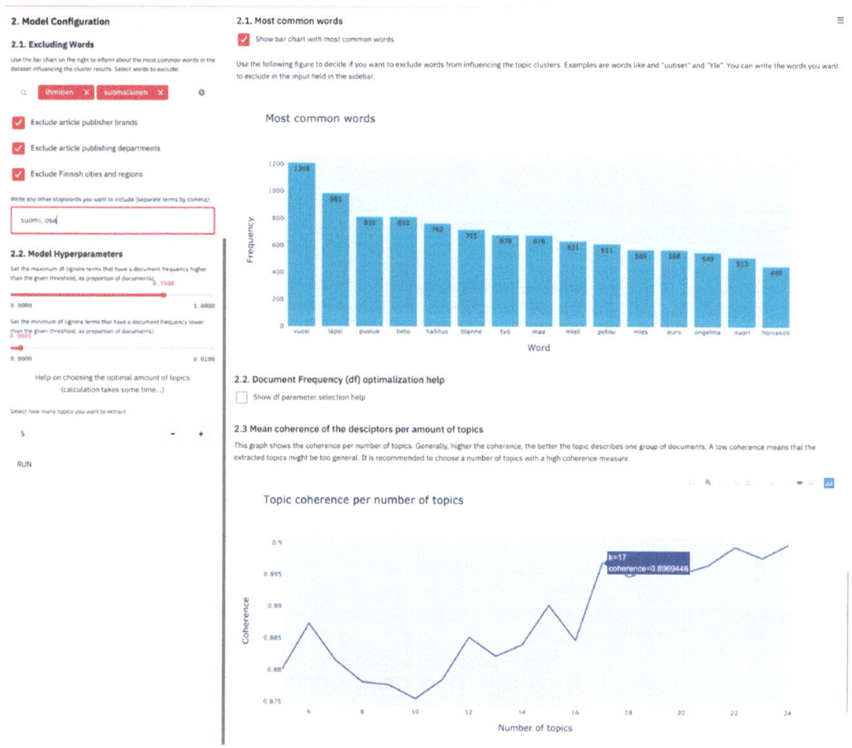

Fig. 3 Screenshot of INTEX's model configuration screen

(i) **Data input selection**. Users can select sources, filter by metadata, and choose a time window. Immediate feedback to user's input is presented either in graphical or tabular form.

(ii) **Model configuration**. The only hyperparameter in INTEX is the number of topics to extract. Since choosing the optimal number of topics beforehand can be challenging, a topic suggestion of 15 topics is provided initially. Topic coherence is computed based on the Word2Vec model [30].

(iii) **Model interpretation and assessment**. Model output is shown as topic-term and document-topic tables, to provide a quick overview of the generated topics. Users can notice what topics are reflected in the input set of documents and can see suggestions on what topics need refinement.

(iv) **Model refinement**. Iterations with focus group sessions resulted in the following set of options: merge, split, and remove keywords from a topic, and rename a topic. INTEX's visualizations reflect the results of these refinements in real time.

(v) **Exploratory data analysis (EDA) in wider context**. Users can see topic development over time and compare topic content production with consumption by

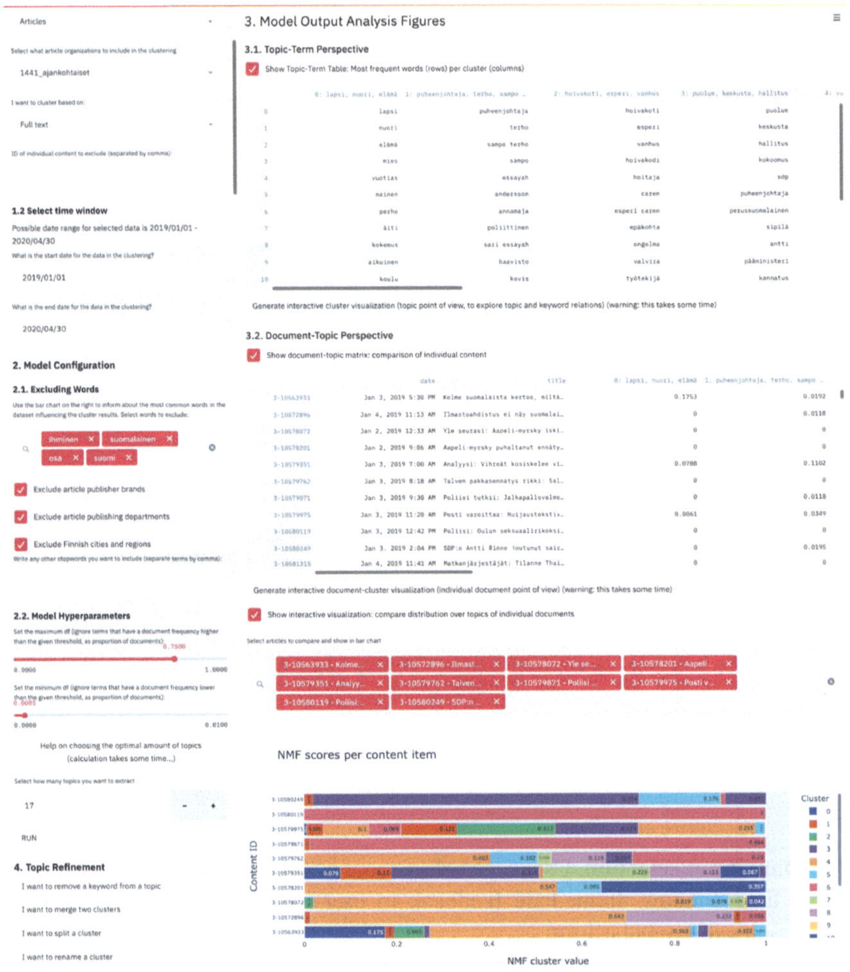

Fig. 4 Screenshot of INTEX's model output screen

different age groups. Data export, including intermediate modeling steps, is also available.

As noted, the workflow in INTEX covers the whole 'user journey', from data selection to exploratory data analysis and exporting the results. The user can follow the five steps explained above both in sequential order or can go back to any earlier step at their own will, such as changing the data input or model configuration after model refinement.

Fig. 5 Screenshot of INTEX's interactive visualizations screen

Fig. 6 Screenshot of INTEX's topic quality screen

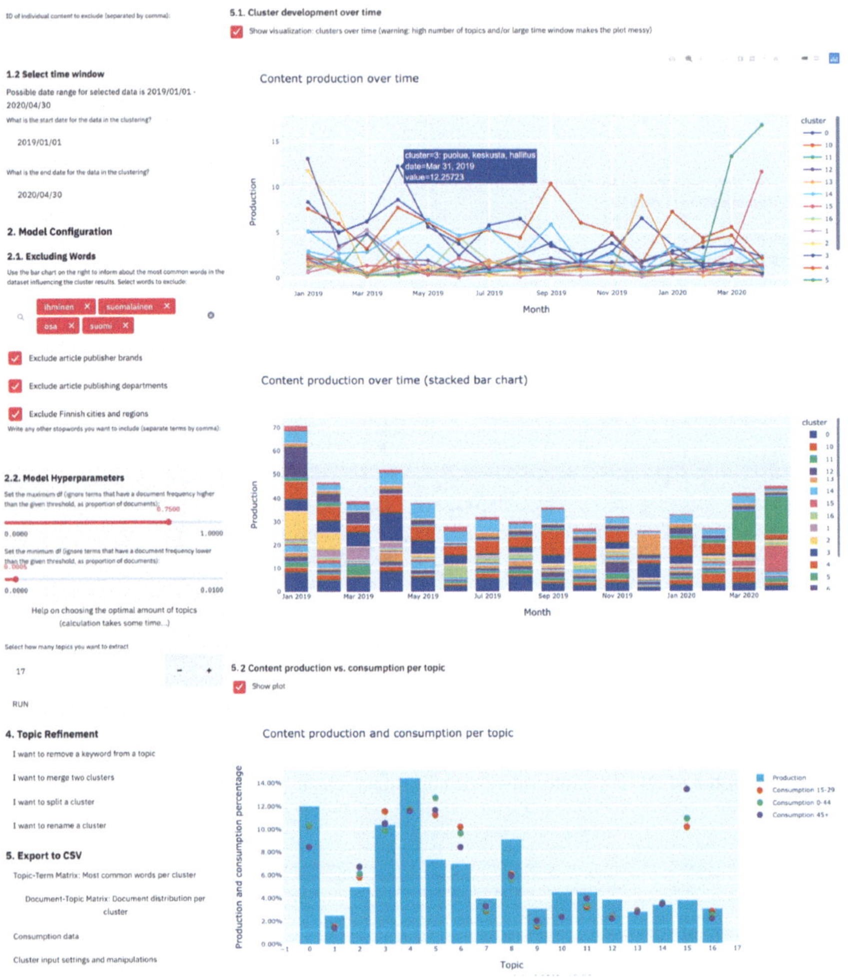

Fig. 7 Screenshot of INTEX's exploratory visualizations screen

3.2 *Implementation*

INTEX is delivered as a web-based single-page application that interacts with the user by dynamically rewriting the current page with new data from a web server, instead of the default method of the browser loading entire new pages. Fast and smooth transitions between pages make the web application feel like a native desktop-based app.

The backend of INTEX uses the Python library Stanza[1] on top of SpaCy[2] to preprocess text documents and apply NMF for topic modeling. The frontend of INTEX is built with the open-source framework Streamlit.[3] Like Jupyter Notebooks, Python scripts for data modeling are the only assets required to build the user interface; the Streamlit framework creates an interactive and user-friendly interface on top of those. But unlike Jupyter notebooks, which require users to run blocks of Python code, Streamlit hides the scripts in the background and presents an interactive interface to the user.

The user interface has two main modules (Fig. 2). A panel on the right displays information in text, tables, and interactive visualizations. A panel on the left takes in the user actions that influence the topic model. Regarding model configuration (Fig. 3), INTEX includes a bar chart of the 15 most prevalent keywords in the document corpus and a table showing the document frequency of each word. Users can control feature extraction by excluding words via keyword filters and sliders. The left panel allows controlling feature extraction by excluding words, either by selecting a popular word using a drop-down menu with the most common words, typing additional words, clicking on checkboxes to exclude predefined sets of words, or changing the minimum or maximum document frequency using sliders.

The user can also select the number of topics to extract and click on a button to initialize the model (Fig. 4). As soon as the topics are derived, the interface allows the user to interpret the model, refine it, explore the resulting data, and export them. Checkboxes are implemented to toggle tables and figures, and buttons are shown to generate additional, more computationally demanding interactive visualizations. The interactive topic visualization to explore relationships between topics and keywords is only generated on demand. This visualization is made using LDAvis[4] which generates an interactive HTML file from the output of a topic model; see Fig. 5. Relations between individual documents and their topics are visualized with the Bokeh library[5] and the UMAP dimensionality reduction algorithm [28].

INTEX allows the user to get an estimation of the topics quality (Fig. 6), by comparing model residuals per topic, and refine topics on demand. Depending on the refinement action, topics and words can be selected from dynamically generated drop-down menus or typing. Note that topics are usually independent from geographical location. Finally, exploratory data analysis and data export options are also available (Fig. 7). The figures for EDA can be accessed after the model has generated the initial set of topics, but the figures are not displayed in detail initially, since the user should focus on topic evaluation and refinement before diving into how the topics can be utilized in wider context.

[1] https://stanfordnlp.github.io/stanza/

[2] https://spacy.io/

[3] https://www.streamlit.io/

[4] https://github.com/bmabey/pyLDAvis.

[5] https://bokeh.org/

4 Evaluation

To derive useful insights about how users perceive and feel about using INTEX, we analyzed the perceived usability (efficiency and satisfaction) and user experience of INTEX via rating scales that were complemented with semi-structured interviews at post-task.

4.1 Dataset

A dataset of 605 news articles were provided by Yle, the Finnish national broadcasting company.[6] Yle's department of Current Affairs ('Ajankohtaiset') selected articles from January 1st 2019 until April 30th 2020. Each article comprises M = 318 words (SD = 231) after text preprocessing. Most articles were familiar to all the participants, thus lowering the barrier to getting introduced to topic modeling.

4.2 Participants

Ten participants (6 female, 4 male) aged 30–39 were recruited from Yle. All participants were Finnish and spoke English fluently. They had various backgrounds regarding data analytics and data science. Seven participants were confident in their ability to use data analytics tools, and the remaining three were self-perceived as neutral. Five participants indicated to have been aware or used some clustering techniques before, but none had done topic modeling.

4.3 Procedure

We conducted individual evaluation sessions that took up to one hour per participant. Each session was conducted remotely with audio and screen-capture recording. Each session started with a walk-through of INTEX. Then, the following task scenario was presented: "You want to make a report about the most important news articles published by Yle's Current Affairs department in the last year. Use INTEX to derive a set of topics that would help you and your target audience to understand the contents that have been covered by such news articles". Participants were instructed to think-aloud during this task. Afterward, a short semi-structured interview was conducted. After the interview, participants completed a survey containing closed questions, addressing their feeling on usability, user experience, and user perception of their interaction with INTEX. See Appendix C for more details.

[6] https://yle.fi/

4.4 Evaluation Measures

We logged task completion time along with the aforementioned post-test survey. Perceived usability was measured in a 1–5 Likert scale (1: 'strongly disagree', …, 5: 'strongly agree') following the System Usability Scale (SUS) [21]. User experience was measured with nine questions adopted from Smith et al. [44]; see Appendix C. The first four questions relate to frustration, trust, task ease, and confidence. The next five questions relate to model adherence, instability, latency, quality, and improvement. Participants answered these questions again on a 1–5 point Likert scale. Finally, the outcomes of the think-aloud protocol were coded thematically.

4.5 Results

Evaluation results are reported in Figs. 8 and 9. Regarding task completion time, participants spent $M = 24$ min ($SD = 7$ min) on the task. This represents a significant improvement of over 50% with regards to manual work, which all participants estimated to be more than one hour at the very least. We should point out that none of the participants had conducted any topic modeling task before, but quickly understood and saw the value of INTEX for their daily work. Regarding system usability and user experience, the average SUS score is 81, which is well above the benchmarked average for websites and web applications [5, 26]. It is worth noting that SUS scores below 50 imply serious usability issues [5], so we can conclude that INTEX is perceived as highly usable.

Participants found the task easy ($M = 4.2$, $SD = 0.8$), trusted INTEX ($M = 4.1$, $SD = 0.7$), felt confident using it ($M = 3.9$, $SD = 0.9$), and did not experience frustration (negative statement, lower is better, $M = 1.8$, $SD = 0.8$). Participants mentioned that INTEX adhered to their input ($M = 4.2$, $SD = 0.9$), had low latency ($M = 4.1$, $SD = 0.9$), and was not unstable (negative statement, $M = 1.8$, $SD = 0.6$).

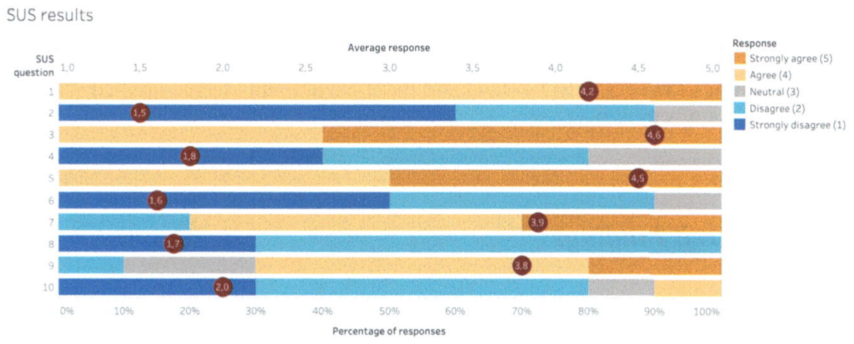

Fig. 8 Results of the SUS questionnaire

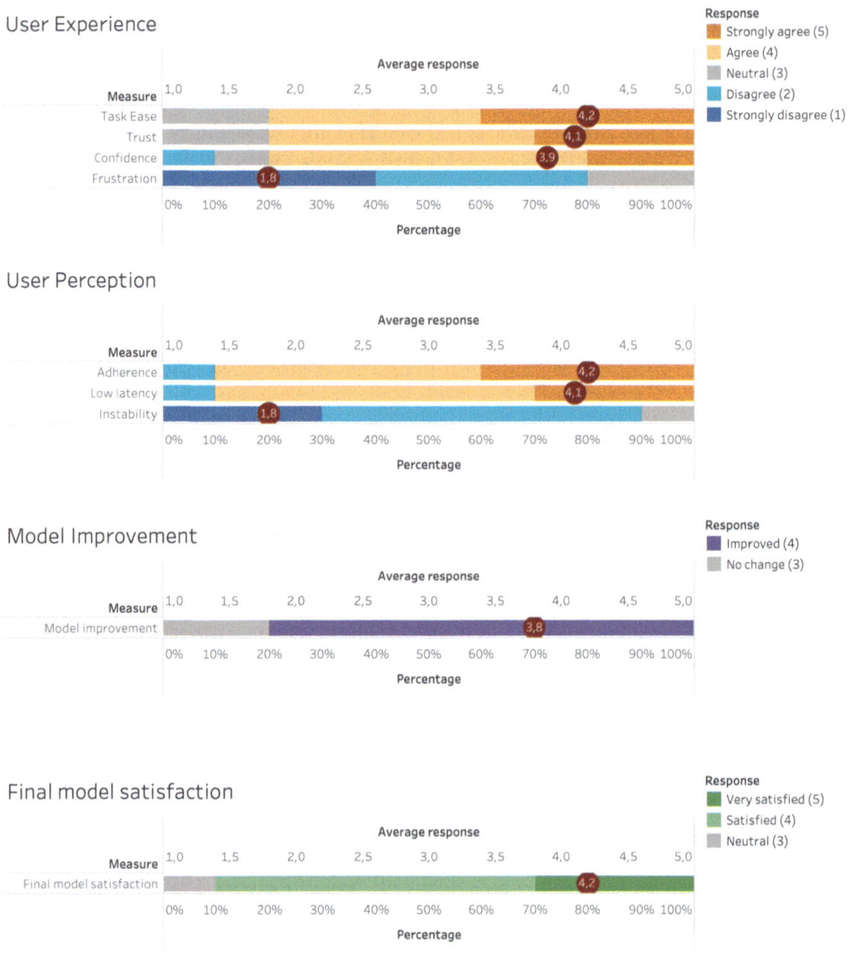

Fig. 9 Results of the post-task questionnaire

In addition, participants argued that the final topics were substantially improved over the initial topics ($M = 3.8$, SD $= 0.4$) and most participants were satisfied with the results ($M = 4.2$, SD $= 0.4$).

4.6 *Research Findings*

In the following, we distil the most relevant findings from the post-task interviews. We hope these will inform other researchers interested in creating ITM applications.

1. **Users do not change the model configuration before an initial run**. Only two participants made changes to the default model configuration before they ran the model for the first time. Three participants made no changes at all. P3 mentioned that they did not change any stopwords or hyperparameters because she wanted to *"see what the model comes up with before manipulating it, so that I can get an idea of how it works and nothing important will be left out"*.
2. **Users are uncertain about the number of topics to extract, but only initially**. Three participants decided to run the model with the default number of 5 and four participants specified from 10 to 20 topics. P5, who chose 10 topics, argued that *"just extracting 5 topics might be too few on this dataset"*, and P6, who chose 20, mentioned that he *"loves to explore a lot of data first to get a general idea on what to specify in the longer run"*.
3. **Users like to explore and try out functionality multiple times**. Seven participants ran the model with at least two different numbers of topics to extract. This suggests that users engaged with INTEX instead of just following the study instructions blindly.
4. **Aligning expectations with system implementation is key, as users' motivation can be quite diverse**. Post-task interviews revealed that individual participants had different interests and use cases in mind, which resulted in differences in user actions and findings. For example, P8 focused a lot on excluding stopwords (*"I don't want common words, that can be part of any subject, to influence my modelling results."*), while P7 used multiple topic refinement operations to *"ensure topics have high quality so I can safely use them later on"*, and P6 spent most of his time exploring the topic results in the EDA plots with topic development over time and consumption rates, which *"helps in micro-segment discovery"*.
5. **Exploratory data visualizations do not only serve as an 'extra' analysis, but also support the users in topic model understanding, evaluation, and refinement**. Four participants have used the visualizations to evaluate individual topic results, and made model refinements based on analyzing these plots. P10 mentioned that she merged two topics on the coronavirus as well as topics on politics, based on trend peaks in the plot of topic development over time: *"The production of articles about politics and elections have a similar development over time, both showing a peak in the spring, so I will merge these two clusters together"*.
6. **Users like the variety and interactivity of the visualizations**. All participants pointed out that they liked the fact that the visualizations are interactive. For example, P6 mentioned: *"When I hover over data in the charts, I see more information on the content and the topic clusters, that is really good"*.
7. **INTEX triggers users' curiosity and encourages them to use the application with other data sources**. When exploring the last plot including consumption data per topic, P5 stated that *"I want to do some analysis on questions that come to my mind. It is great that I can do this analysis with just a few clicks."*
8. **Users like to be in control of the model, but would like to see suggestions and get a sense of its quality**. Users got excited when they see that manual

refinements to the model are implemented and reflected as expected. Users also appreciate recommendations made by the application about which topics to refine. This also holds for customizing model configuration settings, like adding custom stopwords. P8 mentioned that *"it is really handy to see the most common words in the dataset, this makes it intuitive and fast to decide which words to exclude"*.

9. **Users like to see model refinements reflected immediately**. Multiple participants verbally appreciated the results of user and system actions to be directly visible. P3 indicated that *"the value of INTEX is that you get really quickly information on the data"*.
10. **Users without previous modeling knowledge feel confident using INTEX**. Participants indicated that they are amazed by how much they can achieve with this application without having any technical experience. They did not feel the need to completely understand the underlying model, but indicated their confidence in their actions and the final results. P2 said that *"it is fascinating how much you can do with machine learning, although I don't even know how it works"*.
11. **Users like INTEX's user interface**. P5 indicated that *"the left-hand panel stays with the model settings, that is really consistent and really helpful"*. P6 said that he really liked that the interface was designed from a user experience point of view: *"It does not only look good, but it is also very intuitive and functional, it gives a lot of details which are all very understandable"*.
12. **Users like to explore functionalities rather than reading any user manual first**. None of the participants went through the 'how to use' tutorial before they started the modeling task. P10 said: *"I know what the application should be roughly capable of, so I will just explore the functionalities"*. P6 proposed to introduce question marks or info icons with explanations: *"that would help me a lot, because then I do not have to search for the information elsewhere in the application"*.
13. **Users would like to see an 'undo' option**. P1 wanted to revert an action, but was not able to. *"I would like to see an undo option, to revert an action if I made a mistake and want to go back to the previous model results"*. Previous work also flagged the importance of having an 'undo' operation [41], however this is challenging to implement mainly because of the memory cost of keeping track of previous model computations, which are typically very expensive.

5 Discussion

Our results indicate that INTEX indeed helps non-technical end-users with domain expertise perform topic modeling and intervene on the process, without the help of data scientists of NLP experts. According to the Curved Grading Scale of SUS, a score of 81 indicates that the application has a high usability, falling in the top 10% of scores (90th percentile), suggesting that INTEX has 'excellent' performance [26] in terms of effectiveness, efficiency, overall ease of use, and learnability. Results from the additional questionnaires suggest that INTEX provides a high user experience and that users are satisfied with the underlying model and overall functionality of the application. For example, participants indicated that being able to control the model results by the offered refinement options does not only influence their user experience but also has a positive impact on how they perceived the final results.

INTEX's design follows the HCD framework as well as recommendations from previous research. For example, Smith et al. [44] noticed that users want to be in control, they dislike latency, and that model results should be easily interpretable. Our evaluation results indicate that participants indeed perceived INTEX supporting these aspects. In particular, latency has been mentioned as a major user experience limitation in previous applications [2, 25]. While the overall latency of functions in INTEX is very low, some functions such as calculating model coherence or generating visualizations may take a higher computation time. Since these time-consuming computations are explicitly stated in the interface, participants did not mention latency as a problem. We can conclude that the model internals should be transparent to the user, and the actions and computations needed should be made explicit in the user interface.

Previous ITM applications used complicated plots to visualize topic model output. In INTEX, a combination of both simple and advanced plots is implemented, to give the user the option to explore results in detail. We found that participants demand different visualizations, depending on their background and personal interests. None of the participants indicated that there were too many visualizations, or that visualizations were too complicated. Although our participants had mixed expertise, the user experience and perception results are quite stable. The average standard deviation over all questions is 0.71 on a five-point Likert scale, with the highest standard deviation of 0.9 for statements on user confidence, perceived model adherence, and model latency. Observations of user-model interactions during the evaluation task show that participants use simple topic refinement options and avoid changing complex model settings. Complex model refinement options such as changing keyword order or changing their weights were not implemented because they would be hard to understand for novice users, as suggested by Lee et al. [25]. An unexpected insight is that the EDA visualizations, which were implemented as 'extra' analysis figures, supported users in topic model understanding. This finding suggests that users can improve the model and link the results to data that they are familiar with.

5.1 Limitations

INTEX is unique in its combination of use context, data, users, interface design, topic model, and visualization techniques. Currently there are no existing ITM applications for the broadcasting domain, and previous work has not designed with and for domain experts, so we cannot compare INTEX against any competing ITM application. In addition, previous ITM applications have not been evaluated with real users under a similar setting like ours, so it is difficult to compare results across domains. This implies that the results of our user evaluation are indicators of the usability and user experience with INTEX only. INTEX is designed to extract and visualize a relatively small number of topics from a set of documents. From our focus group sessions, we found that users would not be interested in extracting more than 15 topics, but later in our evaluation we found that users would benefit from extracting a larger number of topics, up to 50. Currently, visualizations can easily represent results of up to 15 topics, but may become difficult to interpret or slow to generate when used on a larger number of topics.

5.2 The Past, Present, and Future of ITM

The Past. Topic modeling requires efficient analysis methods and techniques for automatic theme discovery, to automatically group multiple documents into a smaller number of semantically meaningful categories. Classic topic models had two important shortcomings that prevented these models for being usable in practice: (1) the discovered topics were hard to interpret and (2) the models were prone to extracting too many or too few topics, leading to too general or too specific results.

The Present. ITM applications address the previously mentioned key shortcomings of classic Topic Models, incorporating human expertise in the process in a way that users can refine extracted topics and do exploratory data analysis. However, most ITM applications are designed for data scientists and NLP experts, who often lack domain knowledge about the data and its high-level interpretation in a business context.

The Future. INTEX represents the future of ITM applications, as it bridges the gap between NLP experts and domain experts in the broadcasting media, like journalists and data analysts, who have a broader knowledge than NLP experts about the produced and consumed media content, but often lack NLP expertise. All in all, any human-in-the-loop application should be designed according to HCD principles in collaboration with non-technical end-users.

6 Conclusion

INTEX is an interactive topic modeling application for media content production analysis that bridges the gap between domain experts and data scientists. As a practical proof, INTEX has enabled professionals from the Finnish broadcasting company Yle to perform topic modeling on their published media content. Based on a formal user evaluation, we can conclude that INTEX is highly usable, promotes an adequate user experience, and is easy to learn by non-technical domain experts. Our findings suggest that INTEX represents the future of Interactive Topic Modeling applications. INTEX is publicly available at https://github.com/laura-ham/INTEX.

Acknowledgements We thank Yle for their support. This work was supported by the Horizon 2020 FET program of the European Union (grant CHIST-ERA-20-BCI-001) and the European Innovation Council Pathfinder program (SYMBIOTIK project, grant 101071147).

Appendix 1: Stakeholders

The following stakeholders were identified:

1. **End-users** of INTEX: domain experts within the broadcasting company. They are data analysts and describe themselves as data-literate, but do not have an engineering or scientific background. Part of their daily job is analyzing data and making statistical reports, with the help of spreadsheets and interactive data visualization tools like Microsoft Excel and Tableau. The national broadcasting company Yle is the domain of all end-users, which means that they interact with content (article, audio and video) production and consumption across different types of media platforms (television, web pages, mobile applications, social media, etc.), and across various types of audiences (with different demographics, media consumption intentions and behavior, etc.).
2. **Content producers and journalists**: data-literate domain experts who are interested in learning on what topics represent their produced media. They do exploratory data analysis on various sources of data and will consume the output of the topic models, but will not directly interact with the interactive topic modeling application itself.
3. **Production decision-makers and media planners**: they mostly want to be informed about new insights and trends that may influence their decision making process. They will not interact with the application itself, but will consume the results of the subsequent data analysis.
4. **Managers** of the direct users: they play a role from a business point of view. They make decisions based on data reports, and thus benefit from the results of INTEX, given that new insights can be gained. In addition, managers may decide on where their teams spend time on, and thus whether an ITM application may be used in the first place. It is important to assure buy-in from this group of stakeholders.
5. **System administrators and IT**: they offer the infrastructure for deploying and maintaining the product.
6. **Data scientists and engineers**: they are responsible for the technical model, implementation and improvements of the application. Technical questions from all stakeholders about the product will be taken by this group of people.
7. **Product owners**: they are responsible for the final product, its maintenance, and marketing operations.

The first group, the direct end-users of the application, is the only primary stakeholder group. The data-literate producers and journalists mentioned in the second group are secondary users, since they do not interact frequently with the product itself. This group rather uses the product through an intermediary, which is the first user group mentioned. Then, the other stakeholder groups are tertiary users. These users are affected by the system and/or decision-makers. Note that, in this context, individual people can belong to multiple stakeholder groups, since people may have multiple roles in the company. For example, a content producer (group 2) may also be a production decision maker or media planner (group 3). Designing the application is done with taking the different stakeholder groups in mind, rather than different individual persons, since their roles, and thus desires and needs, can be ambiguous.

Appendix 2: Focus Group Sessions

2.1. First Focus Group Session

The first focus group consisted of two potential end-users and one secondary user. One end-user is an analyst at the Yle News Lab,[7] a testing laboratory for data journalism. Another primary user is head of Yle's general data analytics team. The secondary user is a web producer at Yle's department of current affairs. None of the participants have worked with any topic modeling application tool before. The session took one hour, and was held in-person.

After an initial, open discussion on opportunities and wishes from the participants, various models, interaction, visualization and design possibilities were proposed. This informed the participants what was possible from a technical point of view. Participants indicated their preferences among the options provided, which led to a richer set of requirements.

User requirements were extracted from the first focus group session, and also from iterations and theoretical background [13]. Requirements were categorized as application architecture (business), technical topic model implementation (system), and user interface and interactions (design). In addition, we identified the following set of attitudes and desires that should be considered in the design of ITM applications:

- End-users would like to perform the topic modeling 'every few weeks to months', but multiple times with various subsets of a bigger dataset of articles. They want to filter on metadata to achieve this, for example the type of the articles, publishing department of the articles, etc.
- End-users are able to spend time on the total modeling process, from opening to closing the application after completion. As long as the end-user is able to extract meaningful and accurate topics, it is worth the time to explore and refine results.
- The preferred number of topics or themes to extract lies between 5 and 15. This was later updated to 5–50 topics, after conducting interviews with other stakeholders.

[7] https://newslab.yle.fi/

- End-users would like to see some visualization to quickly determine what stopwords to exclude. It was mentioned that it is hard to come up with words to exclude from modeling without seeing which words influence the modeling process.
- End-users and secondary users (the 'data-literate producers') would like to see preliminary visualizations on how the extracted topics can be used. This helps them determine if the extracted topics are meaningful. A visualization was proposed on how topics are represented in the set of input documents over time, and participants would like to see it included in the final application.
- End-users are willing to spend time and effort to interact with the model for the best results, but pointed out that they would rather refine settings that are proposed by the model than manually set parameters from the beginning. This applies to model parameters as well as topic labeling. As a result, the application should propose settings and output labels, and give the user the opportunity to edit these proposed settings and labels.
- The design of a product is not limited to the requirements of the end-users. It became clear that the results of a topic modeling application are likely to be used by the secondary users. Although this user group is not interacting with the modeling application itself, the analysts are using the results of the model, the extracted topics, in exploratory data analysis. Since the primary goal of this group is to gather new insights from this analysis of media topics combined with other data sources, it is important that extracted topics are accurate, meaningful and easy to understand. Additionally, the learned topics should be extracted to a data format that is easy to handle by other data analysis software.

2.2. Recurring Focus Group Sessions

Recurring sessions with two focus groups followed the first focus group session and the first design iteration:

1. The same focus group as the initial user requirement research, with two end-users and one secondary user. Sessions with this group were held every one or two weeks for the course of the two-month design and development cycle. This group had a very active role in the participatory design process. Also concept testing and desirability study methods were applied in some sessions.
2. A focus group with three end-users, one secondary user, and two tertiary users. Sessions with this focus group were less frequent, and started later in the design process. Sessions were less oriented to the design of the platform, but more toward concept and usability testing. Although only a small amount of new requirements was extracted from this group of participants, they confirmed findings from the other focus group sessions. In addition, addressing a second focus group leads to a design for a wider target group and avoids design fixation.

No strict protocol was followed during these sessions. Study methods that were applied during these sessions varied, depending on the design phase in the HCD cycle. In the beginning of the design and development process, sessions were more focused toward participatory design, whereas later more desirability studies were conducted.

An example of a **participatory design** session is finding out whether and which model revision techniques are most desired. A prototype of INTEX was presented to the participants. Participants were asked to interact with a high-fidelity prototype of the first part of INTEX, in which no revision or interaction was possible. The users were thus presented with a topic modeling output, and were asked whether they would like to make any changes to the result, and which changes. After an initial discussion on the users' wishes, the range of possibilities were presented, to give the participants the opportunity to think about those as well.

An example of applying the **concept-testing method** in a focus group session is introducing possible topic model visualizations to the end-user. In early focus group sessions, users were presented with different types of (graphical and textual) visualizations that represent (part of) the model output. Participants were asked to give their preference on visualizations, which they would most use and benefit from during the interactive modeling process. This method was used to understand if users would want or need specific visualizations.

Finally, **desirability study** techniques were applied in some focus group sessions as well. Although desirability studies are principally carried out to find out what visual design alternative is preferred, the method was applied here to find out the most desired option in a set of presented designs. An example is on interactive versus non-interactive visualizations. Data plots that represent the same data but differ in whether they provide interactivity (for example selecting a subset of data to display), were both presented to users, after which they were asked to indicate their preference. Additionally, the following was observed:

- From exploratory data analysis with topic modeling results during testing sessions, the stakeholders showed most interest in two data analysis visualizations. First, how different topics in produced media content relates to its consumption over different age groups. Second, how the representation of topics in produced media develops over time.
- Although wishes, desires, and requirements from both focus groups were mostly complementary, sometimes they conflicted. An example is the number of topics to extract. Group 1 indicated that extracting up to 15 topics would suffice, while group 2 indicated interest in extracting a larger number of topics (close to 50). The possible number of topics influences how the model should be configured for optimal results and also influences the visualizations. For example, increasing the number of extracted topics to 50 makes the visualizations that plot topic development over time a bit messy, while up to 15 topics are much more clear to distinguish in a single plot. Conflicting requirements like this were solved by discussing the concerning requirement with both focus groups, and a decision was made while keeping the technical requirements and capabilities in mind.
- The iterative nature of the design and development process also led to revisions of requirements within the groups. While this is the advantage of HCD, this may also lead to conflicting desires, and requires a well thought out decision. This may

slow down the development, but we believe that this will only benefit the final product.

Appendix 3: Evaluation Study Questionnaires

In the following we provide the list of questions presented to the participants regarding the user experience evaluation and the post-task interviews.

3.1. User Experience and User Perception Questionnaire

1. Using this application to perform the task was frustrating.
2. I trusted that the application would update the clusters of the articles well.
3. It was easy to use this application to perform the task.
4. I was confident in my specified changes to the tool.
5. How satisfied are you with the final topics?
6. How do you think the final topics compare to the initial suggested topics?
7. After my changes, the application updated fast enough.
8. The tool made the changes I asked it to make.
9. The tool made unexpected changes beyond what I asked to make.

3.2. Post-task Semi-structured Interview Questions

1. Why did you choose this number of topics?
2. What do you think about the on-page explanations?
3. Did the visualizations provide you with sufficient information?
4. Was every function and visualization clear?
5. Does this application help you in discovering new insights or new use cases?
6. Are there functions, visualizations, or data that where not implemented but you would like to have seen or used?

References

1. Abdollahi B, Nasraoui O (2018) Transparency in fair machine learning: the case of explainable recommender systems. In: Human and machine learning
2. Arapakis I, Bai X, Barla Cambazoglu B (2014) Impact of response latency on user behavior in web search. In: Proceedings of SIGIR
3. Arora S, Ge R, Moitra A (2012) Learning topic models–going beyond SVD. In: Proceedings of FOCS
4. Bakharia A, Bruza P, Watters J, Narayan B, Sitbon L (2016) Interactive topic modeling for aiding qualitative content analysis. In: Proceeding of the CHIIR
5. Bangor A, Kortum PT, Miller JT (2008) An empirical evaluation of the System Usability Scale. Int J Hum Comput Interact 24(6)
6. Baxter K, Courage C, Caine K (2015) Understanding your users: a practical guide to user research methods. Morgan Kaufmann

7. Blei DM, Ng AY, Jordan MI (2003) Latent Dirichlet allocation. J Mach Learn Res 3
8. Bouma G (2009) Normalized (pointwise) mutual information in collocation extraction. In: Proceedings of the GSCL
9. June-Barlow Chaney A, Blei DM (2012) Visualizing topic models. In: Proceedings of the AAAI
10. Chang J, Gerrish S, Wang C, Boyd-Graber J, Blei D (2009) Reading tea leaves: how humans interpret topic models. In: Proceedings of the NeurIPS
11. Choo J, Lee C, Reddy CK, Park H (2013) Utopian: user-driven topic modeling based on interactive nonnegative matrix factorization. IEEE Trans Vis Comput Graph 19(12)
12. Chuang J, Manning CD, Heer J (2012) Termite: visualization techniques for assessing textual topic models. In: Proceedings of the ACL workshops
13. Clegg D, Barker R (1994) Case method fast-track: a RAD approach. Addison-Wesley Longman Publishing Co., Inc.
14. Deerwester S, Dumais ST, Furnas GW, Landauer TK, Harshman R (1990) Indexing by latent semantic analysis. J Assoc Inf Sci Technol 41(6)
15. Gardner MJ, Lutes J, Lund J, Hansen J, Walker D, Ringger E, Seppi K (2010) The topic browser: an interactive tool for browsing topic models. In: Proceedings of the NeurIPS workshops
16. Goodwin K (2009) Designing for the digital age: how to create human-centered products and services. Wiley
17. Greene D, O'Callaghan D, Cunningham P (2014) How many topics? Stability analysis for topic models. In: Proceedings of the ECML-PKDD
18. Hofmann T (1999) Probabilistic latent semantic analysis. In: Proceedings of the UAI
19. Hoque E, Carenini G (2015) Convisit: interactive topic modeling for exploring asynchronous online conversations. In: Proceedings of the IUI
20. Hu Y, Boyd-Graber J, Satinoff B, Smith A (2014) Interactive topic modeling. Mach Learn 95(3)
21. Jordan PW, Thomas B, McClelland IL, Weerdmeester B (1996) Usability evaluation in industry. CRC Press
22. Kulesza T, Stumpf S, Burnett M, Wong WK, Riche Y, Moore T, Oberst I, Shinsel A, McIntosh K (2010) Explanatory debugging: supporting end-user debugging of machine-learned programs. In: Proceedings of the IEEE VL/HCC
23. Lau JH, Newman D, Baldwin T (2014) Machine reading tea leaves: automatically evaluating topic coherence and topic model quality. In: Proceedings of the EACL
24. Lee H, Kihm J, Choo J, Stasko J, Park H (2012) iVisClustering: an interactive visual document clustering via topic modeling. In: Computer graphics forum, vol 31
25. Lee TY, Smith A, Seppi K, Elmqvist N, Boyd-Graber J, Findlater L (2017) The human touch: How non-expert users perceive, interpret, and fix topic models. Int J Hum Comput Stud 105
26. Lewis JR, Sauro J (2018) Item benchmarks for the System Usability Scale. J Usabil Stud 13(3)
27. van der Maaten L, Hinton G (2008) Visualizing data using t-SNE. J Mach Learn Res 9
28. McInnes L, Healy J, Melville J (2018) UMAP: uniform manifold approximation and projection for dimension reduction. arXiv:1802.03426
29. Meyer R (2016) How many stories do newspapers publish per day? Available at theatlantic.com. Accessed Jan 2022
30. Mikolov T, Chen K, Corrado G, Dean J (2013) Efficient estimation of word representations in vector space. In: Proceedings of the ICLR workshops
31. Moore K (2020) How long would it take to watch all of Netflix? Available at whats-on-netflix.com. Accessed Jan 2022
32. Murdock J, Allen C (2015) Visualization techniques for topic model checking. In: Proceedings of the AAAI
33. O'callaghan D, Greene D, Carthy J, Cunningham P (2015) An analysis of the coherence of descriptors in topic modeling. Expert Syst Appl 42(13)
34. Paatero P, Tapper U (1994) Positive matrix factorization: a non-negative factor model with optimal utilization of error estimates of data values. Environmetrics 5(2)
35. Rohrer C (2014) When to use which user-experience research methods

36. Saeidi AM, Hage J, Khadka R, Jansen S (2015) ITMViz: interactive topic modeling for source code analysis. In: Proceedings of the ICPC
37. Sedlmair M, Meyer M, Munzner T (2012) Design study methodology: reflections from the trenches and the stacks. IEEE Trans Vis Comput Graph 18(12)
38. Sievert C, Shirley K (2014) LDAvis: a method for visualizing and interpreting topics. In: Proceedings of the ACL workshops
39. Simon S, Mittelstädt S, Keim DA, Sedlmair M (2015) Bridging the gap of domain and visualization experts with a liaison. In: Proceedings of the EuroVis, vol 2015
40. Smith A, Chuang J, Hu Y, Boyd-Graber J, Findlater L (2014) Concurrent visualization of relationships between words and topics in topic models. In: Proceedings of the ACL workshops
41. Smith A, Kumar V, Boyd-Graber J, Seppi K, Findlater L (2018) Closing the loop: user-centered design and evaluation of a human-in-the-loop topic modeling system. In: Proceedings of the IUI
42. Smith A, Lee TY, Poursabzi-Sangdeh F, Boyd-Graber J, Elmqvist N, Findlater L (2017) Evaluating visual representations for topic understanding and their effects on manually generated topic labels. Trans Assoc Comput Linguist 5
43. Smith A, Malik S, Shneiderman B (2015) Visual analysis of topical evolution in unstructured text: design and evaluation of TopicFlow. In: Applications of social media and social network analysis
44. Smith-Renner A, Kumar V, Boyd-Graber J, Seppi K, Findlater L (2020) Digging into user control: perceptions of adherence and instability in transparent models. In: Proceedings of the IUI
45. Stevens K, Kegelmeyer P, Andrzejewski D, Buttler D (2012) Exploring topic coherence over many models and many topics. In: Proceedings of the EMNLP
46. Zou C, Hou D (2014) LDA analyzer: a tool for exploring topic models. In: Proceedings of ICSME

Mobile Augmented Reality Gamification Strategies to Promote Social Skills: Case Studies and Future Challenges

Lissette López-Faican, Javier Jaen, and Jorge Montaner

Abstract Empathy is considered a strong predictor of prosocial behaviors, and its teaching is necessary in the educational context to discourage aggressive behaviors and promote positive social attitudes you go in students. Currently, technology makes it possible to create attractive resources for students, motivating them to want to learn instead of having to learn. Along this line, there are games supported by technology, some of which integrate Augmented Reality (AR), a promising technology that allows users to interact with digital content superimposed on the physical world, to capture the interest of students and motivate them to actively participate in the learning activity. Under this context, this chapter presents a review of strategies implemented to date related to the development of social skills with Augmented Reality. Additionally, two case studies with location-based Mobile Augmented Reality (MAR) are also presented to promote social skills in students. Finally, based on the analysis of these results, design guides and strategies are proposed that should be followed to increase the effectiveness of the processes of acquiring empathic and social skills through gamification with Augmented Reality. This chapter aims, therefore, to lay the foundations for the next developments that must be carried out in this field.

L. López-Faican (✉)
Pedagogía de las Ciencias Experimentales Informática, Universidad Nacional de Loja, Av. Pio Jaramillo Alvarado, 110103 Loja, Ecuador
e-mail: lissette.lopez@unl.edu.ec

J. Jaen
Instituto Mixto de Tecnología Informática, Universitat Politècnica de València, Camí de Vera, 46022 Valencia, Spain
e-mail: fjaen@upv.es

J. Montaner
Departamento de Sistemas Informáticos y Computación, Universitat Politècnica de València, Camí de Vera, 46022 Valencia, Spain
e-mail: jormonm5@inf.upv.es

S. Sayago et al. (eds.), *Future Perspectives on Human-Computer Interaction Research*,
https://doi.org/10.1007/978-3-031-71697-3_6

1 Introduction

Prosocial behavior is defined as a voluntary behavior aimed at benefiting or helping others [85]. This ability is related to empathy, which, together with the prosocial response, is essential to cultivating positive interactions and increasing collaboration/cooperation, exchange and helping behaviors between all individuals and groups in society [69]. Hence, it is important in the inclusion of educational programs.

There are various educational strategies in the literature to teach social skills to students, with a special interest in those designed with technology, such as Augmented Reality (AR), which allows for the creation of immersive and stimulating learning experiences through enriched teaching environments [5]. However, as we will see in the next section, from the analysis of the related works, it can be concluded that, on the one hand, a large part of them is focused on single-user environments and, on the other hand, there are few applications benefit from Mobile Augmented Reality (MAR) with markerless and location-based experiences. MAR allows the creation of AR experiences without requiring sophisticated hardware requirements. Additionally, augmentation techniques without physical markers enable the execution of the experience in a variety of real-world locations, which in turn contributes to greater realism and local presence. Finally, from this analysis, it is also concluded that relatively little is known about how innovative gamification technologies, such as MAR, can be applied to the design of multiplayer games to teach social skills.

Therefore, this chapter is a step forward toward location-based gamified MAR strategies for social skills development, detailing two prototypes MAR. The first prototype where the positioning of virtual content in the real world is designed by "spatial anchors", which implements multi-user scenarios for identification and manipulation of basic emotional states for emotional intelligence and social skills evaluated with primary school children. The second prototype is designed with the "Global Positioning System (GPS)", at a single-user and multi-user level that implements help scenarios and narratives aimed at a target character to promote empathy in terms of prosocial behavior, proposals that were evaluated with secondary students. Based on the prototypes and their evaluation results, we have proposed some guidelines to consider in future design of interactive MAR systems for the promotion of social skills in students, which we believe are useful for professionals in the field.

The chapter begins with a discussion of existing educational strategies to date with AR technology (Sect. 3), and Sect. 4 continues with the proposal of a process and conceptual model to promote social skills and describes the design and evaluation of two location-based MAR games. Finally, Sect. 5 lists some design guidelines for future work with MAR technology to promote social skills in students, and Sect. 6 discusses the main conclusions and future work.

2 Augmented Reality in Education

AR is an immersive technology that overlays virtual information in real space interactively and in real time. This combination of the virtual and real world is driven by different technological resources such as mobile devices, glasses (Head-Mounted Display—HMD), projector-based screens, holographic screens, among others, with mobile devices such as smartphones or tablets being the most used for their affordability and common use [13]. Smartphones or tablets use various technologies such as image recognition, object tracking, and sensors to measure location and orientation, which makes it possible for AR to become mobile. This constitutes a practical solution to offer the user an AR experience without sophisticated hardware requirements [26, 32].

Mobile Augmented Reality (MAR) has two standard augmentation techniques, marker-based and markerless. Marker-based MAR uses physical markers that can be special images, QR codes, or other 2D models recognized by the camera to produce virtual content in delete text, still images, video clips, sounds, 3D models, or animations. Markerless MAR, on the other hand, detects a surface in the camera image and produces virtual 3D objects on the detected surface. Marker-based MAR is easier to develop and provides a more stable environment for virtual 3D objects, but using a physical marker makes it less convenient than markerless MAR [39].

MAR addresses various application areas, including education to create immersive and stimulating learning experiences through enriched teaching environments. As Baabdullah [5] mentioned, this MAR-based interaction sparks interest in students to actively participate in the learning process, which, in turn, will make the learning process more enjoyable and fun. In addition, students are more attentive and motivated, which will be reflected in their level of performance.

A key characteristic of MAR is the "perceived realism" or "local presence", which implies the ability of the augmented world to closely mimic the sensations or experiences of the real world [13, 58]. An alternative in MAR applications to lead to greater realism and local presence is location-based games (without physical markers) that position virtual content over a specific real-world location. These games facilitate navigation in delete outdoor and indoor spaces, [33], providing real-time user tracking to anchor virtual objects in the physical space relative to the user's position, and these augmented objects remain fixed while the user moves the device. Also, location-based MAR games may involve one or more players who may be located in the same location or spread across different physical spaces, and where the game may take place in a wide variety of locations and contexts [4].

Location-based MAR games can be implemented using the Global Positioning System (GPS) for open locations, which respond to the player's position in the real world and enrich physical landscapes with digital information through geographic coordinates such as latitude, longitude, and altitude [25]. Some examples are available in the literature, such as a viewer of real building models to help students evaluate their own architectural proposals [62], the application "Mystery at the Lake" for learning environmental science [25], Explorez (single-user) and VdeUVicson (multi-user) for

French language learning [57], WallaMe for artistic education [60] or in the physical activity “Camt comic run” application [31].

Another alternative to consider is spatial anchors, which allow dynamic scanning of a diversity of physical spaces to be used as trackable maps to recognize real-world locations in both outdoor and indoor spaces. Spatial anchoring relative to a physical space, when identified by the camera, positions digital content through x, y, z coordinates and ensures that objects remain in the same place, thus maintaining the illusion of the positioning of virtual objects in the real world [30]. As an example, we have the work of Tsai and others [78] for learning logic programming and the application of Silva and others [70] for developing and learning of new culinary products. Other proposals support indoor navigation such as GuideMe [35] or MRsive [1].

Finally, all these proposals mentioned in this section highlight location-based MAR as a promising technology that is currently revolutionizing educational processes at all levels, from preschool to higher education institutions.

3 Related Works for Social Skills Development

Teaching social skills in educational programs has gained popularity [50, 81], because it is considered a feature to deter problematic behaviors and foster positive social attitudes in children and adolescents. A widely used approach to promote skill learning in education is gamification, game-based learning, or serious games, as it shares the idea of using positive gaming experiences for a serious purpose, such as achieving behavioral change, instead of focusing on entertainment [38].

Along these lines, there are many game-based interventions aimed at promoting social skills in students [6, 22, 40, 53], however, in this paper, we are especially interested in those that are based on AR technology, creating more realistic scenarios and being a technology that is currently revolutionizing educational processes, as demonstrated in the previous section.

To discourage aggressive behaviors, we have the VERA application [56] or PREVER (Prevention of Racial Stigma) [2] that creates interactions between students with competitive dynamics using QR markers to evaluate the existence of bullying. There are also interventions for social skills in people with Autism Spectrum Disorders (ASDs), such as “playing with a cow” based on paper markers [46] and other studies that use smart glasses (Google Glass, Microsoft Kinect), desktop or laptop computers, and smartphones or tablets [11, 16, 36].

Since empathy is linked to prosocial behavior, empathy training is a useful strategy in programs aimed at improving social skills in children and adolescents. In this area, we have contributions to promote empathy toward people with mental illnesses [52, 71] or disabilities [27] using AR glasses and an example is the Schizophrenia Simulator [71]. We also have other approaches to promote effective communication [80] or historical empathy [9, 75].

Emotional intelligence (EI) involves the ability to recognize the meanings of emotions and their relationships and to reason and solve problems based on them, and its influence is recognized in various aspects of human performance, such as empathy, adaptation social/sociability, others [21, 59], which is why there is also a study that evaluates the effectiveness of the popular game Pokémon Go on cognitive performance and emotional intelligence (sociability) [59].

Several literature reviews in this area of work compare AR versus Virtual Reality (VR) in this context. At the level of empathy, a contribution is the work of Paananen and others [54] where they highlight that VR (43%) is the most popular technology to promote this skill, while AR (7%) has been constantly investigated after the launch of the Hololens headset in 2016. Another similar conclusion is the work of Tay and others [77], which analyzes 16 works aimed at people with mental illnesses, where only 1 is AR with smart glasses [71]. To impart social skills, we have a review where they analyze seven proposals, and only one is AR for patients with Autism [51]. Another review [63] spaces that only 3 of 16 works are AR and only 1 is collaborative. At the level of emotional intelligence, we also have a review [55] where they analyze 19 articles, 9 with AR, and a large part of them are based on Glasses or markers and aimed at people with ASD.

A recent review that is important to highlight is the work of Mittmann and others on AR in social skills [50], where they analyze 17 AR applications and conclude that the majority are based on overlay AR. They also highlight that social skills are mainly taught in a single-user environment and a large part of them (10 works) are aimed at children with autism. The researchers suggest that future work could explore ways to improve social skills in pairs or even groups.

These findings suggest that AR technological proposals can effectively promote the learning of social skills in the educational context, but also show that existing efforts have been limited to completely virtual environments and in single-user AR scenarios. There are also a few location-based applications with MAR, where MAR allows the creation of AR experiences without requiring sophisticated hardware requirements [26]. Few works incorporate augmentation techniques without physical markers, enabling the execution of these augmented experiences in a wide variety of real-world physical locations, which in turn adds greater realism to the game scene [4, 33]. Therefore, this work is a step forward toward location-based gamified MAR strategies for social skill development.

4 Case Studies with MAR

A learning model is presented at a process and conceptual level for the acquisition of social skills (see Sect. 4.1), which is implemented in two gamified strategies with Mobile Augmented Reality based on location to promote social skills in students.

The first prototype implements a simplified subset of the learning model in Fig. 1 such as tasks and digital entities, where the positioning of virtual content in the real world is designed by "spatial anchors", which implements multi-user scenarios for

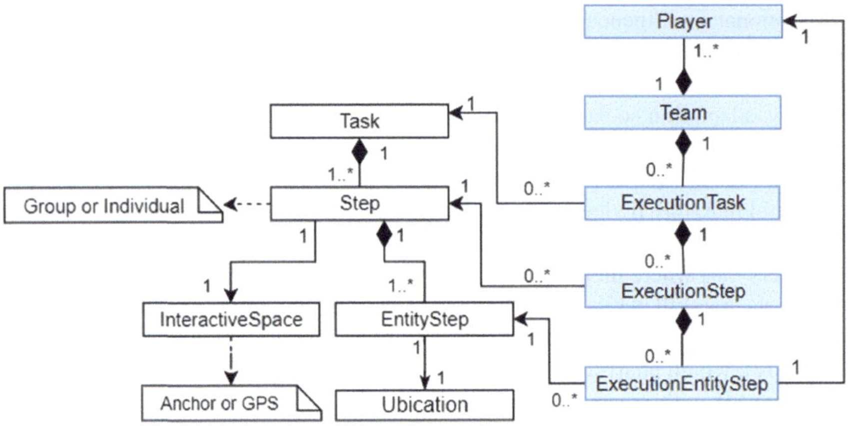

Fig. 1 Conceptual model of tasks and steps

identification and manipulation of basic emotional states for emotional intelligence and social skills evaluated with primary school children (see Sect. 4.2). The second prototype implements the complete learning model in Fig. 1, which is designed with the "Global Positioning System (GPS)", at a single-user and multi-user level that implements help scenarios and narratives aimed at a target character to promote empathy in terms of prosocial behavior, proposals that were evaluated with secondary students (see Sect. 4.3).

4.1 A Process and Conceptual Model for the Acquisition of Social Skills

4.1.1 Process Model

Empathy is oriented toward others, since it encompasses the ability to indirectly experience and understand the feelings of another person [74], where many researchers define various model proposals that attempt to represent the processes and components that intervene and help generate empathy [15, 23, 34, 72].

Given the diversity of models defined for empathy, in this chapter we propose an underlying hybrid model from the literature that combines the main components and processes of this ability. The proposal (see Fig. 2) integrates Keskin's circular process [34] due to its structure in terms of continuous steps, and this is expanded to highlight the intrapersonal (cognitive, affective) and interpersonal results expected of Davis [15], thus ending with directed behaviors toward the goal such as prosocial behavior [43–45]. This combination is justified, given that empathy is considered a strong predictor of prosocial behaviors, defined as voluntary behavior aimed at benefiting or helping others [19, 85]. This hypothesis is also evident in some of the models of empathy that include this ability as a result [15, 64, 72, 86]. Additionally, other researchers suggest that empathy and prosocial response are essential to cultivate positive interactions and increase collaboration/cooperation, exchange, and helping behaviors among all individuals and groups in society [69].

As empathy differs from one person to another and from one experience to another, it is natural not to be able to predict when empathy will arise. However, the chosen model proposes a circular process structured by continuous phases, beginning with the observation of the situation and its meaning. Through imagination, the situation moves toward reality. Subsequently, the cognitive (perspective taking) and affective (feelings) aspects of empathy emerge and, therefore, a person better understands the situation or event to adopt a behavior or actions that benefit the situation or goal, such as prosocial behavior [34].

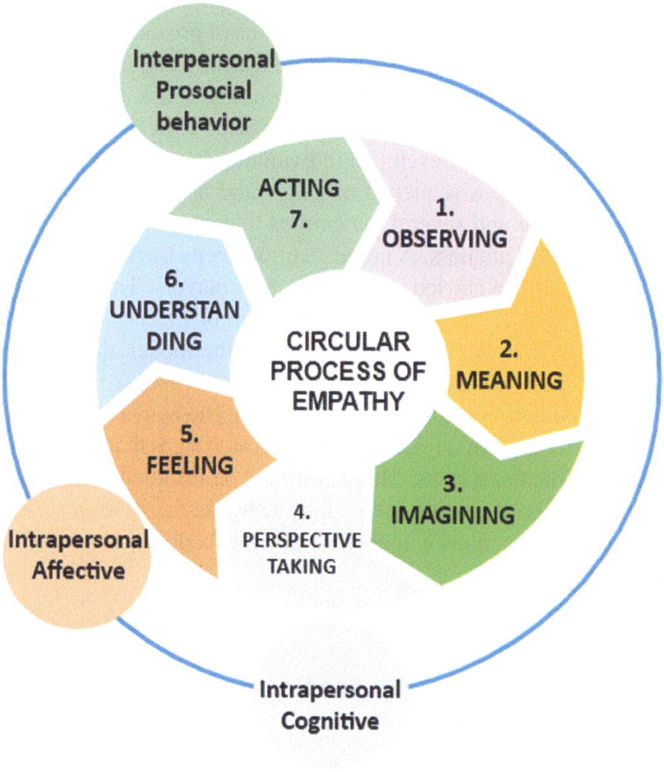

Fig. 2 Theoretical process model for prosocial behavior

4.1.2 Conceptual Model

The circular model to promote empathy processes in terms of prosocial behavior described above requires an operational strategy that allows defining activities that lead children and adolescents to develop these skills. For this operationalization, we propose a gamified learning model based on tasks and steps (see Fig. 1) that represent game themes. Choosing gamification as an operational strategy has multiple advantages that have been widely analyzed in other works [29, 38, 48].

The conceptual model aims to lead the player to execute various stories (tasks) in the real world following the "observation-action" loop, starting with the observation of a specific reflective scenario to culminate with behavioral actions to benefit the objective or situation, being prosocial behavior. Therefore, the cognitive, affective, and behavioral processes of the proposed circular model of empathy (see Fig. 2) arise from these reflective situations (tasks). In this paper, the conceptual model is deployed for a specific skill, being empathy in terms of prosocial behavior; however, its design is oriented to be adaptive for multiple learning contexts.

The model consists of two main conceptualizations: a task configuration (classes with white background) and a task execution (classes with blue background). The configuration of a task can be developed individually (single-user) or group (multi-user) and is structured by a sequence of steps, and a step is the combination of an interactive AR space and several 3D entities that are geolocated either by GPS coordinates or by spatial anchors. A task execution keeps track of the real-time state or progress of a task being carried out by a team of players. The real-time state not only involves the state of the task but also the state of the steps and of the related 3D entities that participate in a step. According to the model, different teams may execute the same task configuration. For extensions reasons, in this chapter, we describe a simplified subset of the complete model. The actual model also includes several relationships between steps, allowing for nested steps that may consist of both mandatory and optional sub-steps. This allows the definition of complex structures or game paths to support varying game designers' needs. Also, a step entity (3D object) can have a list of actions with their respective feedback and rewards, whether positive or negative.

4.2 Emotional Intelligence in MAR with Spatial Anchors

The proposal for a location-based MAR game with "spatial anchors" is presented, with competitive vs. collaborative dynamics, which aims to identify and manipulate basic emotional states for emotional intelligence [42], given its influence on positive skills such as empathy, social adaptation/sociability, others [21, 59]. The proposal was evaluated with primary school children in terms of usability and gaming experience and social skills.

4.2.1 Architecture

The proposal is deployed on Apple iOS 11 smartphones, developed with three main technologies:

- Unity as a game development platform, as it has cross-platform development features on IOS and Android operating systems.
- Photon Unity Networking (PUN) for networked multiplayer gaming infrastructure that provides fast communication methods to synchronize player actions across game scenes.
- Placenote Augmented Reality SDK, which uses an advanced computer vision system to position digital content in the real world through coordinates x, y, z (spatial anchors).

4.2.2 Design

The proposal implements location-based MAR scenarios with spatial anchors, which addresses two networked multiplayer game dynamics, competitive vs. collaborative, where the objective is to encourage players to discover characters in the physical environment that show different emotions such as anger, sadness, joy, or others to act on them, throwing objects that intensify or improve the emotional state of the characters.

The game configuration is given by an initialization file (see Fig. 3) to store various game themes (tasks), in this context based on the recognition and manipulation of basic emotions. Each task is structured by two types of digital entities (3D objects), being actors and projectiles.

- **Actors**: Emotional characters that are captured attached to an initial level of life (see Fig. 3, actors). At the beginning of the game, characters are randomly placed in the physical environment (x, y, z points on the 3D map). Each 3D object has a list of configured projectiles that effect its emotional state, either positively or negatively. Finally, the characters are captured by the players in their inventory of objects when they reach the desired emotional state, as in other games such as the well-known Pokémon Go but allowing the participants to identify and act on the emotional states of the characters.
- **Projectiles**: Objects to be thrown (see Fig. 3, projectiles) to achieve a desired emotional state of a target character (actors). When the player selects a projectile, it is instantiated in the center of the screen as a 3D object, follows the movement of the camera, and is launched in whatever direction the camera is pointed when the player touches the object on the screen.

The projectiles have a single throw, where players must find the objects already thrown in the physical environment and recover them to use them again. Each object can only be thrown by the player who created it in the augmented world, although

```
"task": "emotions",
"projectiles": [
  {"id":1, "path": " projectile_heart",
   "rotationX":0," rotationY":0," rotationZ":0},
  {"id":2, "path": " projectile_smile ",
   "rotationX": 0," rotationY":0," rotationZ":0},
  {"id":3, "path": "projectile_crying ",
   "rotationX": 0," rotationY":0," rotationZ":0}
 ],
"actors": [
  {"id":1,
   "path": "actor_angry", "initial_life":10,
   "initX":10,"initY":5,"initZ":7,
   "projectiles": [
      {"id":1,"units":8},
      {"id":2,"units":2}]
  },
  {"id":2,
   "path": "actor_sad", "initial_life":10,
   "random_position": true,
   "projectiles": [
      {"id":1,"units":6},
      {"id":2,"units":4},
      {"id":3,"units": -1}]
   }
 ]
```

Fig. 3 MAR game, initial configuration

other players can see the object and its trajectory in 3D. This increases awareness about what the other players are doing.

The player, after logging in in the competitive or collaborative mode (see Fig. 4), can access the menu of objects (projectiles) that can be thrown (1), being instantiated in the center of the camera for launch (2), the objective characters to capture (actors) along with their 2D interface that shows the percentage of the final emotion acquired (3), which varies depending on the projectile that is thrown at them and how appropriate it is for the change in emotional state. Also, you can check the total score obtained (4) and the characters already captured, either individually or as a team (5). Both actors and projectiles continually move within the augmented 3D space, encouraging players to get closer to these 3D objects to view them from different perspectives. Additionally, 3D objects are instantiated in a network multiplayer system and synchronized on all players' devices, so that both the positions of the projectiles and the actors along with their emotional state will always be updated in real time in all game scenes.

The competitive mode of the proposal is related to the definition of healthy competition [68], "a short activity in which the winners' prizes are not large and that has to be focused on the learning process instead of the results finals". When a projectile hit a target character (actor), it updates their desired emotional level in a positive,

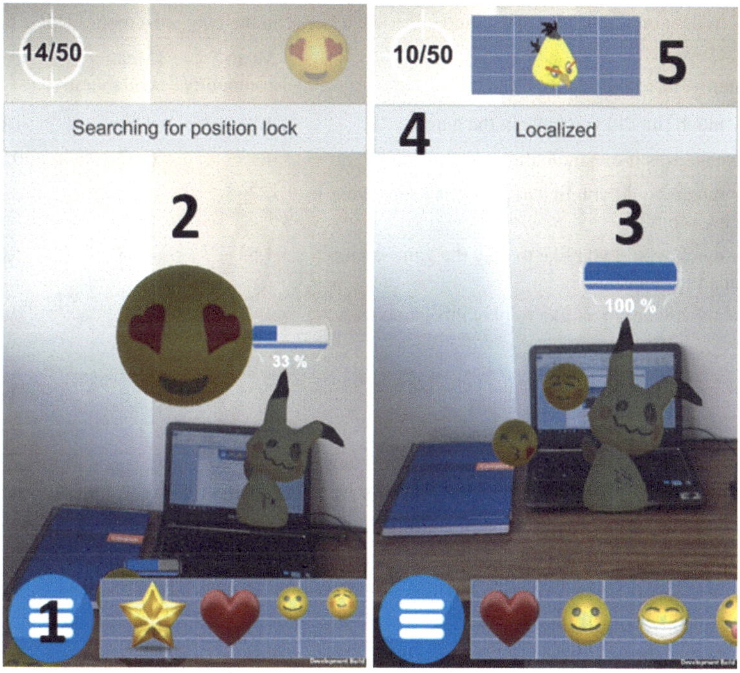

Fig. 4 MAR game, 3D objects instantiated in the real world by spatial anchors

negative, or neutral way. When a character reaches the desired emotional level, it is captured by the player who threw the greatest number of objects suitable for the character to reach the desired final emotional state.

On the contrary, collaborative gameplay requires the joint intervention of two players to capture a character. In this case, a 3D character must be hit by two objects from different players in a time window, which begins when the first object hits the character, forcing the other player to throw another object before the limit time expires. This type of restriction was designed to meet the conditions of collaborative learning [24], such as motivating participants to carry out planning activities (deciding which character to capture, identifying their emotional state, and deciding which objects to throw), coordination (synchronize your launches), and communication (discuss results after coordinated actions).

The game ends when all characters are captured either individually or as a team. If the game is played in competitive mode, the game shows the list of participants with their points earned and the winner; and when it is collaborative everyone wins, the total points obtained as a team are shown.

Table 1 Wilcoxon test results of use and experience between the two game modes (*$P < 0.05$)

Questions (minimum 1, maximum 5)	Mean competitive	Mean collaborative	P-value
1. How much fun did you have in the game?	4.61	4.61	1.000
2. How easy was it to handle the game?	4.13	3.97	0.310
3. How much would you like to play this game again in the classroom?	4.76	4.66	0.356
4. How much would you like to play the game again outside the classroom?	4.55	4.55	1.000
5. How much would you like to play this game with friends?	4.71	4.82	0.102

4.2.3 Evaluation and Results

As a previous step to start the game, the physical location where the learning activity is going to take place must be scanned, where the Placenote infrastructure provides an interface for scanning the physical space and storing it in the cloud. Therefore, prior to the experiment, the classroom space was scanned, and this was done only once before starting the game sessions.

The game was evaluated in a primary school where 38 fifth-grade children aged between 9 and 11 years participated (mean (M) = 10.42, 17 men and 21 women). The children were grouped in pairs with a total of 19 groups. Additionally, consent was obtained from the children to voluntarily participate in the evaluation.

Each pair played in competitive and collaborative mode for an estimated total time of 15 min of play. To obtain the children's opinions about the experience and use of the game [47, 76], a Likert questionnaire was applied to compare both game modes and was applied after finishing each game mode. To the results obtained, the statistical test was applied, where the p-values shown in Table 1 highlight that there are no differences between the two game modes in all the questions evaluated; however, it can be highlighted that all their values are above the intermediate value (3) of the rating scale, minimum 1 and maximum 5.

As a second questionnaire, an observation template was applied to evaluate various events [10] which was completed by two evaluators external to the institution. Table 2 highlights that the collaborative game with significant statistical differences has higher values in affect, physical activity, social interaction, and use of the tool compared to the competitive modality.

4.2.4 Discussion

Our proposal implements a multiplayer game with MAR based on location with spatial anchors, with competitive and collaborative game dynamics for the recognition and manipulation of basic emotional states for emotional intelligence and social skills.

Table 2 Wilcoxon test results of observational data from different events between the two game modes (*$P < 0.05$)

Parameter (minimum 0, maximum 3)	Mean competitive	Mean collaborative	P-value
Affection	1.5570	1.7900	0.000*
Physical activity	1.1012	1.2678	0.026*
Social interaction	0.0437	2.2853	0.000*
Use of the tool	1.4213	1.7200	0.000*
Satisfaction, measured by oral comments made during the activity	1.0087	1.0087	1.000

The competitive and collaborative version differs in the way in which game characters are captured, with the collaborative version being more challenging as communication, collaboration, and synchronization actions with other players are required. Therefore, it is not surprising that children perceived the competitive version as slightly easier (see Table 1, question 2), since this mode involves only individual actions that do not require coordinated actions. However, the results did not show significant statistical differences, indicating that interaction in augmented 3D space was easy for primary school children for both game modes.

At the level of game experience, both modes have high levels of fun, given that their values are above the intermediate value (see Table 1). The cognitive challenges of our game were aligned with producing in the players' feelings of ability to meet the stated objective, which resulted in the children showing no signs of boredom or frustration during the learning activity. Children were willing to return to playing with their friends not only in their school environment but also outside the classroom, demonstrating the potential of MAR games to support learning scenarios in many outdoor contexts. Signs of satisfaction (see Table 2) were not expressed verbally in both modalities. According to the observers, they were focused on the task and did not make explicit comments of satisfaction until the final goal was achieved. However, given that the activity was not carried out repeatedly, nor were the children's interventions very long, these results must be taken with some caution, which is why its impact remains to be studied by developing larger play sessions.

The collaborative game version had a greater impact on emotional affect, promoting physical activity, social interaction, and motivated children to explore the tool with more interest than in the competitive version (see Table 2). This reveals the importance of creating collaborative activities that motivate participants in a fun way to commit to the learning activity. Also, collaboration is a viable alternative for the acquisition of communication skills and allows for the creation of mutual social bonds since it eliminates individualized play and motivates children to create dialogues and interact as a team to achieve a common goal. As mentioned [18], collaboration has the potential to create rules agreed upon by all participants, which leads to creating threads of communication between them.

Finally, a contribution of our study is to show that both competitive and collaborative modalities with MAR can foster intrinsically rewarding learning scenarios, providing educators with an innovative and low-cost technological tool to implement new educational scenarios. Also, our proposal involves the visualization of a single augmented world shared on all the players' devices, without the need for physical markers so as not to limit its deployment in real spaces, another advantage of this proposal.

4.3 Empathy in MAR with GPS Positioning

The proposal of a location-based MAR game with GPS geographic positioning is presented in a single-user version for an individual learning approach [44] and its multi-user extension for a team learning approach [45], supporting the development of empathy in terms of prosocial behavior.

The proposal implements the complete gamified model of learning tasks and steps (see Fig. 1) through help scenarios directed toward a target character. The multi-user version expands the help scenarios to allow teamwork with dynamic collaborative, competitive, and narrative execution through directed dialogues.

The single-user and multi-user versions were evaluated with secondary students in terms of the Interpersonal Reactivity Index (IRI) of empathy and prosocial behavior (PBQ). Different participants are used to evaluate the single-user and multi-user version. At the MAR technology level, qualitative results were also obtained in terms of usability and gaming experience.

4.3.1 Architecture

The proposal implements the gamified learning model of tasks and steps (see Fig. 1) made up of two final applications that interact with each other, being the location-based AR mobile game (client) and a web application (server). Each one was designed for specific purposes (see Fig. 5), so that the web application is intended for the configuration of the gamified learning model of tasks and steps, while the mobile game deployed on Android mobile devices executes said model.

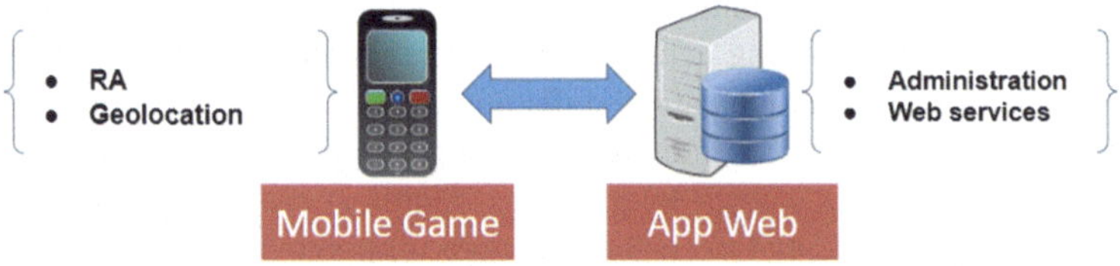

Fig. 5 Location-based MAR game architecture with GPS

The implementation of the game in this section refers to the positioning of geolocated scenarios by GPS coordinates; however, the proposed model has support for various types of location that can take place in a wide variety of physical locations in the real world and that can be implemented for various learning contexts.

For the client, (1) unity was used as the game design framework, (2) AR foundation for the use of Augmented Reality, and (3) AR location for the positioning of the virtual content by coordinates (GPS), being latitude, longitude, and altitude. At the server level, the (4) Django framework was used to configure the gamified learning model of tasks and steps and (5) Django REST framework to create the web services as a communication channel between the two applications.

Additionally, the web application is designed to listen to the changes or actions executed by each player, providing a shared global state of 3D object locations in all players' scenes, creating a multiplayer experience of placing and capturing 3D objects.

4.3.2 Design

The proposal implements MAR scenarios based on GPS location, organized around a central challenge or mission (task) that leads the player to execute various stories individually (single-user) or group (multi-user) for the development of specific skills, being in this particular context for empathy in terms of prosocial behavior.

To start the execution of the tasks available in the MAR game, these must be previously configured in the web application and assigned to the players for execution accordingly. The MAR game starts showing the tasks that the user must execute in session, whether individual or group. If the tasks are group tasks, the players must coordinate as a team the order of the tasks to be executed. When players select the task to solve, the game shows the current step that must be executed along with the physical space where they must move to start the activity as a team or individually.

After initiating a step, its 3D objects are instantiated at real-world GPS positions and appear at the corresponding physical location when the user arrives at that location, where Fig. 6a shows a scenario of a distressed child, where each 3D object can have an animation to give greater realism to each scene. Then, the player must explore the real world to find the 3D objects and perform actions on them such as capture and deposit (b), to achieve the central objective or mission, thus ending the current step. Additionally, each action has its respective feedback (c).

Each 3D object displayed in the augmented world can have positive or negative rewards, which can be captured based on the player's actions, which can be prerequisites to continue with other steps. Negative rewards in these scenarios play the role of distracting entities that do not serve the purpose of the current step. Finally, a task is accomplished when players complete all steps either individually or as a team.

Fig. 6 MAR game, 3D object instantiated in the real world by GPS

4.3.3 Evaluation and Results

The proposal at a single-user and multi-user level was evaluated with secondary students between 12 and 15 years old to measure the impact of the gamified strategy in terms of the level of empathy and prosocial behavior. At the beginning and at the end of the program, students answered two questionnaires. The first was the Interpersonal Reactivity Index (IRI), which is made up of four dimensions of empathy: fantasy, perspective taking, empathic concern, and personal distress rated on a scale of 1–28 [14] and the Prosocial Behavior Questionnaire (PBQ) as a second questionnaire [83] rated on a scale of 1–3. Furthermore, after completing the experiment, a qualitative evaluation was carried out with unstructured interviews with the participants to find out their opinions related to the usability and experience of the game.

Additionally, prior to the experiment, permission was asked from the school and the students were informed that they could leave the study at any time and that the administration of the questionnaires would be anonymous.

An Individual Learning Approach

They were defined four tasks to be solved individually, where players must face a situation in which they must provide help to an objective (see Table 3, where an extract related to an example task is shown). The reason behind the context of providing help is that previous work [66, 69] has shown that tasks related to providing helping promote altruism and prosocial behaviors.

Since a task is made up of steps, Fig. 6 shows as an example Step 1 "Find Maximo" instantiated in the real world. Since a step can be composed of optional steps, Fig. 7 (left) shows an example of an optional step "Find Máximo's friends so they can comfort him" from Task 1 (see Table 3), where several fantastic animated characters are found. Also, in this step some distracting elements are shown that have negative rewards, in this example being angry and unfriendly avatars (see Fig. 7, right). These

Table 3 Task 1, help Maximo who is distressed and crying

Steps	Individual optional steps
Look for Máximo	
What action would you take to help Maximo?	Find Maximo's friends so that they can comfort him
	Look for positive emotions to insert into Maximo's emotional state and minimize his anguish
	Look for sweets to share with him and reduce his distress
Deposit the captured objects near Maximo	

Fig. 7 Task 1, optional step find Maximo's friends so that they can comfort him, friends (left)—angry avatars (right)

Table 4 Single-user MAR game, applied sessions

Sessions	Tasks
Session 1	Task 1 y 2
Session 2	Task 3 y 4
Session 3	Task 1 y 3
Session 4	Task 2 y 4

virtual elements in the physical space help the user understand antisocial and non-empathetic behaviors. When all steps have been completed, the task is complete, and players can see the positive or negative rewards in their inventory of captured items.

The evaluation was carried out with a group of 15 secondary students from the eighth and ninth grades (mean (M) = 13.00, 10 men and 5 women). Each student completed four sessions in one session per day, and in each session, two tasks were completed aimed at providing help to an objective defined in Table 4. Since the tasks were repeated throughout the sessions, for sessions 1 and 2 the tasks were designed for one physical space (court A), and for sessions 3 and 4, they were designed for another physical space (court B), so that the GPS positions of the 3D objects were different.

Table 5 Single-user MAR game, results of the Wilcoxon Signed Rank test for IRI (*$P < 0.05$)

IRI	Mean (pre)	Mean (post)	*P*-value
Fantasy	15.20	18.33	0.012*
Perspective taking	14.53	15.47	0.444
Empathic concern	14.13	18.47	0.001*
Personal distress	15.27	13.47	0.156

Table 6 Single-user MAR game, results of the Wilcoxon Signed Rank test for PBQ (*$P < 0.05$)

PBQ	Mean (pre)	Mean (post)	*P*-value
Prosocial behavior	2.1433	2.3167	0.344

At the beginning and at the end of the program, students answered the Interpersonal Reactivity Index (IRI) questionnaire for empathy and the Prosocial Behavior Questionnaire (PBQ). For the results obtained from the IRI questionnaire, was applied the statistical test presented in Table 5, which shows a significant statistical difference in two dimensions of empathy such as fantasy and empathic concern.

For the PBQ, Table 6 shows that the level of prosocial behavior after completing the sessions improved in the students; however, the results lack significant statistical differences.

In addition to the quantitative results, the qualitative user experience was also obtained when interacting with a product [8] and receives comments and feedback on the game proposal. In general, all participants mentioned that they really liked the game and commented on its usefulness. For example, P1 said: "I recommend it to a friend because it is a very friendly game to learn about help, honesty, etc.". From a feedback point of view, other players recommended some points to further improve the gameplay dynamics such as: greater diversity of characters with more tasks or missions and multiplayer scenarios. As P2 said: "If it were for two people, it would be much better". Some players also suggested that tasks should not be repeated in sessions and that there should be more physical space to move. For example, P3 said, "It is repetitive and has no new stories", while P4 commented, "The physical space should be expanded and there should be more tasks to solve".

A Team Learning Approach

To have a greater contribution to the learning of empathy in terms of prosocial behavior, there are group activities that allow participants to improve the skills of building trust, conflict management, communication, and collaboration, which leads to positively influencing development of positive relationships and social behaviors [24, 79].

Under this justification, the study expands the individual help tasks, to be solved as a team with competitive and collaborative dynamics. To these tasks, four additional ones were added to create collaborative directed dialogues, thus having eight multi-user tasks differentiated in two contexts: (a) a context in which the players face a situation in which they must provide help to an objective as a group, and (b) a narrative context in which a dramatization is proposed through dialogues that users have to verbalize as if they were actors related to a situation that requires empathetic behavior.

The reason behind the narrative context is that using the think-aloud method, that is, asking people to speak out loud while carrying out a task, facilitates the acquisition of knowledge [65]. According to Van Someren and others [82], this approach is used in the context of many cognitive processes, including the manifestation of empathy. In addition, there are studies that conclude that the method of thinking aloud through collaborative scenarios facilitates social interaction [65].

- *Task 1, Help Maximo, who is distressed and crying*

  Helping tasks combine healthy competition and collaboration. For the task presented as example in Table 3, the players for steps 1 and 3 must "collaborate" with each other to find the 3D objects in the real world and perform actions such as "search" or "deposit" in order to finish as a team the current step.

  Step 2 shows players the optional steps available, so they can choose as a team the step they want to solve. This step implements the competitive dynamic, where players must "compete" to "capture" the greatest number of 3D objects individually. When a 3D object is captured by a player, the object is deleted from the scenes of the other players who are part of the team; this is intended for the game to maintain a global state or scene of 3D object locations by making the players visualize from different positions in the real world the same game scene.
- *Task 2, Narrative about bullying Jorge*

  Since a 3D object of a task can have a list of actions and each action gives feedback (see Fig. 1), a narrative model was implemented that allows players to dramatize a situation to verbally exercise empathic skills thanks to the existence of a "theatrical prompter" appearing as text in augmented physical space. Table 7 shows an excerpt from a narrative proposal.

At the level of execution of the narrative task in the MAR game, Fig. 8 shows the dialogue of Player A, who initiates the narrative in Step 1 of Task 2, "Start the dialogue" (see Table 7). In this step, the system displays a 3D object (chest) that represents the beginning of the dialogue and shows the actions and feedback according to its configuration.

Continuing with Step 1 in Task 2, the narrative continues with Player B responding to Player A's dialogue. In this step, the system shows a 3D object (question) that represents the answer in the dialogue. This 3D entity displays its list of actions (possible answers to give). The user is therefore free to direct the narrative and receive positive or negative feedback based on their decisions (see Fig. 9).

The group task proposal was evaluated with a group of 34 secondary students in the ninth and tenth grades (mean $(M) = 13.79$, 21 men and 13 women). Based on the eight available tasks, the evaluation was designed so that each group of two students

Table 7 Task 2, narrative about bullying Jorge

Steps	Player A (starts dialogue)	Player B (responds to dialogue)
Start the dialogue	Accompany him with facial gestures/tone of voice to give more realism, tell your friend "I'm angry and I'll take it out on Jorge"	What should your friend do? Select an option: "Take away his anger somehow so he's okay": It is not correct, the man who cultivates kindness never thinks of harming anyone "Don't hurt innocent people": Tell your friend, "Don't be filled with anger or violence, these are conditions that make it impossible to live happily"
Take perspective, put yourself in Jorge's place	Accompany him with facial gestures/tone of voice that determines anger or friendship, tell your friend "There's Jorge, let's go see him"	What does your friend plan to do? Select an option: "Harassing Jorge": This is not correct; bullying is a rare event and usually does more harm than good "Talk with Jorge": Tell your friend "Remember, friendship doubles the joys and divides the anguish"
Choose the final scenario	What do you plan to do? Select an option: "Harass Jorge": It's not right, abuse is horrible, it poisons you, but only if you let it "Chat with my friend Jorge": Tell your friend "You're right, friendship is the development of mutual respect"	Tell your friend "Remember, life is based on good deeds" Congratulations, you have reflected on bullying

Fig. 8 Task 2, Step 1, Player A starts the dialogue

Fig. 9 Task 2, Step 1, Player B responds to the dialogue

Table 8 Multi-user MAR game, *t*-test results for related samples IRI (*$P < 0.05$)

IRI	Mean (pre)	Mean (post)	*P*-value
Fantasy	14.00	17.68	0.000*
Perspective taking	15.00	17.06	0.001*
Empathic concern	15.03	18.74	0.000*
Personal distress	12.88	14.21	0.226

Table 9 Multi-user MAR game, *t*-test results for related samples PBQ (*$P < 0.05$)

PBQ	Mean (pre)	Mean (post)	*P*-value
Prosocial behavior	2.0324	2.4838	0.000*

develops four sessions, one session per day, and in each session, they execute two tasks, starting with the help tasks and culminating with the narrative tasks.

At the beginning and at the end of the program, students answered the same questionnaires from the individual learning approach. For the IRI, the results presented in Table 8 show that there is a significant statistical difference in the dimensions of fantasy, perspective taking, and empathic concern.

For the PBQ questionnaire (see Table 9), significant results were obtained at the level of prosocial behavior after completing the experiment.

Through the interview applied at the end of the program, qualitative opinions related to the usability and experience of the game were obtained. Regarding the usability of the system, some participants gave positive opinions, as P1 said "I don't have any observations, I think it's perfect", although other users pointed out some concerns related to the display of the 3D content. P2 said, "I wish the graphics were more visible", and P3 said, "In sunlight conditions, it was sometimes difficult to see the screen". These problems would be avoided in future experiments if high-resolution OLED displays are used.

Regarding the experience of the proposed game, some users said that they would like to have more challenging tasks as well as more realistic content as P4 said: "I would like to see more realistic characters, like real people". Also, participants enjoyed the narrative style. As P5 stated, "I really liked the chest" and P6 said "I liked the dialogues".

4.3.4 Discussion

The game proposal with MAR based on location with GPS positioning, structured in a conceptual model of tasks and steps, allowed the implementation of reflective scenarios so that students work individually or in teams to develop certain skills, such as empathy in terms of prosocial behavior.

The team learning approach is an improved version of the individual approach, thanks to feedback suggested by students. Individual tasks of providing help to a target were expanded with collaborative and competitive group dynamics. Duplication of tasks was also avoided, thus providing new and more challenging scenarios for all sessions. Additionally, since the students requested greater diversity of 3D objects, the 3D objects of the optional steps were expanded so that there is greater diversity of objects to capture.

Quantitative Results

The individualized game had a positive impact as a learning strategy only in two dimensions of the Interpersonal Reactivity Index (IRI) of empathy, being fantasy and empathic concern; however, the multi-user proposal as team learning improved these results, promoting three dimensions of the IRI such as fantasy, perspective taking, and empathic concern and, in turn, prosocial behavior.

The students observed "3D objects for thinking" in the game scene displaying different animations in the augmented world to represent reflective situations such as bullying, crying, emergency situations or poverty, and the manipulation and exploration of these tangible artifacts in the real world facilitated that the participants reflect and identify with the fictional characters in the scene, thus helping to intensify the sensation of fantasy.

A characteristic of MAR is "perceived realism" [13], which led to our proposal being able to show help scenarios in the real world, trying to get as close as possible to reality, leading the player to get involved in the situation with all your skills to overcome the proposed challenge. These immersive characteristic generated feelings of concern, compassion, and caring in the students that led them to want to help the target avatar (empathic concern). The immersion of our game is also justified by the work of Georgiou and others [25], which mention that location-based AR contexts provoke immersion due to a set of unique characteristics such as: they employ mobile and location-based interfaces that combine physical and digital spaces, allowing the activity to be extended beyond the limits of the traditional digital space, which encourages players to explore the physical world in different directions.

Perspective taking is a complex and continuous process that requires motivation and practice [17], which is why it is recommended that future training programs can be continuous to allow participants to experience situations from different perspectives. In our proposal at the single-user level, the lack of significant statistical difference in perspective taking could have been affected by the duplicated tasks, since the students knew the scenarios in the subsequent sessions, failing to generate new perspectives in the participants. On the contrary, the multi-user version executed non-repetitive scenarios which led to improved results. Additionally, the narrative style through the "think aloud" technique to construct meaning of the stories presented contributed to the improvement of this dimension, which motivated the participants to adopt different roles to imagine the situations from different perspectives.

Personal distress was not affected by any approach, whether at the single-user or multi-user level. It would be interesting in future to evaluate factors that may affect this ability, such as feelings of loneliness [12], others, in order to design technological resources conducive to controlling this feeling, which is more associated with selfish motivation, rather than altruistic one [20].

At the level of prosocial behavior, the multi-user version seems to improve the level of prosocial behavior in students immediately after the gaming activity with significant statistical differences. This is argued by the collaborative and competitive dynamics of the MAR game, which allowed the players to generate planning, communication, and collaboration activities to develop the assigned task as a team, which in turn lead to positively influence the development of positive relationships and skills social, as also argued by previous works [24]. However, our evaluation does not ensure that the learning of these skills lasts over time. A long-term study would be necessary to evaluate its impact for prolonged learning.

Qualitative Results

Implementing the task and step learning model in our MAR game enabled step-driven navigability, which guided players in the augmented world to meet the assigned goal. Our proposal also unites the real and virtual world into one to give players a degree of realism, being a feature that positively affects gameplay [61].

To further improve the dynamics of the game, it is necessary to highlight some qualitative characteristics resulting from the training. Some users said that they would like to have more challenging tasks in which time restricted actions need to be done or hidden content needs to be found by solving puzzles and mysteries. This brings out an important issue when designing these types of environments. Young players who are used to playing challenging games on mobile devices expect this level of difficulty and complexity in serious games as the one described in this work. This feedback is important for us to create future scenarios designed with difficulty levels according to the capabilities and skills of each student.

Another interesting issue raised by some participants was the need for more realistic content, without a cartoon style. This shows that for some participants, having synthetic and non-realistic 3D characters made them feel less emotionally attached. This point should not be ignored because a serious AR-based game that aims to improve players' prosocial attitudes needs to establish both cognitive and emotional links between the game characters and the players. If players feel that the characters shown are unrealistic and see them as artificial artifacts, then they will not perceive them as real elements of the game and empathy processes may be hindered. In our future implementations, we plan to solve this problem by avoiding some of the non-human characters that were used in this experiment. This problem can also be an argument in favor of scenarios with a narrative design in which real people (the players) are complemented with 3D content instead of having virtual characters that simulate the presence of people. These design decisions still need to be evaluated in future experiments.

Regarding the style of the game, it was surprising to the research team that the participants enjoyed the narrative style. When users were asked why they liked the "chest", they responded that it helped them think about possible responses that could occur in a similar real-world situation. Therefore, it seems that these scenarios helped participants engage in self-reflective thoughts, which aligns with other works where they mention that narrative is a useful intervention to promote empathy and self-reflection, which would eventually lead to more prosocial behavior [37].

The narrative context also raises an important question that was not evaluated in this work. It remains to be seen whether narrative scenarios involving more than two players would provide additional benefits. In this case, some participants might express aggressive antisocial behaviors, while others might select appropriate prosocial narrative statements to counteract the incorrect behaviors expressed by some classmates. It would be interesting to evaluate whether the coexistence of these two antagonistic behaviors interpreted/simulated by real individuals would be more effective than the narrative schemes evaluated in the present work.

5 Design Guidelines for Future Work with MAR

The two proposals for games with MAR based on location were evaluated in the educational context; therefore, based on the quantitative and qualitative results that emerged from the evaluations, some design guidelines for location-based MAR games are defined on the design requirements of AR experience and social skills learning in education.

Game time management (DG1): Our gamification proposal did not use time as an additional challenge. However, as they demonstrated good usability skills with MAR, it is feasible to introduce time as a game challenge to evaluate its impact on achieving goals. Educational games should also incorporate a time limit to control this resource [84].

Skill and balanced challenge (DG2): Integrate difficulty levels into the game according to the capabilities or expectations of each player for a total immersion experience "flow". As Ben and others mention [7], when skill and challenge are balanced, an optimal immersive experience can occur (flow).

Mixed competitive-collaborative mode (DG3): Define collaborative multi-user activities to compete between groups, to encourage students to communicate and collaborate further to win the game against other groups. These dynamics allow students to work on their strengths, develop critical thinking, validate their ideas, and appreciate a variety of learning styles, abilities, preferences, and individual perspectives [84]. Collaboration also allows working in groups with a common objective to develop planning, communication, and collaboration skills, where the literature argues that these skills lead to positively influencing the development of positive relationships and social skills [24, 79].

Face-to-face game (DG4): Multi-user educational games must create a physical interaction between players, where users meet face to face to execute a given game session [3], which will allow students to put into practice emotional and social skills. In a face-to-face context, it is also possible to have much more control over when and where students interact with the game [84], thus minimizing the risks of addiction.

Choice of augmented scenarios (DG5): Provide diversity of tasks to give players the option to choose the challenge or mission, where this choice gives players the feeling of being in control of the game [73]. Therefore, our gamified model based on tasks and steps is designed to be adapted to multiple learning contexts for the development of specific skills in education.

Support active learning (DG6): The themes of the game can be diverse; however, the context must provide opportunities for exploration, problem-solving, and inquiry, which will allow students to evaluate ideas, apply strategies, obtain feedback, and practice and consolidate your learning [84]. Furthermore, previous research [24] confirmed that providing these opportunities creates learning environments driven by intrinsic motivation.

Global 3D Object Space (DG7): AR location-based games allow the game to take place in a wide variety of real-world physical locations, which leads to creating a global space of placement and capture of multi-user 3D objects, displaying the same scenery to all participants.

Dynamic 3D objects to add to realism (DG8): 3D objects in augmented space are attractive to students but could incorporate additional functions to make the MAR game even more dynamic and attractive, as several students suggested after finishing the game. This could include more explicit visual changes to game characters to reflect their emotional state more vividly, contributing to realism perceiving AR. Also instantiate realistic-looking avatars in the augmented world to generate a greater contribution to immersion. In this sense, Daassi and others [13] maintain that "perceived realism" is a component that contributes to immersion. These aspects are related to intrinsic motivation [73], which involves simulations, fun challenges, a sense of wonder and curiosity, leading students to want to learn instead of having to learn.

3D objects for thinking (DG9): Provide avatars in the augmented world with animations representing different situations, so that students observe, manipulate, and explore tangible artifacts serving as a bridge to reflect on the experiences of others. This theory is applicable from previous gaming work [17, 28].

Augmented space with help and feedback actions (DG10): Integrate dialogue-driven narrative into help tasks, where 3D objects instantiated in the real world can react with reflective phrases to create short dialogues whether player–avatar or player–player, since the narrative adds value to empathy along with prosocial behavior [37, 67].

"Think-aloud" directed dialogues (DG11): To execute guided dialogues between participants, implement the "think-aloud" method to construct meaning from the presented text, encouraging participants to promote the adoption of roles to better understand the stories presented and reflect on them.

Fictional narrative connected to reality (DG12): Design AR scenarios connected to real experiences of vulnerable groups or specific groups in society to encourage self-reflection and thereby promote social skills.

Reinforce Knowledge (DG13): Introduce specific self-reflection strategies at the end of each session to help students reflect on their decisions made in the game. It is important to highlight that the strategies implemented by games for the acquisition of knowledge must be complemented with traditional learning techniques to provide an adequate academic balance [41]. Additionally, this feedback can improve students' concentration levels, thus providing opportunities for long-term learning [73].

Finally, all these recommendations will help create dynamic and attractive AR multiplayer scenarios to improve students' degree of involvement in a learning activity.

6 Conclusions and Future Works

Teaching social skills in educational programs has gained popularity because it influences the positive development of students and prevents an upward trajectory of aggressive behaviors. One approach to promote learning in education is gamification or game-based learning since it improves students' motivation to learn, participation, and satisfaction in the learning activity, even more so in those ubiquitous games that enrich the real environment of the user with digital content to transmit gaming experiences to the real world, as AR does [41]. In fact, the study of situated learning in physical spaces with accessible technology such as MAR and location-based with respect to the development of social skills in education is still in early stages.

Given that empathy is related to prosocial behavior, a theoretical model is proposed that unifies the main components and processes of empathy, ending with actions on the target such as prosocial behavior. The model was transformed into operational game dynamics that lead the player to experience a variety of reflective situations following the "observation-action" loop. For this, a gamified learning model based on tasks and steps was designed that leads the player to execute various reflective stories (observation) organized around a central challenge or mission, developed individually (single-user) or group (multi-user), seeking to promote positive emotions such as empathy in terms of prosocial behavior (action). These scenarios are augmented in the real world by GPS coordinates or by spatial anchors (previously scanned physical space). Additionally, the learning model can be adapted to multiple learning contexts.

Two location-based multi-user MAR game proposals were developed. The first with "spatial anchors" designed at a multi-user level with competitive dynamics vs. collaborative that implements scenarios for identifying and manipulating basic emotional states for emotional intelligence. The proposal was evaluated with primary school students, and the results indicate that both modalities motivated the participants to get involved in the learning activity and also collaboration had a greater contribution to the children's social interaction. The second proposal supported the Global Positioning System (GPS), which implemented the gamified model of learning tasks and steps through help scenarios aimed at a target character, at a single-user and multi-user level. Additionally, the multi-user version added narratives executed through collaborative directed dialogues that require the emission of empathetic responses. The effectiveness of the proposal in single-user and multi-user versions was evaluated by secondary students, where the individualized game had a positive impact as a learning strategy only in two dimensions of the Interpersonal Reactivity Index (IRI) of empathy: fantasy and concern empathic. The multi-user version as team learning expanded these results, promoting three dimensions of the IRI: fantasy, perspective taking, and empathic concern and, in turn, prosocial behavior. It was also evident that the narrative approach of the multi-user version contributed positively to these results.

The two location-based MAR game proposals were intrinsically satisfactory at the level of usability and game experience in the students, so we consider that these strategies are innovative techniques that enhance the motivation in the participants to learn specific skills, such as empathy in terms of prosocial behavior. In future work, we recommend integrating difficulty levels that match the student's skills and abilities to drive an optimal immersion experience "flow" [7]. Also evaluate if these levels can be adaptive for goals developed as a team with competitive and collaborative dynamics. Also, we highlight that gamified strategies to promote a skill must be complemented with traditional learning techniques to provide an adequate academic balance [41], to also support a long-term learning effect.

At a comparative level of the techniques used to create location-based AR games, it could be seen that "spatial anchors" provide greater positioning accuracy for 3D objects than GPS-based solutions. Additionally, spatial anchors are adapted to work in both outdoor and indoor spaces. The second option is being the "Global Positioning System (GPS)", functional only in open spaces given its low performance indoors due to the imprecision of the GPS satellite signals [33]. GPS also has precision limits to position 3D objects in the real world, either due to weather conditions or the precision of the smartphone's GPS, where these results agree with other researchers who highlight this inaccuracy [49]. However, an advantage of this placement technique is the ability to anchor augmented objects to a global spatial reference remotely, rather than having to be physically on site to anchor such content (spatial anchors). In future, it would be useful to explore other technological proposals to try to address the inaccuracy of geolocation data using GPS, for example, the ARCore geospatial API or complementing satellite navigation with real-time kinematic positioning (RTK). This is also in order to analyze the feasibility of designing collaborative tasks to perform actions on the same 3D object in real time, approaching the Photon Unity Networking (PUN) solution being a networked multiplayer game infrastructure, implemented in our proposal with space anchors.

Finally, we have also proposed in this work several guidelines to consider in the design of interactive MAR systems for the promotion of social skills in students, which we believe are useful for professionals in the field. There are also lines of research that should be addressed in future, and we hope that this manuscript can serve as a basis for continuing to explore how MAR technology can provide opportunities to support the learning of specific skills in education.

References

1. Al Rabbaa J, Morris A, Somanath S (2019) MRsive: an augmented reality tool for enhancing wayfinding and engagement with art in museums, pp 535–542. https://doi.org/10.1007/978-3-030-23525-3_73
2. Álvarez-Bermejo JA, Belmonte-Ureña LJ, Martos-Martínez A, Barragán-Martín AB, del Mar Simón-Marquez M (2016) System to detect racial-based bullying through gamification. Front Psychol 7. https://doi.org/10.3389/fpsyg.2016.01791
3. Ang CS, Avni E, Zaphiris P (2008) Linking pedagogical theory of computer games to their usability. Int J E-Learn 7(3):533–558. https://www.learntechlib.org/p/24229
4. Arango-López J, Collazos CA, Gutiérrez Vela FL, Castillo LF (2017) A systematic review of geolocated pervasive games: a perspective from game development methodologies, software metrics and linked open data, pp 335–346. https://doi.org/10.1007/978-3-319-58637-3_27
5. Baabdullah AM, Alsulaimani AA, Allamnakhrah A, Alalwan AA, Dwivedi YK, Rana NP (2022) Usage of augmented reality (AR) and development of e-learning outcomes: an empirical evaluation of students' e-learning experience. Comput Educ 177:104383. https://doi.org/10.1016/j.compedu.2021.104383
6. Bachen CM, Hernández-Ramos P, Raphael C, Waldron A (2016) How do presence, flow, and character identification affect players' empathy and interest in learning from a serious computer game? Comput Hum Behav 64:77–87. https://doi.org/10.1016/j.chb.2016.06.043
7. Ben Itzhak N, Franki I, Jansen B, Kostkova K, Wagemans J, Ortibus E (2023) Usability and user experience of an individualized and adaptive game-based therapy for children with cerebral visual impairment. Int J Child-Comput Interact 35:100551. https://doi.org/10.1016/j.ijcci.2022.100551
8. Bernhaupt R (2010) User experience evaluation in entertainment, pp 3–7. https://doi.org/10.1007/978-1-84882-963-3_1
9. Çakiroğlu Ü, Aydin M, Köroğlu Y, Ayvaz Kina M (2023) Looking past seeing present: teaching historical empathy skills via augmented reality. Interact Learn Environ 1–13. https://doi.org/10.1080/10494820.2023.2174142
10. Carrion-Plaza A, Jaen J, Montoya-Castilla I (2020) HabitApp: new play technologies in pediatric cancer to improve the psychosocial state of patients and caregivers. Front Psychol 11. https://doi.org/10.3389/fpsyg.2020.00157
11. Cheng Y, Bololia L (2023) The effects of augmented reality on social skills in children with an autism diagnosis: a preliminary systematic review. J Autism Dev Disord. https://doi.org/10.1007/s10803-022-05878-4
12. Cudo A, Kopiś N, Zabielska-Mendyk E (2019) Personal distress as a mediator between self-esteem, self-efficacy, loneliness and problematic video gaming in female and male emerging adult gamers. PLoS ONE 14(12):e0226213. https://doi.org/10.1371/journal.pone.0226213
13. Daassi M, Debbabi S (2021) Intention to reuse AR-based apps: the combined role of the sense of immersion, product presence and perceived realism. Inf Manag 58(4):103453. https://doi.org/10.1016/j.im.2021.103453
14. Davis MH (1980) A multidimensional approach to individual differences in empathy. JSAS Catalog Sel Doc Psychol 10:85

15. Davis MH (1994) Empathy. A social psychological approach. Published 2018 by Routledge. https://books.google.com.ec/books?id=fC1NDwAAQBAJ
16. Dechsling A, Orm S, Kalandadze T, Sütterlin S, Øien RA, Shic F, Nordahl-Hansen A (2022) Virtual and augmented reality in social skills interventions for individuals with autism spectrum disorder: a scoping review. J Autism Dev Disord 52(11):4692–4707. https://doi.org/10.1007/s10803-021-05338-5
17. Dishon G, Kafai YB (2020) Making more of games: cultivating perspective-taking through game design. Comput Educ 148:103810. https://doi.org/10.1016/j.compedu.2020.103810
18. Dunleavy M, Dede C, Mitchell R (2009) Affordances and limitations of immersive participatory augmented reality simulations for teaching and learning. J Sci Educ Technol 18(1):7–22. https://doi.org/10.1007/s10956-008-9119-1
19. Edele A, Dziobek I, Keller M (2013) Explaining altruistic sharing in the dictator game: the role of affective empathy, cognitive empathy, and justice sensitivity. Learn Individ Differ 24:96–102. https://doi.org/10.1016/j.lindif.2012.12.020
20. Eisenberg N, Fabes RA (1990) Empathy: conceptualization, measurement, and relation to prosocial behavior. Motiv Emot 14(2):131–149. https://doi.org/10.1007/BF00991640
21. Engelberg E, Sjöberg L (2004) Emotional intelligence, affect intensity, and social adjustment. Pers Individ Differ 37(3):533–542. https://doi.org/10.1016/j.paid.2003.09.024
22. Ferreira PC, Veiga Simão AM, Paiva A, Martinho C, Prada R, Ferreira A, Santos F (2021) Exploring empathy in cyberbullying with serious games. Comput Educ 166:104155. https://doi.org/10.1016/j.compedu.2021.104155
23. Feshbach ND (1978) Studies of empathic behavior in children. Prog Exp Pers Res 8:1–47. http://www.ncbi.nlm.nih.gov/pubmed/360290
24. Garcia F, Jurdi S, Jaen J, Nacher V (2018) Evaluating a tactile and a tangible multi-tablet gamified quiz system for collaborative learning in primary education. Comput Educ 123:65–84. https://doi.org/10.1016/J.COMPEDU.2018.04.011
25. Georgiou Y, Kyza EA (2018) Relations between student motivation, immersion and learning outcomes in location-based augmented reality settings. Comput Hum Behav 89:173–181. https://doi.org/10.1016/j.chb.2018.08.011
26. Ghasemi Y, Jeong H, Choi SH, Park K-B, Lee JY (2022) Deep learning-based object detection in augmented reality: a systematic review. Comput Ind 139:103661. https://doi.org/10.1016/j.compind.2022.103661
27. Guarese R, Pretty E, Fayek H, Zambetta F, van Schyndel R (2023) Evoking empathy with visually impaired people through an augmented reality embodiment experience. In: 2023 IEEE conference virtual reality and 3D user interfaces (VR), pp 184–193. https://doi.org/10.1109/VR55154.2023.00034
28. Holbert N, Wilensky U (2019) Designing educational video games to be objects-to-think-with. J Learn Sci 28(1):32–72. https://doi.org/10.1080/10508406.2018.1487302
29. Höyng M (2022) Encouraging gameful experience in digital game-based learning: a double-mediation model of perceived instructional support, group engagement, and flow. Comput Educ 179:104408. https://doi.org/10.1016/j.compedu.2021.104408
30. Ifrim A-C, Moldoveanu F, Moldoveanu A, Grădinaru A (2021) LibrARy—enriching the cultural physical spaces with collaborative AR content, pp 626–638. https://doi.org/10.1007/978-3-030-77599-5_43
31. Intawong K, Puritat K (2021) A framework of developing mobile gamification to improve user engagement of physical activity: a case study of location-based augmented reality mobile game for promoting physical health. Int J Online Biomed Eng (IJOE) 17(07):100. https://doi.org/10.3991/ijoe.v17i07.22349
32. Irshad S, Rohaya Bt Awang Rambli D (2014) User experience of mobile augmented reality: a review of studies. In: 2014 3rd international conference on user science and engineering (i-USEr), pp 125–130. https://doi.org/10.1109/IUSER.2014.7002689
33. Janarthanan R, Annapoorani A, Abhilash S, Dinesh P (2022) Implementation of gamified navigation and location mapping using augmented reality, pp 265–276. https://doi.org/10.1007/978-981-19-2347-0_20

34. Keskin SC (2014) From what isn't empathy to empathic learning process. Procedia Soc Behav Sci 116:4932–4938. https://doi.org/10.1016/j.sbspro.2014.01.1052
35. Khayyat M, Yahya S, Alsharabi M, Aljahdali A, Alshehri A (2020) Implementation success of an indoor navigation with location-based augmented reality. Int J Recent Technol Eng (IJRTE) 8(6):367–373. https://doi.org/10.35940/ijrte.E4915.038620
36. Khowaja K, Al-Thani D, Banire B, Salim SS, Shah A (2019) Use of augmented reality for social communication skills in children and adolescents with autism spectrum disorder (ASD): a systematic review. In: 2019 IEEE 6th international conference on engineering technologies and applied sciences (ICETAS), pp 1–7. https://doi.org/10.1109/ICETAS48360.2019.9117290
37. Koopman EM (Emy), Hakemulder F (2015) Effects of literature on empathy and self-reflection: a theoretical-empirical framework. J Lit Theory 9(1). https://doi.org/10.1515/jlt-2015-0005
38. Krath J, Schürmann L, von Korflesch HFO (2021) Revealing the theoretical basis of gamification: a systematic review and analysis of theory in research on gamification, serious games and game-based learning. Comput Hum Behav 125:106963. https://doi.org/10.1016/j.chb.2021.106963
39. Lee L-K, Chau C-P, Tsoi K-N, Yang NL, Wu N-I (2019) A mobile game for learning English vocabulary with augmented reality block builder, pp 116–128. https://doi.org/10.1007/978-981-13-9895-7_11
40. Lim MY, Leichtenstern K, Kriegel M, Enz S, Aylett R, Vannini N, Hall L, Rizzo P (2011) Technology-enhanced role-play for social and emotional learning context—intercultural empathy. Entertain Comput 2(4):223–231. https://doi.org/10.1016/j.entcom.2011.02.004
41. López JA, Collazos CA, Velas FLG, Moreira F (2018) Using pervasive games as learning tools in educational contexts: a systematic review. Int J Learn Technol 13(2):93. https://doi.org/10.1504/IJLT.2018.092094
42. López-Faican L, Jaen J (2020) EmoFindAR: evaluation of a mobile multiplayer augmented reality game for primary school children. Comput Educ 149:103814. https://doi.org/10.1016/j.compedu.2020.103814
43. López-Faican L, Jaen J (2021) Designing gamified interactive systems for empathy development. In: Companion publication of the 2021 ACM designing interactive systems conference, pp 27–29. https://doi.org/10.1145/3468002.3468236
44. López-Faican L, Jaen J (2023) Design and evaluation of an augmented reality cyberphysical game for the development of empathic abilities. Int J Hum Comput Stud 176:103041. https://doi.org/10.1016/j.ijhcs.2023.103041
45. López-Faican L, Jaen J, Montaner J (2023) Exploring augmented reality in multiplayer game design to promote empathy and prosocial behavior. In: XXIII international conference on human computer interaction, pp 1–8. https://doi.org/10.1145/3612783.3612794
46. Lorenzo G, Gómez-Puerta M, Arráez-Vera G, Lorenzo-Lledó A (2019) Preliminary study of augmented reality as an instrument for improvement of social skills in children with autism spectrum disorder. Educ Inf Technol 24(1):181–204. https://doi.org/10.1007/s10639-018-9768-5
47. Lund AM (2001) Measuring usability with the USE questionnaire. Usability Interface 8(2):3–6
48. Luo Z (2022) Gamification for educational purposes: what are the factors contributing to varied effectiveness? Educ Inf Technol 27(1):891–915. https://doi.org/10.1007/s10639-021-10642-9
49. Mercier J, Chabloz N, Dozot G, Ertz O, Bocher E, Rappo D (2023) BiodivAR: a cartographic authoring tool for the visualization of geolocated media in augmented reality. ISPRS Int J Geo Inf 12(2):61. https://doi.org/10.3390/ijgi12020061
50. Mittmann G, Zehetner V, Hoehl S, Schrank B, Barnard A, Woodcock K (2023) Using augmented reality toward improving social skills: scoping review. JMIR Serious Games 11:e42117. https://doi.org/10.2196/42117
51. Mukkawar VV, Netak LD (2022) Technological evaluation of virtual and augmented reality to impart social skills, pp 62–73. https://doi.org/10.1007/978-3-030-98404-5_6
52. Nakazawa A, Iwamoto M, Kurazume R, Nunoi M, Kobayashi M, Honda M (2023) Augmented reality-based affective training for improving care communication skill and empathy. PLoS ONE 18(7):e0288175. https://doi.org/10.1371/journal.pone.0288175

53. Orm S, Vatne T, Tomeny TS, Fjermestad K (2021) Empathy and prosocial behavior in siblings of children with autism spectrum disorder: a systematic review. Rev J Autism Dev Disord. https://doi.org/10.1007/s40489-021-00251-0
54. Paananen V, Kiarostami MS, Lik-Hang L, Braud T, Hosio S (2024) From digital media to empathic spaces: a systematic review of empathy research in extended reality environments. ACM Comput Surv 56(5):1–40. https://doi.org/10.1145/3626518
55. Papoutsi C, Drigas A, Skianis C (2021) Virtual and augmented reality for developing emotional intelligence skills. Int J Recent Contrib Eng Sci IT (IJES) 9(3):35. https://doi.org/10.3991/ijes.v9i3.23939
56. Pérez-Fuentes M del C, Álvarez-Bermejo JA, Molero M del M, Gázquez JJ, López Vicente MA (2015) Violencia Escolar y Rendimiento Académico (VERA): aplicación de realidad aumentada. Eur J Investig Health Psychol Educ 1(2):71. https://doi.org/10.30552/ejihpe.v1i2.19
57. Perry B (2021) Gamified mobile collaborative location-based language learning. Front Educ 6. https://doi.org/10.3389/feduc.2021.689599
58. Rauschnabel PA, Felix R, Hinsch C, Shahab H, Alt F (2022) What is XR? Towards a framework for augmented and virtual reality. Comput Hum Behav 133:107289. https://doi.org/10.1016/j.chb.2022.107289
59. Ruiz-Ariza A, Casuso RA, Suarez-Manzano S, Martínez-López EJ (2018) Effect of augmented reality game Pokémon GO on cognitive performance and emotional intelligence in adolescent young. Comput Educ 116:49–63. https://doi.org/10.1016/j.compedu.2017.09.002
60. Sáez-López J-M, Sevillano-García-García ML, Pascual-Sevillano M de los Á (2019) Application of the ubiquitous game with augmented reality in Primary Education. Comunicar 27(61):71–82. https://doi.org/10.3916/C61-2019-06
61. Sánchez JLG, Vela FLG, Simarro FM, Padilla-Zea N (2012) Playability: analysing user experience in video games. Behav Inf Technol 31(10):1033–1054. https://doi.org/10.1080/0144929X.2012.710648
62. Sánchez Riera A, Redondo E, Fonseca D (2015) Geo-located teaching using handheld augmented reality: good practices to improve the motivation and qualifications of architecture students. Univ Access Inf Soc 14(3):363–374. https://doi.org/10.1007/s10209-014-0362-3
63. Scavarelli A, Arya A, Teather RJ (2021) Virtual reality and augmented reality in social learning spaces: a literature review. Virtual Reality 25(1):257–277. https://doi.org/10.1007/s10055-020-00444-8
64. Segal EA (2011) Social empathy: a model built on empathy, contextual understanding, and social responsibility that promotes social justice. J Soc Serv Res 37(3):266–277. https://doi.org/10.1080/01488376.2011.564040
65. Seng GH (2007) The effects of think-aloud in a collaborative environment to improve comprehension of L2 texts. Reading 7(2)
66. Şengel A, Gur K (2018) Effects of the 'Social Responsibility for Health' program on adolescents' empathic skills, altruistic and health perception. Marmara Med J 6–11. https://doi.org/10.5472/marumj.371278
67. Shaffer VA, Bohanek J, Focella ES, Horstman H, Saffran L (2019) Encouraging perspective taking: using narrative writing to induce empathy for others engaging in negative health behaviors. PLoS ONE 14(10):e0224046. https://doi.org/10.1371/journal.pone.0224046
68. Shindler J (2009) Transformative classroom managemen.
69. Silke C, Brady B, Boylan C, Dolan P (2018) Factors influencing the development of empathy and pro-social behaviour among adolescents: a systematic review. Child Youth Serv Rev 94:421–436. https://doi.org/10.1016/j.childyouth.2018.07.027
70. Silva F, Ferreira R, Castro A, Pinto P, Ramos J (2022) Experiments on gamification with virtual and augmented reality for practical application learning, pp 175–184. https://doi.org/10.1007/978-3-030-86618-1_18
71. Silva RD de C, Albuquerque SGC, Muniz A de V, Filho PPR, Ribeiro S, Pinheiro PR, Albuquerque VHC (2017) Reducing the schizophrenia stigma: a new approach based on augmented reality. Comput Intell Neurosci 2017:1–10. https://doi.org/10.1155/2017/2721846

72. Singer T, Lamm C (2009) The social neuroscience of empathy. Ann N Y Acad Sci 1156(1):81–96. https://doi.org/10.1111/j.1749-6632.2009.04418.x
73. Spencer J (2017) Five ways to boost student engagement with flow theory. http://www.spencerauthor.com/flow-theory/
74. Stevens F, Taber K (2021) The neuroscience of empathy and compassion in pro-social behavior. Neuropsychologia 159:107925. https://doi.org/10.1016/j.neuropsychologia.2021.107925
75. Sweeney SK, Newbill P, Ogle T, Terry K (2018) Using augmented reality and virtual environments in historic places to scaffold historical empathy. TechTrends 62(1):114–118. https://doi.org/10.1007/s11528-017-0234-9
76. Takatalo J, Häkkinen J, Kaistinen J, Nyman G (2010) Presence, involvement, and flow in digital games. In: Evaluating user experience in games, pp 23–46. https://doi.org/10.1007/978-1-84882-963-3_3
77. Tay JL, Xie H, Sim K (2023) Effectiveness of augmented and virtual reality-based interventions in improving knowledge, attitudes, empathy and stigma regarding people with mental illnesses—a scoping review. J Pers Med 13(1):112. https://doi.org/10.3390/jpm13010112
78. Tsai C-Y, Lai Y-C (2022) Design and validation of an augmented reality teaching system for primary logic programming education. Sensors 22(1):389. https://doi.org/10.3390/s22010389
79. Tsay M, Brady M (2012) A case study of cooperative learning and communication pedagogy: does working in teams make a difference? J Scholarsh Teach Learn 10(2):78–89. https://scholarworks.iu.edu/journals/index.php/josotl/article/view/1747
80. Valente A, Lopes DS, Nunes N, Esteves A (2022) Empathic AuRea: exploring the effects of an augmented reality cue for emotional sharing across three face-to-face tasks. In: 2022 IEEE conference on virtual reality and 3D user interfaces (VR), pp 158–166. https://doi.org/10.1109/VR51125.2022.00034
81. Van Noorden THJ, Haselager GJT, Cillessen AHN, Bukowski WM (2015) Empathy and involvement in bullying in children and adolescents: a systematic review. J Youth Adolesc 44(3):637–657. https://doi.org/10.1007/s10964-014-0135-6
82. Van Someren M, Barnard YF, Sandberg J (1994) The think aloud method: a practical approach to modelling cognitive, vol 11. Academic, London, pp 29–41
83. Weir K, Duveen G (1981) Further development and validation of the prosocial behaviour questionnaire for use by teachers. J Child Psychol Psychiatry 22(4):357–374. https://doi.org/10.1111/j.1469-7610.1981.tb00561.x
84. Whitton N (2009) Learning with digital games. a practical guide to engaging students in higher education. Routledge. https://doi.org/10.4324/9780203872987
85. Wu X, Lu X (2021) Musical training in the development of empathy and prosocial behaviors. Front Psychol 12. https://doi.org/10.3389/fpsyg.2021.661769
86. Yu C-L, Chou T-L (2018) A dual route model of empathy: a neurobiological prospective. Front Psychol 9. https://doi.org/10.3389/fpsyg.2018.02212

From Past to Present: Human–Machine Interfaces Evolve Toward Adaptivity

Angela Carrera-Rivera, Felix Larrinaga, Ganix Lasa, Daniel Reguera-Bakhache, and Gorka Unamuno

Abstract Human–machine interfaces (HMI) facilitate communication between humans and machines, and their importance has increased in modern technology. However, traditional HMIs are often static and do not adapt to individual user preferences or behavior. Adaptive User Interfaces (AUIs) have become increasingly important in providing personalized user experiences. Machine-learning techniques have gained traction in User Experience (UX) research to provide smart adaptations that can reduce user cognitive load. This chapter focuses on the development of adaptive HMIs within industrial contexts, offering a structured framework. It provides an overview of the past and present of HMIs and AUIs, while also outlining prospects for future research. The framework, enhanced by user interactions and Context-Aware Recommendation Systems (CARS), aims to provide tailored adaptations, thereby improving overall UX. A case study highlights real-time remote monitoring in smart factories, improving the ease of use and ease of decision making. The study demonstrates the framework usage in addressing real-world HMI, discussing results, challenges, and limitations.

A. Carrera-Rivera (✉) · F. Larrinaga
Software and System Engineering and Computer Science Department, Faculty of Engineering, Mondragon Unibertsitatea, Loramendi 4, 20500 Arrasate, Spain
e-mail: aicarrera@mondragon.edu

F. Larrinaga
e-mail: flarrinaga@mondragon.edu

G. Lasa
Design Innovation Center (DBZ), Mondragon Unibertsitatea, Loramendi, 4, 20500 Arrasate-Mondragon, Gipuzkoa, Spain
e-mail: glasa@mondragon.edu

D. Reguera-Bakhache
Data Analysis and Cybersecurity Department, Faculty of Engineering, Mondragon Unibertsitatea, Loramendi 4, 20500 Arrasate, Spain
e-mail: dreguera@mondragon.edu

G. Unamuno
IDEKO, Basque Research and Technology Alliance, Arriaga Kalea, 2, 20870 Elgoibar, Spain
e-mail: gunamuno@ideko.es

S. Sayago et al. (eds.), *Future Perspectives on Human-Computer Interaction Research*,
https://doi.org/10.1007/978-3-031-71697-3_7

Keywords Adaptive User Interface · Framework · Recommendation system · Context awareness · Human–machine interface

1 Introduction

Human–Machine Interfaces (HMIs) serve as cognitive and communicative platforms for humans and machines, facilitating the transmission of information [19]. Research on User Experience (UX) in this domain aims to enhance not only usability and performance but also overall user satisfaction, by considering the user's motivational goals during an interaction. According to Aranburu et al. [5], users are motivated by a sense of autonomy and competence in their work environment. To enhance UX, manufacturing companies should consider the factors intrinsic to these motivators, such as the system's ability to facilitate intuitive and rapid task completion, as well as its capacity to anticipate user needs. Anticipation of user needs is closely linked to the user cognitive capacity, influencing the memory required to complete a task [14].

Adaptation is defined as the capacity of systems to fit individual user physical and mental abilities, as well as the context of use and platform capabilities [51]. Since the early days of Human–Computer Interaction (HCI), Adaptive User Interface (AUI) have played a central role and have been considered a key characteristic of smart UX [37]. The use of AUI can provide personalization, individually tailored instructions, and assistance, which cannot only improve the performance of the user but also enhance UX and acceptance of use [12].

This chapter focuses on the creation of adaptive HMIs in industrial contexts, employing a structured framework. Section 2 presents the correspondent background on HMI and AUI. In Sect. 3, we introduce the framework, which facilitates the integration of technological aspects, such as Context-Aware Recommendation System (CARS), with design elements, ensuring the consideration of dimensions influencing user interaction [42]. In this approach, the exploitation of user interactions, coupled with CARS, aims for personalized and targeted adaptations, aligning with user preferences.

On the current landscape of smart factories, decentralized mobile and computer applications have become the standard, offering advantages like accessibility, real-time monitoring, and on-the-go information for workers. The case study in Sect. 4 focuses on supervisory tasks, particularly real-time remote monitoring of machines to improve visibility in smart factory production processes [30]. Given the high cognitive load associated with these tasks from extensive data and visual complexity during monitoring and control [31], the adaptation goal is to tailor feature presentations based on user contextual information. This case study demonstrates the framework use in enhancing user experience and addressing real-world challenges. Next sections discuss the results, challenges, and limitations in Sect. 5, culminating in the conclusion.

2 Background

2.1 Human–Machine Interfaces (HMIs), Past, and Present

An HMI represents the means of communication between humans and machines. These interfaces have become increasingly important in modern technology, allowing users to interact with complex systems and devices intuitively and efficiently. Over the years, HMIs have evolved significantly, from simple command-line interfaces to sophisticated interfaces [45] that can take many forms, such as graphical user interfaces, voice interfaces, touchscreens, and augmented reality displays.

HMIs in manufacturing evolve with each industrial revolution [31]. In the first industrial revolution, individual machines operated independently without integrated control systems, posing challenges in overseeing manufacturing processes. Simple machine functions led to basic HMIs with mechanical input controls such as levers and analogue dials [24]. The transition to Industry 2.0 brought about electrified mass production, enabling data supervision and control in manufacturing. This shift increased the demand for HMIs, leading to the development of integrated supervisory systems in dedicated control rooms at manufacturing sites [24, 45]. However, the complexity of tasks and information also increased. To address this, researchers introduced HMIs like the Command-Line Interface (CLI) and Text-Based Interface (TBI). CLI used punch cards and machine codes for sequential command-based control, demanding substantial learning effort due to cryptic commands [30]. In contrast, TBI simplified operations with text-based commands, enhancing learning and reducing cognitive load. TBI, using natural language commands, proved more user-friendly than CLI, overcoming the learning curve associated with the latter.

In Industry 3.0, a digital revolution introduced computerized robots and automation to manufacturing [40], generating extensive data beyond the capacity of electromechanical-based HMIs. This led to a transition to computer-based HMIs, enabling graphical information presentation and complex system management [30]. Graphical User Interfaces (GUIs) played a transformative role for supervising automated production processes, offering comprehensive information and control. Although more user-friendly than TBIs, GUIs at this stage had limitations in presenting SCADA-based graphics in mobile devices, which are used for monitoring and controlling processes in industries [40].

In the fourth industrial revolution, also known as Industry 4.0, Cyber Physical Systems (CPS) lead manufacturing transformation by integrating all production elements. This evolution gives rise to smart factories with advanced HMIs overseeing multiple shopfloors. These HMIs, equipped with IoT technologies, support teleworking and incorporate various interaction modalities such as voice, Virtual Reality (VR), and Augmented Reality (AR) [31].

Smart HMIs, capable of understanding and adapting to individual user preferences, needs, or contexts, are crucial for optimal user performance. Furthermore, HMIs fulfill multiple functions on the current smart factory environment. Kumar and

Lee [30] identified four types of functions: operation and supervision, management, maintenance service, and cybersecurity.

The lack of adaptivity of HMI can lead to a steep learning curve, reduced efficiency, and a poor UX. This is precisely where an Adaptive User Interface (AUI) can be helpful, offering intelligent user interaction methods to enhance the overall user experience.

2.2 Adaptive User Interface (AUI)

An Adaptive User Interface (AUI) serves as a dynamic component, capable of altering interface characteristics and functionality based on user requirements. Also referred to as "Intelligent User Interface" in more recent studies [10], AUIs have played a central role in the realm of Human–Computer Interaction (HCI) since its inception [38]. In a comprehensive literature review conducted by Miraz et al. [37], one of the fundamental challenges identified in the domain of AUIs is the absence of a clear definition regarding the constituents of user interface adaptation. Table 1 presents various definitions found in the literature. Based on this, we conclude that an AUI is an intelligent UI that utilizes artificial intelligence techniques, such as machine learning, recommendation systems, natural language processing or others, to dynamically adjust one or more UI elements in real-time. It responds to the current context of use with the goal of enhancing usability.

The three pillars of AUI development are Artificial Intelligence (AI), User Modeling, and Human–Computer Interaction (HCI) (Fig. 1).

AI landscape encompasses a diverse array of tools, techniques, and algorithms. Various AI approaches come into play in the development of AUIs. An early example

Table 1 Definitions adaptive user interface (AUI)

Definitions	References
"...and intelligent and adaptive means to implement the proper response techniques. Furthermore, the intelligent interface can learn about the subject's lifestyle and adapt the interaction style/mode accordingly."	[43]
"Human–machine interfaces that have the objective of improving the effectiveness, naturalness and the efficiency of interaction (human machine interactions) by reasoning (involving artificial intelligence methods), representing and modeling the users, tasks, device and context."	[54]
"...by their capability to adapt at run-time and make several communication decisions concerning'what','when','why' and'how' to communicate."	[59]
"Human–machine interfaces that aim to improve the efficiency, effectiveness, and naturalness of human–machine interaction by representing, reasoning, and acting on models of the user, domain, task, discourse. They use artificial intelligence (AI), human–computer interaction (HCI), software engineering (SE) and other techniques to promote more natural and usable human–machine interaction"	[20]

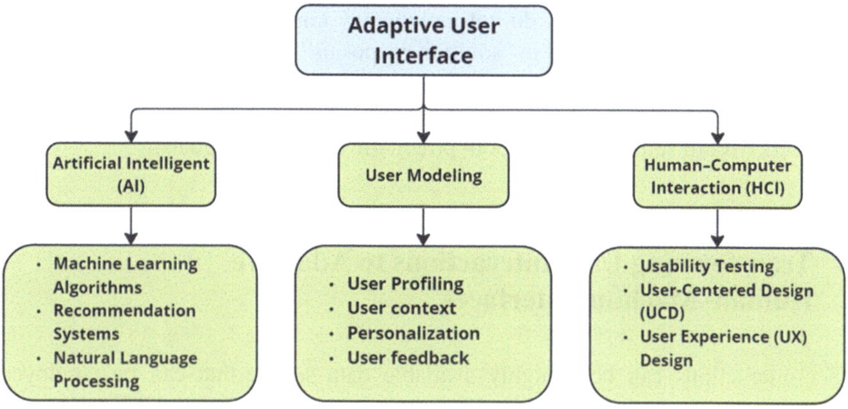

Fig. 1 Adaptive user interface pillars

is the "AVANTI" system presented by Stephanidis et al. [52]. This system introduced a conceptual framework aimed at dynamically adjusting the user interface to individual user needs, particularly in terms of accessibility, using a rule-based approach.

Machine-learning techniques and rule-based systems stand out as two of the most common approaches in AUI development. These systems rely on predefined rules to govern how the interface should adapt under specific conditions. For instance, Hussain et al. [22] introduced a rule-based AUI tailored for a wellness application. Their methodology/system is centered on contextual data and an authoring tool, allowing for personalized interface adjustments that provide users with an enhanced and tailored experience.

Similarly, Khan and Khusro [28] presented a model-based and context-aware approach for smart cars. This AUI aimed to mitigate driving distractions by considering contextual information in the model and user interactions to create rules. In a different vein, Stefanidi et al. [50] developed a context-aware AUI for augmented reality interfaces, specifically designed to assist law enforcement agents. Their system leveraged user contextual data and semantic reasoning through Semantic Web Rule Language (SWRL), and delivered dynamic adaptations that improved usability.

Alternatively, some AUIs adopt a recommendation-based strategy. These systems rely on Recommendation Systems (RS) and Context-Aware Recommendation System (CARS) that often integrate machine-learning algorithms. They analyze user behavior and context to offer recommendations for interface adaptations, which users are able to accept or decline.

A current challenge to adaptation is that there is no unified software architecture to support lifecycle development of AUI. Brdnik et al. [10] presented a thorough systematic mapping review on the topic of intelligent user interfaces and AUI, from 2012 to early 2022. From the 212 studies reviewed, only ten corresponded to frameworks and four to methodologies (Table 2). As the table shows, nine of the fourteen described studies do not include any kind of UX or usability evaluation. These studies correspond to "solution proposals" or "validation research". The remaining five include either UX or usability evaluation, but not both. Usability evaluation focuses on task-related aspects such as effectiveness and efficiency, while UX considers overall satisfaction and both pragmatic and hedonic goals.

3 Transforming User Interactions to Adaptive Human–Machine Interfaces

User interactions can be a highly available data source that can be employed for the creation of adaptive HMI. Analyzing interactions during HMI usage can generate valuable information about actions, preferences and behaviors, enriching responsiveness and personalization [11]. This data-driven approach creates interfaces that dynamically adjust to user needs, enhancing intuitiveness and efficiency by implementing machine-learning algorithms and user models. This transformation empowers users with interfaces that align with their preferences and contributes to the ongoing evolution of user-centric technology. The literature suggests a need for methodologies and frameworks that integrate technological implementations of AUI with corresponding design elements [10].

In this section, we aim to explore each of the stages in the creation of adaptive user interfaces in the context of industrial HMI through the framework presented in Fig. 2. Employing a framework offers the advantage of providing a structured approach with predefined components and guidelines, which is crucial for ensuring a seamless integration of technology and design elements. The design for the adaptability of user interfaces requires meticulous consideration of various dimensions impacting user interaction [42].

From a technical standpoint, the framework leverages the exploitation of user interactions and other general sources of context, utilizing CARS as an AI technique.

Recommendation systems, in general, are intelligent algorithms that analyze user preferences and behavior to provide personalized suggestions or recommendations for products, services, or content [26]. Recognizing the significance of context in enhancing UX, it is imperative to incorporate contextual factors into recommendation systems. CARS ensures more personalized and targeted suggestions aligned with user preferences [61]. Therefore, this mechanism serves as the engine for producing the required adaptations.

Subsequent subsections will explain the various aspects of the design and technical implementation, providing a comprehensive understanding of the framework application in the development of adaptive user interfaces for industrial HMIs.

Table 2 Frameworks (F) and methodologies (M) published in the Adaptive User Interface (AUI) literature

Study	Solution offered	Research type	Domain	Intelligent entity	UX	Usability	Method
Stefanidi et al. [50]	M	Evaluation research	Software	Interface	Yes	No	Expert based evaluation, User testing
Gil et al. [17]	F	Evaluation research	Software engineering	Interface	No	Yes	User testing, Questionnaire
Abrahão et al. [1]	F	Solution proposal	Human–computer	Interface	N/A	N/A	
Berman et al. [8]	F	Validation research	3D printing	Interface	No	Yes	User testing, Questionnaire
Gan et al. [16]	F	Validation research	Human–computer	Other model	N/A	N/A	Interaction research
Wallace [60]	F	Validation research	Software engineering	Interface	Yes	No	Automated testing research
Johnston et al. [27]	F	Solution proposal	Software engineering	Interface	N/A	No	
Stumpf [53]	F	Solution proposal	Human–computer	System	No	No	Interaction research
Tan et al. [55]	F	Validation research	Software engineering	System	No	No	Interaction research
Landowska et al. [32]	M	Validation research	Software engineering	System	N/A	N/A	
Zhou et al. [62]	F	Validation research	Human–computer	N/A	N/A	N/A	
Peck et al. [46]	F	Solution proposal	Software engineering	System	No	No	
Fernandez-Garcia et al. [15]	M	Solution proposal	Software engineering	Interface	No	No	
Mezhoudi et al. [36]	M	Validation research	Human–computer	Interface	No	Yes	Interaction research

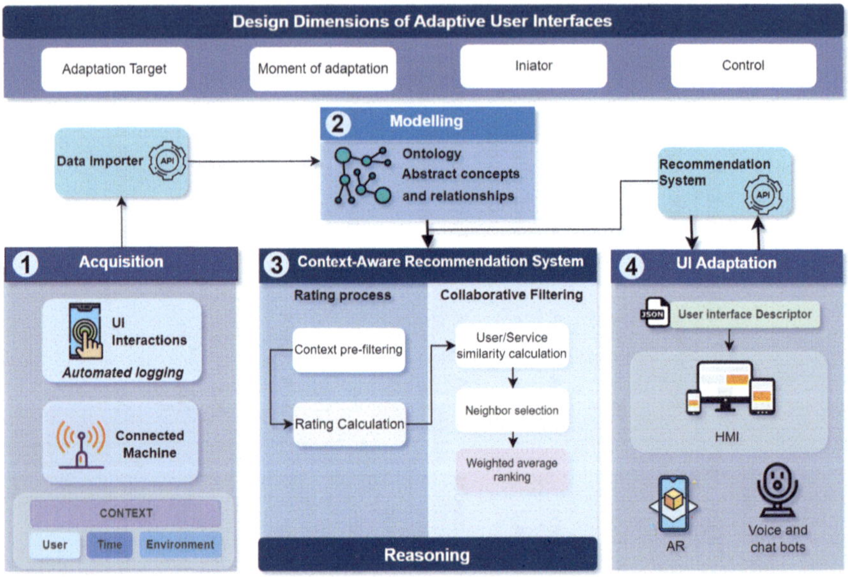

Fig. 2 Framework for the transformation of user interactions to adaptive human–machine interfaces

3.1 Design of Adaptive User Interfaces (AUIs)

The first step is to define the goal of the adaptation process. As discussed previously, modern HMI in smart factories serve diverse functions and perform various tasks. Furthermore, interaction modalities have also evolved over time. Decentralized mobile and computer applications represent the current and present standard of smart factories. These interfaces offer advantages such as accessibility, real-time monitoring, and the ability to provide workers with information on the go. The framework focuses on the **"Supervision"** function that involves real-time remote monitoring of machine parameters to enhance visibility and handle situations in smart factory production processes [30]. The nature of these tasks imposes a high cognitive load on users due to the vast volume of data involved. Moreover, the higher visual complexity contributes to increased reaction time and cognitive load during monitoring and controlling tasks [31].

Therefore, the goal of the adaptation of the HMI is to tailor the presentation of features and options based on the user's contextual information. Considering this, other aspects of the design are discussed below:

i. **Adaptation Target**

Establishing adaptation targets is a fundamental step in HMI adaptation. The primary objective of customizing the UI, based on outputs from the recommendation engine,

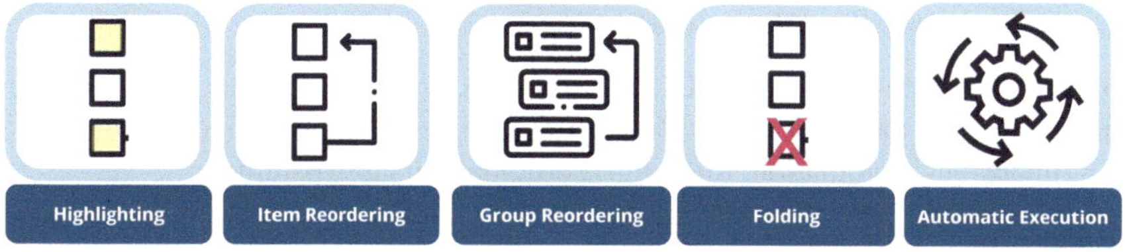

Fig. 3 Adaptation styles

involves modifying layout elements (e.g., messages, cards, and buttons) which represent recommended functions or features of the machine(s), particularly in mobile and web applications.

Adaptation targets are related to specific UI elements that will be adapted in line with the recommendations. The way in which these adaptations are presented to the user constitutes the next step, which underscores the significance of adaptation styles. Adaptation styles play a role in the visual presentation of the selected UI targets (Fig. 3). Adaptation styles described in the literature include [18]:

- **Highlighting**: This involves the strategic use of a contrasting background color to draw attention to specific elements of the interface. For example, messages or cards representing recommended features and options can be highlighted, thereby enriching user navigation and comprehension [57].
- **Item/Feature Reordering**: The repositioning of selected items provides a streamlined approach to information presentation. This is beneficial for ensuring quick access to frequently used or popular features, enhancing efficiency, and reducing cognitive load [37].
- **Group Reordering**: Beyond individual items, entire groups can be reordered within menus, boxes, etc. In this way, related content or functionalities can be clustered, giving rise to a more intuitive and organized user interface.
- **Folding**: Truncating items with lower priority or relevance—commonly referred to as folding, declutters the visual space. This simplifies the user interface and guarantees that pertinent information is presented to the user, contributing to a more focused and efficient interaction [6].

ii. Initiator of the Adaptation and Moment of Adaptation

The *Initiator of the Adaptation* refers to the mechanism and data employed to start the process of adaptations, which, in this case, involves a recommendation-based and context-aware framework. This framework relies on user interactions as the primary data source, but it also requires selecting meaningful contextual sources for delivering features and options. These contextual sources can pertain to the user, device, task, time, or environment and are input into the system.

The *moment of the Adaptation,* dictates when the UI adjustment will occur. In the proposed framework, two moments are considered: (i) when the user starts a session on the HMI or platform, contextual data is retrieved, and (ii) when contextual data changes.

iii. **Control Over the Adaptation**

To analyze the design of the AUI, the amount of control that the user has when interacting with the platform needs to be determined. This is defined by the three sub-dimensions: automation, (decision) participation, and visibility.

In this framework, adaptations are expected to occur autonomously and without specific user input, as changes in selected contextual data serve as triggers for UI adjustments. This falls within a medium level of automation, as it does not explicitly require user input. However, the framework does not automatically identify when more automation might be necessary; for instance, it does not automatically add new contextual sources.

User participation is derived from explicit and implicit forms, such as accepting or declining recommendations. Therefore, for adaptation to function effectively, the framework requires high user participation.

In terms of visibility, the recommendation-based approach presents a high level of transparency in most cases. However, the perception of visibility of the adaptations can be influenced by the chosen adaptation style. For instance, styles such as "highlighting" or "group reordering" are more visually prominent to users, whereas styles like "re-ordering" or "folding" may be less noticeable. Moreover, the automatic execution of options might go entirely unnoticed by users. Consequently, the latter can feel more natural and may only be noticed if it is not working properly. For instance, if adaptations do not fulfill the needs of the user, and/or no communication is received as to how to modify or revert these changes, the user can suffer negative feelings. This emphasizes the importance of feedback mechanisms and communication in the adaptation process.

3.2 *Technical Implementation*

Four steps are considered for the technical implementation, which align with the lifecycle of context-aware applications [47].

3.2.1 Data Acquisition

Acquisition of human–machine interactions is a process that will vary according to how the user interacts with the machine. Interactions are usually linked to visual elements of the interfaces (i.e., buttons, tabs, knobs). Automated logging of user interactions was chosen as the approach for data acquisition in this framework. This approach has several advantages over other data collection methods, including being non-intrusive, capturing data in real-time, and reducing errors associated with manual data entry. Automated logging can be achieved using specialized software such as Matomo or Google Analytics for web or mobile apps, or by building custom logging tools directly onto the system. In some cases, automated logging can be implemented at the interface level without requiring access to the system's internals. However, this approach can be challenging, especially for complex interfaces, and may require access to the underlying code of the system being studied, which is not always possible. For example, Zhou et al. [63] presented an approach for monitoring back-office staff using a screen-mouse-key logger that captured images, mouse, and key actions, along with timestamps, and was transformed into a UI log through image-analysis techniques.

However, capturing user interactions can also raise privacy concerns if personal data is inadvertently captured or if users are not aware that their interactions are being logged. Additionally, the use of machine data is a valuable source of contextual information at the moment to provide the adaptation [13], since alarms, status, and measures of sensors and actuators can potentially change how the user will interact with the machine.

3.2.2 Modeling

The modeling refers to the process of representing data in meaningful elements. This method typically involves the analysis of multiple data sources, to define entities (distinct objects or elements within the system), properties (attributes or characteristics of these entities), relationships (connections or associations between entities) and dependencies [9]. To achieve this, in this framework we employ ontologies, which are used to formally model concepts from a specific domain by providing a detailed specification of entities, their properties, and their relationships [21]. The resulting ontology was created in Protégé[1] and an overview of the general structure is presented in Fig. 4. To visually represent the components of the ontology, we divided the entities into three groups: HMI-Machine functions, Context, and Interaction.

HMI-Machine functions: To effectively display machine information on the HMI, it is crucial to represent each individual feature. Drawing inspiration from Maleki et al. [35], we model each feature using a specific pattern that establishes a connection between the feature and the necessary information. Features, in turn, may serve to group related options, with each option representing a distinct and specific function of the machine.

Context: The second group further extends the ontology to incorporate context-specific entities and relationships. Context refers to any data that can be used to understand the current state, whether situational or locational, of an entity [41]. Iqbal et al. [23] presented an ontology with a specific focus on context modeling for adaptive mobile devices. This ontology encompassed four major sources of contextual information: device, user/identity, environment, and time. Since contextual data is dynamic, most of the contextual data will need to be created as instances, where attributes permit the creation of new types of contextual information.

Interaction: The last group define the entities related to the human–machine interactions and their relationships with the features of the machine and contextual

[1] https://Protege.Stanford.Edu/

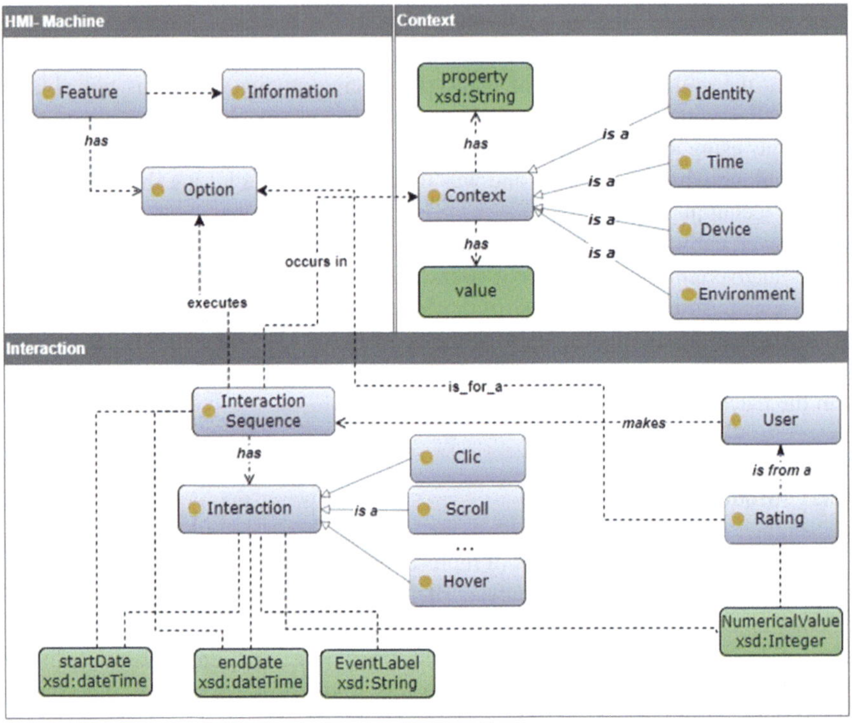

Fig. 4 Model

data within the ontology. Interaction sequences represent an ordered set of individual interactions performed by users within the system and are linked to a specific feature or option. Interactions can take various forms (i.e., click, scroll, hover) and have the ability to trigger events [11]. To enhance the understanding and analysis of these events, it is crucial to name them appropriately and assign a numerical value that quantifies the level of significance associated with each event. Once these elements are incorporated into the ontology, a comprehensive representation of user interactions and their connections to the system behavior and functionality is achieved.

3.2.3 Reasoning—Recommendation System

The reasoning stage entails processing user and contextual data from HMI usage to create AUIs. To this end, CARS are employed, which have been proven to provide better customization and improve recommendation accuracy [61]. The employed recommendation technique is Collaborative Filtering (CF), a prevalent method that relies on available data containing user preferences and ratings to identify similarities between users or items [44]. User-based CF algorithms predict preferences by considering similarities in reported preferences, generating recommendations for HMIs features [44].

However, in contrast to traditional CF scenarios, where ratings are obtained from users more commonly (e.g., star ratings in e-commerce), for a work and industrial setting this option could be more difficult to achieve, and ratings can be primarily obtained based on user interactions (e.g., clicks, views, etc.) that reflect the level of engagement with the digital features provided by the machine. This approach allows for the generation of implicit ratings, which can be used to uncover similarities between users and/or features. This is only possible by using the model previously defined that allows the creation of instances of features and options available on the HMI. Achieving this requires utilizing the previously defined model, allowing the instantiation of features and options available for the HMI.

In this work, the implicit ratings, generated through these interactions, are then utilized in the K-Nearest Neighbor algorithm (kNN). kNN is widely employed in recommendation systems for CF. It identifies similar users by measuring the similarity of their ratings. By considering a weighted average of the preferences of the k most similar users, the kNN algorithm predicts a user's preference for a specific feature or option [29]. To implement the kNN algorithm, a matrix containing the computed ratings resulting from both user interactions and explicit feedback serves as the input. The process of generating these ratings will be explained in the following subsection.

Context Pre-filtering and Rating Calculation

This work adopts the contextual pre-filtering technique that is compatible with recommendation algorithms that do not inherently incorporate context awareness [49]. In this approach, context awareness is achieved by transforming the input of the classical recommendation algorithm and employing user-based collaborative filtering.

Context pre-filtering is a technique that involves using values of contextual attributes as constraints for selecting ratings that will be used in a recommendation system's user-feature/option space [29]. An important initial aspect to consider in this work is the "context generalization´, where contextual attributes are assigned into broader categories [49]. As presented in the ontology, four contextual sources were defined, including identity, device, environment, and time. From these sources, contextual values can be grouped together to represent broader contextual categories. For example, specific user demographics (such as age, or job type) can be grouped together to represent a broader category of "user profile". Similarly, specific time periods can be grouped together to represent a broader category, such as "season" or "shift". Generalizing contextual attributes in this way allows for reducing the dimensionality of the contextual space, and the data sparsity.

Moving forward, as presented in Fig. 5, the RS API receives a set of generalized contextual data in a JSON format. A query is sent to the ontology. In this way, interactions that are irrelevant to the recommendation system are filtered out beforehand. As defined in the ontology, a single Interaction may occur in multiple Context instances (Fig. 4). Therefore, the filter parameters used in the query are non-exclusive to avoid significantly reducing the available data points.

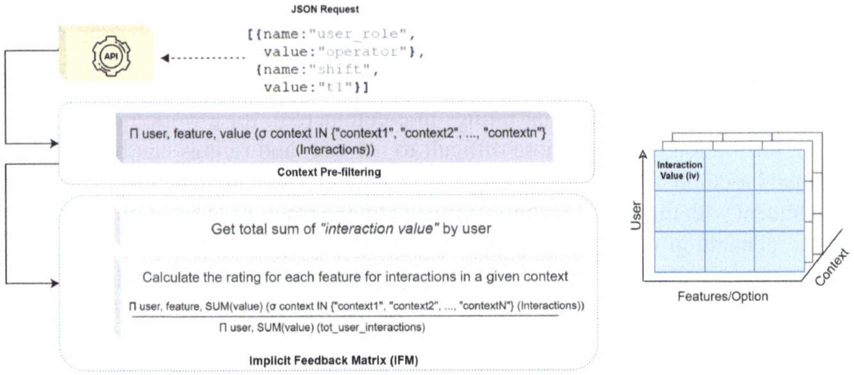

Fig. 5 Rating calculation

Implicit feedback is derived from user actions and behavior, each type of interaction is considered a form of implicit feedback and represented as a binary value that is later used to summarize and calculate the ratings. Positive implicit feedback is given a value of 1 that represents a positive engagement with an option [33]. The rating is a measure of user engagement that represents the ratio of the total sum of interaction value a user has made across a given set of contexts to the number of interactions they have made for an individual feature or option. In relational algebra this can be expressed as:

$$\frac{\prod \text{user, feature, SUM(value)}(\sigma \text{ context IN}\{\text{ context1, context2}, \ldots, \text{contextN}\} \text{ (Interactions))}}{\prod \text{user, SUM(value)(tot user interactions)}}$$

This provides a normalized measure of user activity that considers the user broader range of interactions, allowing for more accurate comparisons between users and features/options. As stated before, interactions can occur in multiple contexts. Therefore, if the same interaction occurs in more than one context within the set of contexts being filtered, the rating for the feature will be calculated as if there were separate interactions. This can result in a higher rating for features that fulfill more than one of the contexts [39]. This approach can help with "cold-start" when there is not relevant information for a specific set of context and reduce the data sparsity problem associated with context pre-filtering. The data become less sparse as each interaction is associated with multiple ratings, which increases the probability that features will be accurately represented in the data. Moreover, this allows to generate more data points, which can help to mitigate sparsity by providing additional information that can be used to better estimate the true value of the interactions.

The next step is to compute the similarities among users to predict a recommendation of options. For that purpose, cosine similarity, Euclidean distance and Pearson correlation factor are used in this approach. We incorporate the kNN algorithm using as input the 2D combined matrix that represents contribution of implicit ratings for each feature/option. Then, limit the neighborhood to predict the weighted average rating s using the rating given to s by users most similar to u and returning the k more relevant options, ranked by the calculated rating.

$$\text{Predicted Rating} = \frac{\sum \left(\text{sim}(u, s) * r_{u,s}\right)}{\sum \text{sim}(u, s)}$$

3.2.4 UI Adaptation

From the technical perspective, a User Interface Descriptor (UID) can be used to define the structure and composition of the UI. These descriptors act as data representations to describe UI elements and their layouts and can be written in standardized data exchange formats such as JSON or XML. According to REST application principles, basic UIDs consist of a name, an optional description, and a list of UISections, which are self-consistent modules of the UI, populated by UI element objects [7]. As a result, each feature or featured options for the machine functions is linked to a UID. They guide the translation of recommendation engine outputs into specific user interface components.

The proposed framework employs a Server-driven UI design pattern to build the AUI. This approach relies on UIDs sent from the server to the client for rendering, taking advantage of cloud computing technology [1]. This design pattern offers flexibility by allowing the server to generate the descriptors and dynamically adapting them based on user context and preferences [56]. To support this approach, the framework includes an API (see Fig. 2), which receives recommended features and generates the descriptors for the HMI based on a schema. This facilitates the process of adapting user interfaces that are rendered in a mobile environment without needing to redeploy, which allows for a real-time adaptability. This is particularly useful considering that HMIs are often multi-platform and work on different devices or are even built into the machine. The client-side should include a rendering mechanism that interprets the UID received from server and generates the appropriate visual elements and layout. Additionally, the client-side manages user input and events like clicks or swipes, transmitting them to the server for processing.

The schema to generate the UID is presented in Fig. 6. The schema introduces the IUIElement interface, which captures common properties of UI elements such as idElement, label, type, but can also receive featureInformation. The IUIContainer interface represents containers or panels holding child UI components. The UITemplate type defines a template structure with an idUserInterface, a root container (IUIContainer), which represents a panel that can have multiple elements; and an array of template sections (UITemplateSection). The UITemplateSection represents a section within a UI template, which can hold multiple UIElements. Specific implementations can be created from these abstract types. For instance, Stack is a concrete

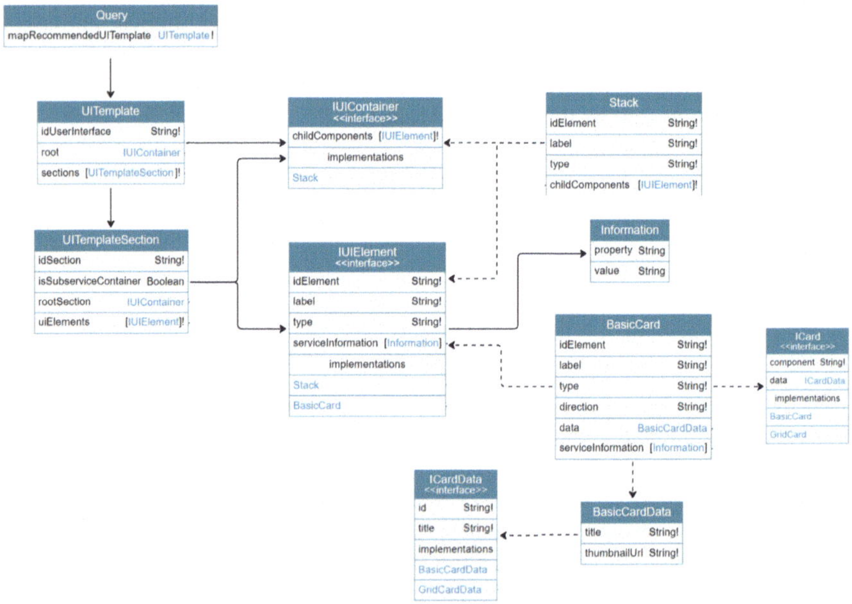

Fig. 6 Schema server-driven UI

type of container or panel that is both IUIElement and IUIContainer. BasicCard is a concrete implementation of an IUIElement. Beyond individual UI elements, the schema addresses the connection with Features and Options presented on the ontology since each of them would be related to a specific UITemplate.

4 Case Study

The "Timeseries Visualizer", developed by a research center in the Basque Country, Spain, served as the platform for this case study. The application, developed under AngularJS,[2] has the primary objective of facilitating the monitoring of grinding machines through the collection of multiple signals. Users have the flexibility to filter information based on specific time periods. The dashboard caters to various company clients. The user roles include researchers, testers, and maintenance operators, with specific roles tailored to the requirements of each client.

The framework was integrated into the existing web application for monitoring grinding machines. The views when adaptations where implemented are the following:

[2] http://angularjs.org/

- Machine Selection: In this view, users can choose specific grinding machines for monitoring from multiple shop-floors, as illustrated in Fig. 7.
- Dashboard: The dashboard view features a left-side navigation bar and presents visual representations, including line plots from various signals received from the grinding machines. The information presented on the dashboard depends on the company and machine selected and additional filters available as shown in Fig. 8.

In Fig. 9, we present the software architecture. As depicted in the figure, the HMIs are external entities to the framework and adaptations are created by deploying the framework into the HMI.

The automated logging of user interactions is implemented using third-party apps (GA4 and Tag Manager). Data acquisition is performed through an API, which

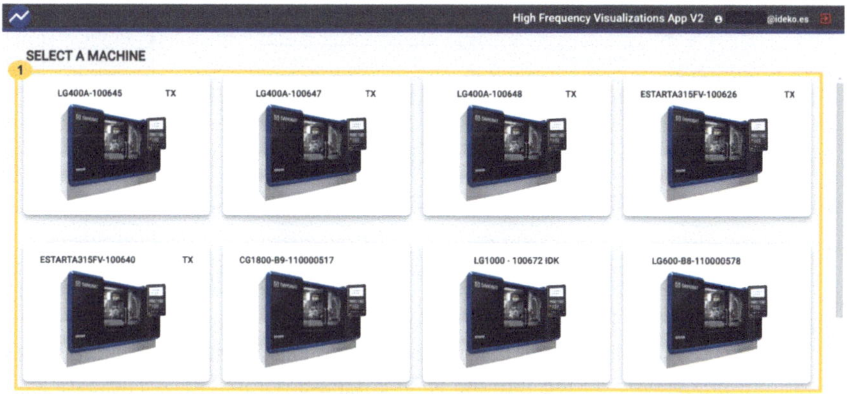

Fig. 7 Machine selection "Time Series Visualizer"

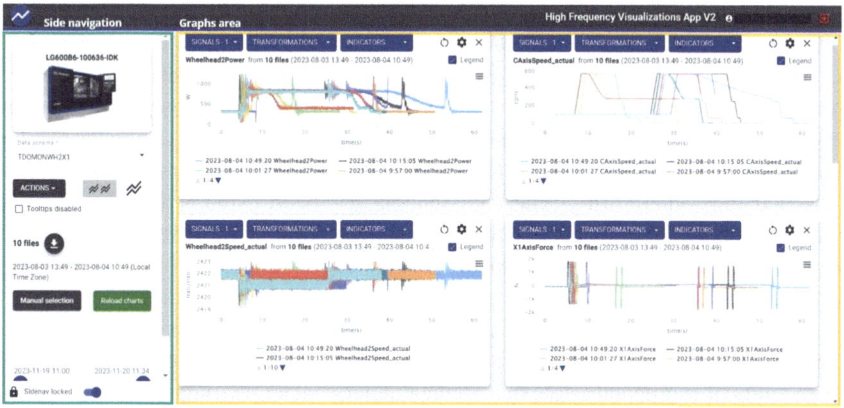

Fig. 8 Dashboard panel "Time Series Visualizer"

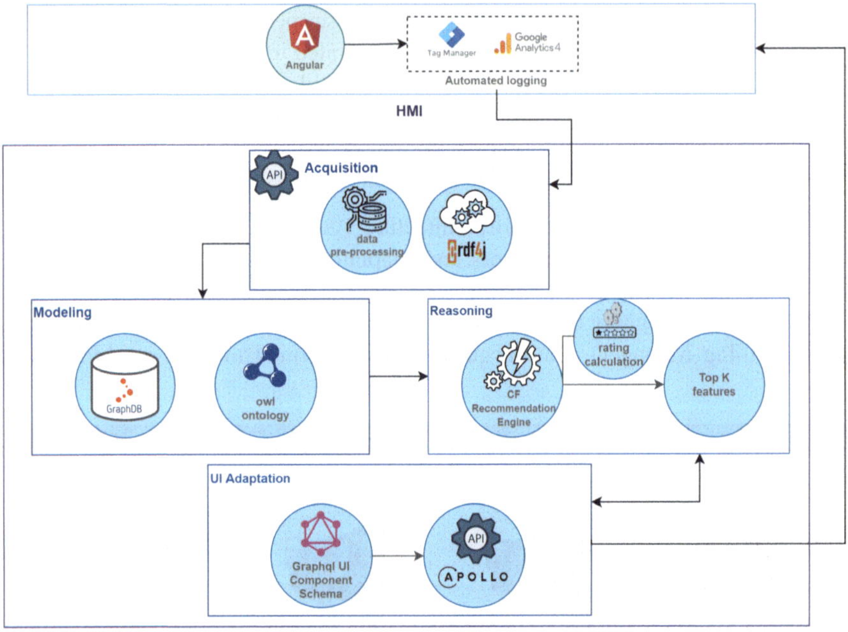

Fig. 9 Architecture of the implemented framework

utilizes Java and RDF4J. It is responsible for receiving user interactions and contextual data selected to intervene in the process of UI generation. The data are subsequently pre-processed and fed into the RDF database (GraphDB[3]). These data are used to train the CARS model used as the "reasoning" engine of the framework.

The second API is developed to create the visual interface shown to the user using Apollo GraphQL 4. The schema for UI generation (depicted in Fig. 6) is created in GraphQL. This tool was selected because it provides a clear and concise way to express the data model of an application and the operations that can be performed on that data. It serves as a contract between the client and the server, specifying how data can be requested and what shape the response will take. The schema in GraphQL is written in the GraphQL Schema Definition Language (SDL), and the results are received on JSON format. However, the same schema could be translated into other forms. The data schema has been explained on Sect. 3.2.4. While the application serves multiple clients, this case study specifically focused on internal users researchers from the center. The interactions of 10 users were systematically recorded over a 48-day period. (Table 3) Prior to participation, explicit consent was obtained from each user, confirming their willingness to have their interactions recorded within the application. The dataset comprises a total of 7906 interactions. It is crucial to note that all data underwent anonymization, and does not contain any sensitive user information.

[3] https://graphdb.ontotext.com/

Table 3 Participants demographics

Attribute	Item	Freq	Attribute	Item	Freq
Gender	Male	8	Occupation	NDT Researcher	2
	Female	2		Grinding Researcher	3
				General Researcher	3
				Precision Researcher	2
Total users	10				

4.1 Case Study Methodology

To better understand the process followed for the implementation of this case study, Fig. 10 presents a visual representation. The process initiates with the selection of adaptation targets, leading to two task paths:

In the bottom path, the framework implementation begins with selecting contextual features and capturing user interactions. These processes may be limited to the initially chosen adaptation targets, as further detailed in the next section. The interactions play a crucial role for calculating implicit ratings for features and options chosen for HMI, contributing to the training of a collaborative filtering model (see Sect. 3.2.3).

The top path involves the selection of adaptation styles and the creation of UI templates utilizing the schema, as detailed in Sect. 4.1.2. The schema, coupled with the recommendation engine allows the generation of the Adaptive HMI when selected contextual features change.

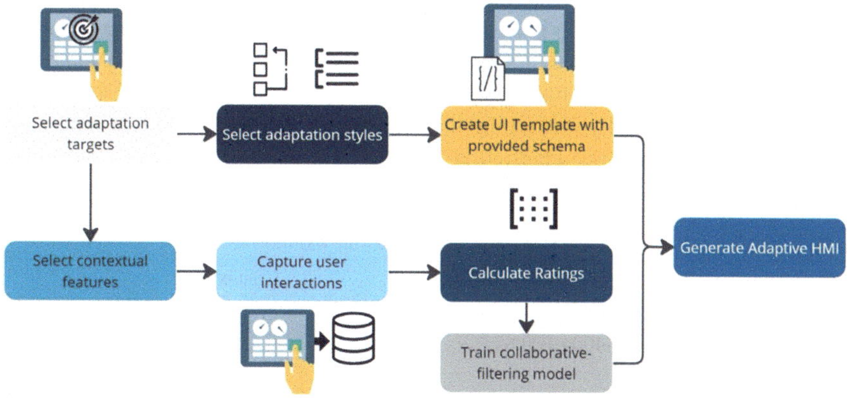

Fig. 10 Case study methodology

4.1.1 Analysis and Technical Implementation of Data Acquisition and Modeling

To start this case study, an analysis was conducted for both the data acquisition and modeling stages within the framework, as these stages are highly interdependent. The first step in the implementation involves selecting options and features within the HMI for the adaptation. Table 4 presents the selected features for this case study, along with an example of the group of options related to each one. Furthermore, it was important to identify the contextual information required to produce the adaptations. In general, for the framework and the process of contextual pre-filtering, contextual data was treated as inclusive information. An inclusive parameter can be defined as a parameter or set of parameters that are considered relevant and actively contribute to a process or system. Inclusion of these parameters enhances the overall functionality. Aspects related to identity and temporal context are seen as "inclusive".

However, for this case, some contextual information needed to be treated as exclusive. An exclusive parameter is a type of parameter or set of parameters that serve as constraints or limitations within the process. Exclusion or restriction of these contextual data helps narrow options or specify conditions within the context. In this case, these parameters reduce options. Specifically, this contextual data is related to the company clients and machine specifications. Then, this information was uploaded into the ontology to create the corresponding individuals for the Context entity.

For the acquisition of user interaction data, an auto-logging methodology is employed to capture user interactions without disrupting the normal functionality of the application. For this case study, Google Tag Manager (GTM) is utilized, integrated with Google Analytics (GA4). Interactions are systematically logged and subsequently stored in a Big Query data warehouse. Table 5 describes the more pertinent fields within the captured dataset, supplemented by illustrative data examples.

To establish a relationship between the individuals instantiated in the ontology and their corresponding interactions, an event label is transmitted as a personalized field within Google Tag Manager. This label incorporates {feature ID: option ID} in a JSON format, thereby facilitating the correlation between individuals and their associated interactions with a particular feature.

Table 4 Features and options of HMI for grinding machine monitoring

Feature	Examples of options	Context
Machine monitoring	Machine LG4004-100,645 Machine LG4004-100,647 …	Company (exclusive) User Role (inclusive) Shift (inclusive)
Signal monitoring	Signal Wheelhead2Power Signal CAxisSpeedActual …	MachineSchema (exclusive) User Role (inclusive) Shift (inclusive)

Table 5 Raw interaction data for features and options in the monitoring of grinding machines

Column	Description	Example
interaction_id	Sequential id	1
user_id	Unique identifier for the user	ggx45gsd
ga_session_id	Google Analytics session id	1,695,633,755
operating_system	User's operating system	Windows
os_version	Version of the operating system	Windows 10
web_info_browser	User's web browser	Chrome
web_info_hostname	Hostname of the web server	idz-dev-docker.ideko.es
date timestamp	Timestamp of the interaction	2023–09-25 09:49:37.390751 UTC
event-timestamp	Timestamp of the event	1.69564E + 15
event_name	Description of the event	selectMachine LG4004-100,645-click
event_date	Date of the event	20,230,925
event_label	Additional information to match event to feature/option feature_ID: option_ID	"machine_ monitoring":"LG4004-100,645"
page_location	URL of the web page	http://idz-dev-docker.ideko.es/
dayofweek	Day of the week when the interaction occurred	2
hour	Hour of the day when the interaction occured	9

4.1.2 Analysis for the Implementation of the Adaptive User Interface

In the process of adapting the user interfaces of the TimeSeries Visualizer, a correlation between the UI components and the previously defined features was established. The identified UI elements now function as the adaptation targets. The adaptation styles were chosen based on the existing UI elements on the user interface. Table 6 provides a concise overview of the adaptation approach, displaying the selected adaptation targets and their corresponding styles. In the case of Machine Monitoring, the identified target is a horizontal container that presents each machine available for monitoring as cards, with no specific order. The adaptation style for this involves reordering the machines and highlighting the first machine within the recommendation selection given by the framework engine as presented in Fig. 11.

In the case of Signal Monitoring, which involves the presentation of charts combined with combo-boxes to select signals, the dashboard currently presents all signals available (>10 charts depending on the machine) to the user with no specific order. Therefore, for the adaptation style in this case, through the analysis of interactions and sequence generation, it was observed that in majority of sequences the

Table 6 Adaptation targets and styles of features

Feature	Adaptation target	Adaptation style
Machine monitoring	HBox and Cards	Item reordening Highlighting
Signal monitoring	Charts and Drop-down list	Folding Reordening

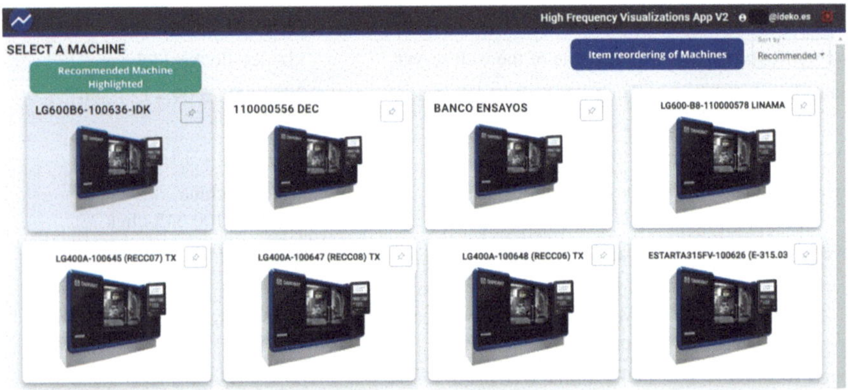

Fig. 11 Machine selection

top-3 of interactions within a sequence was a set of deleteChartN click events. Consequently, the decision was made to fold irrelevant charts, reorder the charts and signals based on the results of the recommendation component, as presented in Fig. 12.

After analyzing the "Adaptation Targets", the additional dimensions for implementing the adaptive interface align with the overall framework description. For example, the adaptation moment occurs automatically in response to contextual changes, based on the context variables established previously on this chapter. Concerning to the user control level over adaptation and their explicit participation, users have the choice of using or not recommended options. Users have an implicit participation as their interactions with the application are captured. The visibility of adaptations is presented through the graphical elements of the interface chosen as adaptation targets. Evidently, users could have greater participation involvement by having the ability to activate or deactivate the visualization of the adaptations and even disconnect the capture of their interactions from the app. These changes would be critical for carrying the changes of this implementation of the framework for an adaptive user interface in a productive environment for end-customers.

From a technical perspective, the use of UI templates is limited to sections where adaptations occur. A JSON response of the API is presented in Fig. 13. In this case, the JSON response is created based on the template for the schema monitoring feature. This section contains a label and dropdown list created from the recommended feature/options. Each of the selected features has its own templates,

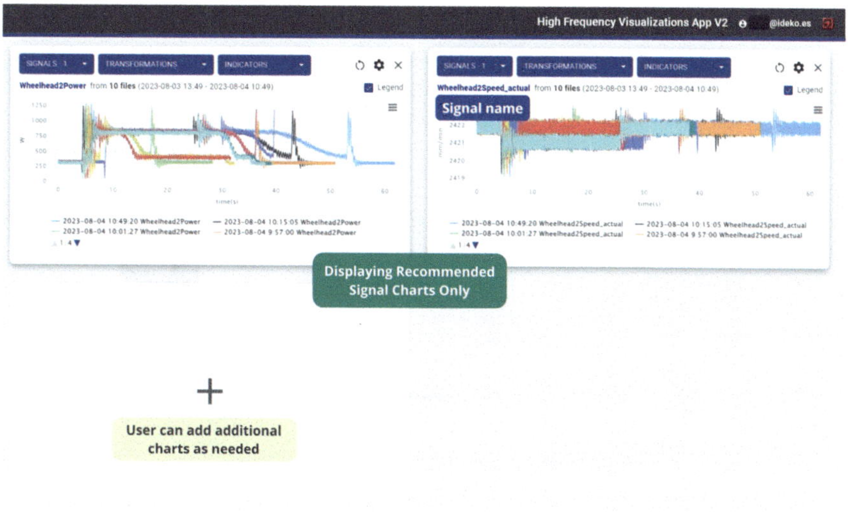

Fig. 12 Dashboard for signals chart presenting adaptations based on recommendations

allowing the generation of the UID based on the recommendations. The advantage of the data schema is its ability to include additional UI elements.

4.2 Recommendation Component Evaluation

Each interaction for a feature and option is given a binary value, whether it represents a positive engagement (1) or a negative engagement (0). To obtain the ratings, we adhere to the process described on Sect. 3.2.3.

The evaluation of the recommendation component follows this protocol: Each set of experiments was repeated 20 times using different randomly selected training and test sets each time (70–30 ratio, respectively), then the average values were taken for each of the metrics. The primary objective is to evaluate the effectiveness of incorporating contextual information in improving recommendation accuracy. The metrics to evaluate are Precision@K, and MAE. Precision scores, measured at different k values (1, 2, and 3) and utilizing various distance metrics (cosine, Euclidean, and Pearson), serve as the key performance indicators.

The first experiment compares the precision@k without using contextual data with a kNN model using Pearson's correlation factor, and cosine and Euclidean distance metrics. The precision@K scores were evaluated at $k = 1, 2$, and 3 as demonstrated in Fig. 14. Precision@1, ranging from 0.53 to 0.58 across different distance metrics, indicates that approximately 53–58% of the top recommendations are accurate. As k increases to 2 and 3, there is a marginal decline in precision values, suggesting a potential trade-off between the number of recommendations provided and their

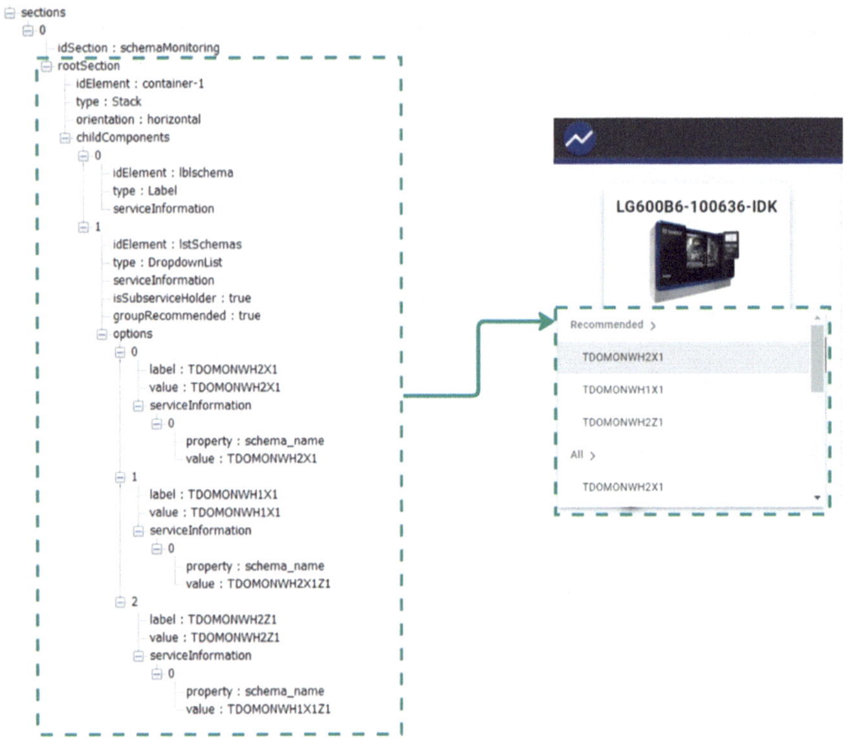

Fig. 13 JSON response from schema monitoring feature/options

accuracy. Notably, the Euclidean distance metric consistently has the least favorable results, while cosine and Pearson distances present a comparable performance.

The second experiment presents the results of precision@k using contextual data are presented in Fig. 15, and in Table 7. In contrast, the context-aware approach demonstrates a significant improvement in precision scores at $k = 1{,}2$. precision@1

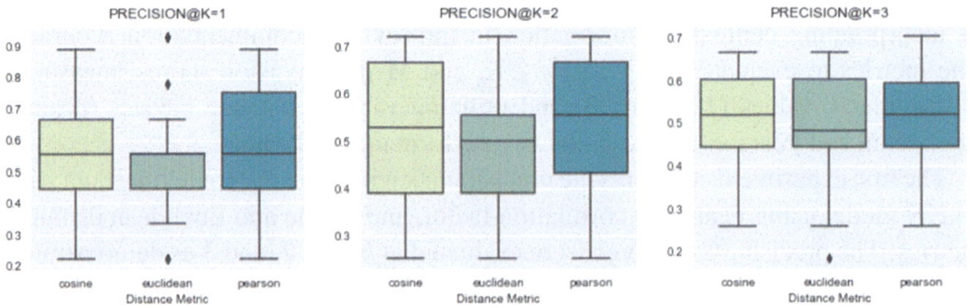

Fig. 14 Precision@K without context

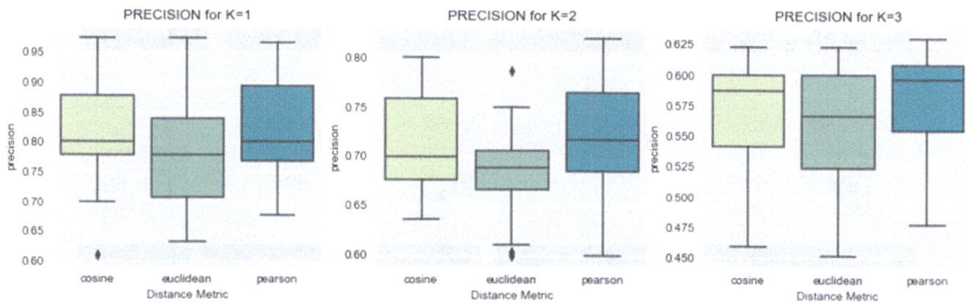

Fig. 15 Precision@K results with context-aware approach

Table 7 Results of Precision@K and MAE

	No context			With contextual data		
	Cosine	Euclidean	Pearson	Cosine	Euclidean	Pearson
Precision@1	0.574074	0.535292	0.586420	0.819886	0.777916	0.825485
Precision@2	0.516889	0.488389	0.533556	0.714912	0.687281	0.717982
Precision@3	0.514815	0.496296	0.516667	0.565278	0.554681	0.571751
MAE	0.138819	0.146843	0.141979	0.079356	0.106063	0.074199

experiences a high improvement, reaching approximately 0.82, signifying a noteworthy enhancement in the precision of the top recommendation. As k increases, precision values decreases. But the results still represent an enhancement than the no-context approach underscoring the benefits of context-awareness.

Complementing the precision analysis, the MAE serves as a quantitative measure of the predictive accuracy of the recommendation system. Lower MAE values indicate more accurate predictions. In Table 7, the "With Contextual Data" approach present lower MAE values compared to the "No Context" scenario for all three distance metrics. This reduction in MAE represent the effectiveness of incorporating contextual data, as the predicted ratings align more closely with the actual ratings, leading to improved accuracy in the recommendations. In the "With Contextual Data" scenario achieves the lowest MAE with the Pearson distance. Although the difference with cosine is not statistically significant. However, a clear result is that Euclidean is outperformed from cosine and Pearson in both precision and MAE. This can be due to the limitations when dealing with high dimensional data [26].

4.3 Validation of the UX

To assess the UX of the framework implementation, the followed protocol is depicted in Fig. 16. Participants engaged in one-to-one 30-min sessions, with 6 out of 10 users registered participating in the evaluation. Prior to executing the planned tasks, users were briefed on the experiment's nature and completed a consent form.

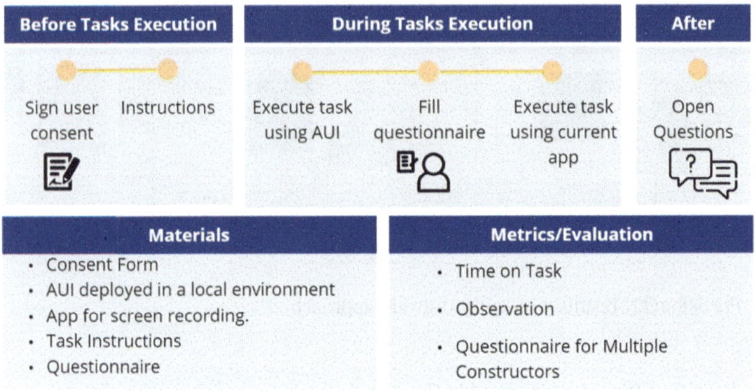

Fig. 16 Experiment protocol followed for case study

During the session, users interacted with the AUI generated through the implementation of the framework on the monitoring system and deployed in a local environment. The participants also needed to fulfill a specific task. Following this, participants filled out the questionnaire, evaluating their experience with the AUI. After that, users proceeded to perform a control task using the current interface without adaptations. This control task, which featured slight alterations, served as a baseline for time comparison. Post-task completion, participants engaged in open-ended questions, asking them about issues or to share observations and express any uncertainties they may have encountered. The materials employed for this evaluation included a consent form, app deployed in a local environment, and software for screen recording as presented on Fig. 17. User were given a general task instructions, while feedback and evaluation were gathered using the questionnaire and observation.

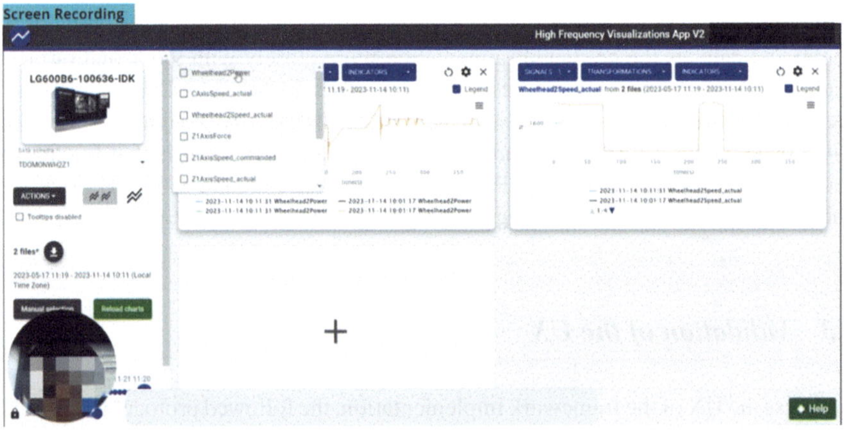

Fig. 17 Experiment set-up: participants task evaluation

The research question for this analysis is: *Do users who engage with the AUI present a reduction in task completion time compared to those who do not follow the recommendations?*

The effectiveness of AUI was evaluated by comparing user interactions with both the current user interface for the monitoring service and the AUI proposed. Table 8 presents the results of the Time on Task metric of the six participants (P1 to P6), each representing distinct roles and varying frequencies of usage with the application.

As stated on the protocol, the decision to start the task execution with the AUI followed by the task execution on the current application was deliberated. By initiating the session with the AUI, we aimed to capture user initial interactions without introducing a learning advantage that could potentially influence their subsequent engagement with the traditional interface. This deliberate approach seeks to mitigate the risk of users becoming overly familiar with the task, thus preserving the authenticity of the experiment. An analysis of the time spent by participants in both interfaces revealed an average reduction of approximately 39.72 s of the Time on Task when using the AUI. This reduction indicates a potential efficiency gain in user interactions, supporting the notion that AUI could contribute positively to the overall UX.

$$\mathrm{Average Reduction} = \frac{\mathrm{Sum of individual Reductions}}{\mathrm{Number of Participants}}$$

$$\mathrm{Average Reduction} = \frac{(31.73 - 29.76 + 92.18 + 11.10 + 69.90 + 63.17)}{6}$$

$$\mathrm{Average Reduction} \approx 39.72\mathrm{s}$$

Users also provided their feedback through a questionnaire. The questionnaire was developed based on the user-centric evaluation framework proposed by Pu et al. [48], specifically tailored to the context of recommendation systems to evaluate the quality of the UX. To capture user responses effectively, a 5-point Likert scale ranging from "strongly disagree" (1) to "strongly agree" (5) was employed for each question [13]. The questions and results summarized in Table 9 and Fig. 18, present an overall

Table 8 Participants time-on-task evaluation

Participant	Role	App usage	Time in current web app	Time in AUI web app
P1	NDT researcher	Seldom	3:11.26	2:39.53
P2	General researcher	Seldom	1:51.07	2:20.83
P3	NDT researcher	Regular	2:57.04	1:24.86
P4	Grinding researcher	Regular	1:25.15	1:14.05
P5	General researcher	Seldom	4:34.09	3:24.19
P6	Grinding researcher	Regular	2:48.04	1:44.87

high level of satisfaction with the suggested changes that take into account their work context, as evidenced by a mean score of 4.00 under the "Behavioral Intentions" construct. This represent a willingness to keep using the application with the adaptations. The "Ease of use" construct, particularly "Ease of Decision Making" (Mean: 4.83), suggests a positive user experience with streamlined recommendations. However, in contrast with the "Ease of Initial Learning" (Mean: 3.83) this could indicate challenges for new users despite perceived ease over time. There is a moderate positive feedback regarding user's ability to find recommended features and options (Mean: 3.83). This result implies that certain presentation styles for system adaptation were more effective than others, generating greater notice from users.

In the "Perceived Usefulness" construct, users express a moderate level of agreement (Mean: 3.50) regarding feeling supported in finding the options they need with the application. This suggests a need for further exploration into user expectations and the perceived utility of the application's features to align more closely with user needs. In the "Quality" construct, users positively rate the accuracy of finding the desired machine (Mean: 5.00) and the relevance of recommended indicators (Mean: 4.17) and transformations (Mean: 4.00) to their work. These high scores indicate a positive result in the user perception of delivering accurate and relevant results.

Then, the "Context Compatibility" construct reveals positive feedback on the relevance of the dashboard to users' tasks (Mean: 4.33) and its consideration of personal context and requirements (Mean: 4.17). These results affirm that the application effectively aligns with user work context, providing a tailored and supportive environment.

5 Discussion

This section will discuss the findings and limitations of the results. The study investigated the impact of implementing the proposed framework for adaptive HMI.

For the analysis of performance and usability, these two are tightly correlated with the efficiency and ease of use according to Pu et al. [48]. Users strongly agreed, as indicated in Table 9, that the use of recommended options saved them time in their task.

The ease of use can be seen as a form of efficiency, minimizing the cognitive load and effort needed for decision-making. This observation finds support in the collected data, indicating a reduction in the time spent on tasks. Integrating task completion time with user feedback offers a more comprehensive understanding of user behavior.

An HMI that enables users to quickly and conveniently access features and options for their work tasks is not only tied to the quality of the recommendations but also to how well they are presented to the user. Therefore, interaction adequacy plays a role that can even affect the perceived accuracy and usefulness of the AUI.

Table 9 Questions and survey results

Construct	Subclass	Question	Mean	SD
Behavioral intentions	–	I would continue using the application with	4.000	0.894
		these changes that take into account my		
		work context		
Ease of use	Ease of decision making	Using the recommended options streamlines the use of the application	4.833	0.408
	Ease of initial learning	If it were the first time I use the application, I think it is intuitive and easy	3.833	0.753
		to navigate to find what I need		
Interaction adequacy	–	I easily found the recommended features and options	3.833	1.169
		I would like that the application provides a suitable way to express my preferences	4.167	1.329
Perceived usefulness	Perceived usefulness	I feel supported in finding the options I need with the application	3.500	1.516
Quality	Accuracy	I easily found the machine I wanted to work with	5.000	0.000
		The recommended indicators in the app are relevant to my work	4.166	0.983
		The recommended transformations in the app are relevant to my work	4.000	0.894
	Context compatibility	The dashboard showed relevant graphs for my task	4.333	0.816
		The dashboard takes into account my personal context and requirements	4.167	0.408

Regarding user satisfaction, as indicated by behavioral intentions assessing users' willingness to continue using the presented adaptive HMI, there is a relationship between their satisfaction level and the likelihood of returning to the product. The average score reflects a notably high level of agreement, averaging at 4.00. Accuracy and context compatibility are factors that positively contribute to the satisfaction. The perceptions of users around these constructs align with the evaluation of the

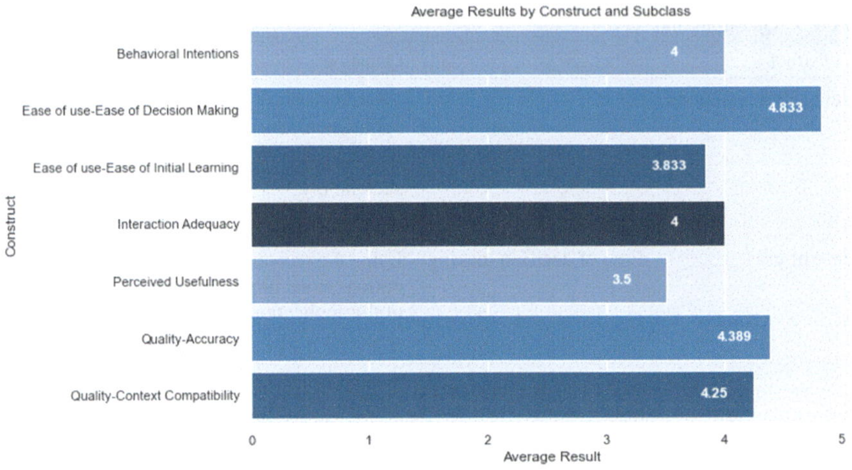

Fig. 18 Results of constructs for evaluation of user perceptions

recommendation component that demonstrate an improvement when selecting the context-aware approach.

These results highlight the importance of considering the system as a whole, where a user-friendly interface and seamless user experience contribute to satisfaction, alongside accurate and compatible adaptations for user interfaces.

While this evaluation provided valuable insights, there are limitations. The sample of 6 participants may be considered small, mostly due to availability constraints. However, we believe the case study remains relevant for its intended purpose. In Jakob [25], it was demonstrated that only 5 users are needed to identify 80% of usability problems, additional research aimed at testing several numbers of users sample has indicated that usability tests with a total of 6 to 8 participants can be just as effective as tests with 12–15 users, allowing for the identification of both minor and major issues [4, 34]. In the context of this study, it builds upon an already designed web-app that users already known at some degree. It specifically focuses on the evaluation of adaptations and the interaction adequacy of this web-app, centered around a well-defined task. The user group for these features shares the same profile; therefore, the results can still be considered useful in gathering the perceptions of this particular user profile.

In regards on the precision of the approach, the results using contextual data improved the recommendations compared to the regular approach. However, we emphasize the need for methods for selecting contextual factors and how this can be integrated into the framework, since the contextual data selected highly influences the recommendation results. This is particularly noticeable when reading users' opinions on how tasks, user identity, or time affect their decision-making. In this case study, we considered user role, shift, and task as sources of context to generate recommendations, as explained in previous sections.

5.1 *Future Work and Opportunities for Research*

- **Functions and Applications of HMIs in Smart Factories**

As presented, HMIs currently can be used for four main functions present in a smart factory environment: operations and supervision, management, maintenance, and cybersecurity. In the previous industrial revolutions, factory functions were performed by completing various tasks that were not traceable from a single device or machine, and functions were also not well connected with each other. There were no interoperable functions, and real-time data collection and control were possible for only a few functions [30]. Within the operations function, the assembly task has received more attention in the context of AUIs. In this work, we have focused on the supervision function and monitoring task, understanding other issues from different functions can be further researched.

- **Emerging Trends in Multimodal Interfaces and Interaction Modes**

Multimodal User Interfaces integrate multiple modes of interaction, allowing users to engage with the machine using a combination of different input and output methods. These can include touch, voice, gestures, keyboard, or mouse. These types of hybrid interfaces that include natural modes of interaction like voice or eye gaze are quickly becoming a new standard. Therefore, understanding how to integrate conversational and voice commands and instructions with those made using a mouse or gestures is important since the use of mobile and web applications is unlikely to disappear entirely.

Looking to the future, the coexistence and integration of HMIs with emerging technologies such as Virtual Reality (VR) and Augmented Reality (AR) will open up new possibilities for interaction and adaptation. Incorporating VR and AR into HMIs can enhance visualization and simulation capabilities, facilitating immersive training and prototyping experiences. Additionally, advancements in natural language processing and machine learning will enable HMIs to better understand and respond to user commands, leading to more intuitive and user-friendly interfaces.

- **Human–Robot Collaboration**

Nowadays, collaborative robots (cobots) are becoming more prevalent in industries. Cobots are designed to work alongside humans, sharing a common workspace and collaborating on tasks in close proximity. In this scenario, HMIs should offer clear and intuitive interfaces that enable operators to easily program cobots, adjust parameters, and intervene when necessary to ensure safety and optimize performance. The role of adaptive HMIs in these scenarios should be further explored, focusing on providing relevant information about cobot behavior, intentions, and status to human operators, serving as a mediator of human–robot collaboration [58] and reducing the risk of accidents or errors.

- **Ethical and Social Implications**

As HMIs continue to advance and integrate into several aspects of daily life, it becomes important to address the ethical and social implications. The use of smart and adaptive HMIs may raise questions about human autonomy, as reliance on automated systems could diminish individual decision-making power. Therefore, as stated in Section 3.1, an important aspect to explore in more detail is the control over the adaptation dimension that a user might have, and how this could affect their UX.

Nowadays, concerns also revolve around job displacement and automation. While HMIs have the potential to enhance efficiency and productivity in industries, historical precedent shows that automation has often displaced human workers at the task level (i.e., in specific job functions such as manufacturing assembly lines) [2], that can result in unemployment and economic disparities, particularly during the initial stages of industrial revolutions. Consequently, there is a need to examine the evolving role of humans in this new era, considering the emergence of new job opportunities and the requisite skills and training needed to adapt to changing technological landscapes, as many studies imply the displacement of jobs [3]. To address these challenges, proactive measures are essential, including robust reskilling and upskilling programs to facilitate the transition of displaced workers into new roles or industries. Additionally, policymakers must prioritize initiatives that ensure equitable access to training and employment opportunities, particularly for marginalized or vulnerable communities.

6 Conclusions

This article presented a general view on HMI and AUI, and introduced a framework for the development of adaptive HMI. A case study was presented with a hands-on development approach to demonstrate the practical implementation of the framework in an industrial environment, considering technological aspects and utilizing appropriate tools. The case study demonstrated the possibilities of implementation in a real-world scenario, focusing on different sections of the HMI. The results demonstrated an improvement on the precision of the recommendations using a context-aware approach. Even when a more extensive analysis of the dimensions of the visual elements on the interface is beyond the scope of the framework, this highlights that the use of AUI and AI technologies does not replace the need for a thorough understanding, analysis of user requirements, and the importance of the design of the HMI. Still, the framework serves as a toolbox that allows for considering multiple design implications since the choice of adaptation target and styles will affect interaction adequacy and ease of initial learning.

Acknowledgements This project is funded by the Basque Government's Department of Education, Universities, and Research (project Ikerketa Taldeak) and the European Union's Horizon

2020 program (Marie Sklodowska-Curie Grant No. 814078). Daniel Reguera-Bakhache is part of Mondragon Unibertsitatea's Intelligent Systems for Industrial Systems research group (IT1676-22), supported by the Basque Government. Angela Carrera-Rivera and Felix Larrinaga are part of the Software Engineering research group (IT1519-22).

References

1. Abrahão S, Insfran E, Sluÿters A, Vanderdonckt J (2021) Model-based intelligent user interface adaptation: challenges and future directions. Softw Syst Model 20(5):1335–1349
2. Acemoglu D, Restrepo P (2020) Robots and jobs: evidence from us labor markets. J Polit Econ 128(6):2188–2244
3. Aghion P, Antonin C, Bunel S, Jaravel X (2023) The effects of automation on labor demand. In: Robots and AI, pp 15–39
4. Alroobaea R, Mayhew PJ (2014) How many participants are really enough for usability studies? In: 2014 Science and Information Conference, pp 48–56. IEEE
5. Aranburu E, Lasa G, Kepa Gerrikagoitia J (2018) Evaluating the human machine interface experience in industrial workplaces. In: Proceedings of the 32nd International BCS Human Computer Interaction Conference, vol 32, pp 1–5
6. Bailly G, Lecolinet E, Nigay L (2016) Visual menu techniques. ACM Comput Surveys (CSUR) 49(4):1–41
7. Belli L, Cirani S, Gorrieri A, Picone M (2015) A novel smart object-driven UI generation approach for mobile devices in the internet of things. In: Proceedings of the 1st International Workshop on Experiences with the Design and Implementation of Smart Objects, pp 1–6
8. Berman A, Thakare K, Howell J, Quek F, Kim J (2021) Howdiy: towards meta-design tools to support anyone to 3d print anywhere. In: 26th International Conference on Intelligent User Interfaces, pp 491–503
9. Bettini C, Brdiczka O, Henricksen K, Indulska J, Nicklas D, Ranganathan A, Riboni D (2010) A survey of context modelling and reasoning techniques. Pervas Mobile Comput 6(2):161–180
10. Brdnik S, Heričko T, Šumak B (2022) Intelligent user interfaces and their evaluation: a systematic mapping study. Sensors 22(15):5830
11. Carrera-Rivera A, Reguera-Bakhache D, Larrinaga F, Lasa G, Garitano I (2023a) Structured dataset of human-machine interactions enabling adaptive user interfaces. Sci Data 10(1):831
12. Carrera-Rivera A, Reguera-Bakhache D, Larrinaga F, Lasa G (2023b) Exploring the transformation of user interactions to adaptive human-machine interfaces. In: Proceedings of the XXIII International Conference on Human Computer Interaction, pp 1–7
13. Carrera-Rivera A, Larrinaga F, Lasa G, Martinez-Arellano G, Unamuno G (2024) AdaptUI: a framework for the development of adaptive user interfaces in smart product-service systems. User Model User Adap Inter. https://doi.org/10.1007/s11257-024-09414-0
14. Champiri ZD, Mujtaba G, Salim SS, Chong CY (2019) User experience and recommender systems. In: 2019 2nd International Conference on Computing, Mathematics and Engineering Technologies (iCoMET), pp 1–5. IEEE
15. Fernandez-Garcia AJ, Iribarne L, Corral A, Wang JZ (2015) Evolving mashup interfaces using a distributed machine learning and model transformation methodology. In: On the Move to Meaningful Internet Systems: OTM 2015 Workshops: Confederated International Workshops: OTM Academy, OTM Industry Case Studies Program, EI2N, FBM, INBAST, ISDE, META4eS, and MSC 2015, Rhodes, Greece, October 26–30, 2015. Proceedings, pp 401–410 (2015). Springer
16. Gan R, Liang J, Ahmad BI, Godsill S (2020) Modeling intent and destination prediction within a Bayesian framework: predictive touch as a usecase. Data-Centric Eng 1:12
17. Gil Y, Garijo D, Khider D, Knoblock CA, Ratnakar V, Osorio M, Vargas H, Pham M, Pujara J, Shbita B et al (2021) Artificial intelligence for modeling complex systems: taming the

complexity of expert models to improve decision making. ACM Trans Interact Intell Syst 11(2):1–49
18. Gobert C, Todi K, Bailly G, Oulasvirta A (2019) Sam: a modular framework for self-adapting web menus. In: Proceedings of the 24th International Conference on Intelligent User Interfaces, pp 481–484
19. Gong C (2009) Human-machine interface: design principles of visual information in human-machine interface design. In: 2009 International Conference on Intelligent Human-Machine Systems and Cybernetics, vol 2, pp 262–265. IEEE
20. Gonçalves TG, Rocha ARC (2019) Development process for intelligent user interfaces: an initial approach. In: Proceedings of the XVIII Brazilian Symposium on Software Quality, pp 210–215
21. Guarino N, Oberle D, Staab S (2009) What is an ontology? In: Handbook on ontologies. Springer, Berlin, pp 1–17
22. Hussain J, Ul Hassan A, Muhammad Bilal HS, Ali R, Afzal M, Hussain S, Bang J, Banos O, Lee S (2018) Model-based adaptive user interface based on context and user experience evaluation. J Multimod User Interf 12:1–16
23. Iqbal MW, Ch NA, Shahzad SK, Naqvi MR, Khan BA, Ali Z (2021) User context ontology for adaptive mobile-phone interfaces. IEEE Access 9:96751–96762
24. Ivergard T, Hunt B (2008) Handbook of control room design and ergonomics: a perspective for the future. CRC Press, Boca Raton
25. Jakob N (2000) Why you only need to test with 5 users. Nielsen Norman Group, Nielsen
26. Jannach D, Zanker M, Felfernig A, Friedrich G (2010) Recommender systems: an introduction. Cambridge University Press, Cambridge
27. Johnston V, Black M, Wallace J, Mulvenna M, Bond R (2019) A framework for the development of a dynamic adaptive intelligent user interface to enhance the user experience. In: Proceedings of the 31st European Conference on Cognitive Ergonomics, pp 32–35
28. Khan I, Khusro S (2020) Towards the design of context-aware adaptive user interfaces to minimize drivers' distractions. Mobile Inform Syst 2020:1–23
29. Kulkarni S, Rodd SF (2020) Context aware recommendation systems: a review of the state of the art techniques. Comput Sci Rev 37:100255
30. Kumar N, Lee SC (2022) Human-machine interface in smart factory: a systematic literature review. Technol Forecast Soc Chang 174:121284
31. Kumar, N., Prajapati, S.: Challenges for interface designers in designing sensor dashboards in the context of industry 4.0. International Journal of Industrial and Manufacturing Engineering 13(8), 539–542 (2019)
32. Landowska A, Szwoch M, Szwoch W (2016) Methodology of affective intervention design for intelligent systems. Interact Comput 28(6):737–759
33. Li G, Wang L, Ou W (2016) Robust personalized ranking from implicit feedback. Int J Pattern Recognit Artif Intell 30(01):1659001
34. Lindgaard G, Chattratichart J (2007) Usability testing: what have we overlooked? In: Proceedings of the SIGCHI Conference on Human Factors in Computing Systems, pp 1415–1424
35. Maleki E, Belkadi F, Boli N, Van Der Zwaag BJ, Alexopoulos K, Koukas S, Marin-Perianu M, Bernard A, Mourtzis D (2018) Ontology-based framework enabling smart product-service systems: application of sensing systems for machine health monitoring. IEEE Internet Things J 5(6):4496–4505
36. Mezhoudi N, Khaddam I, Vanderdonckt J (2015) Toward usable intelligent user interface. In: Human-Computer Interaction: Interaction Technologies: 17th International Conference, HCI International 2015, Los Angeles, CA, USA, August 2–7, 2015, Proceedings, Part II 17. Springer, pp 459–471
37. Miraz MH, Ali M, Excell PS (2021) Adaptive user interfaces and universal usability through plasticity of user interface design. Comput Sci Rev 40:100363
38. Mitchell J, Shneiderman B (1989) Dynamic versus static menus: an exploratory comparison. ACM SigCHI Bull 20(4):33–37

39. Nguyen L et al (2016) A new aware-context collaborative filtering approach by applying multivariate logistic regression model into general user pattern. J Data Anal Inform Process 4(03):124
40. Noyes J, Bransby M (2001) People in control: human factors in control room design, vol 60. IET
41. Ochoa W, Larrinaga F, Pérez A (2023) Context-aware workflow management for smart manufacturing: a literature review of semantic web-based approaches. Future Generation Comput Syst (2023)
42. Oestreich H, Heinz-Jakobs M, Sehr P, Wrede S (2022) Human-centered adaptive assistance systems for the shop floor. In: Human-Technology Interaction: Shaping the Future of Industrial User Interfaces, pp 83–125. Springer, Berlin
43. Orghidan R, Gordan M, Danciu M, Vlaicu A (2013) A prototype for the creation and interactive visualization of 3d human face models. Adv Eng For 8:45–54
44. Papadakis H, Papagrigoriou A, Panagiotakis C, Kosmas E, Fragopoulou P (2022) Collaborative filtering recommender systems taxonomy. Knowl Inf Syst 64(1):35–74
45. Papcun P, Kajáti E, Koziorek J (2018) Human machine interface in concept of industry 4.0. In: 2018 World Symposium on Digital Intelligence for Systems and Machines (DISA), pp 289–296. IEEE
46. Peck EM, Easse E, Marshall N, Stratton W, Perrone LF (2015) Flyloop: a micro framework for rapid development of physiological computing systems. In: Proceedings of the 7th ACM SIGCHI Symposium on Engineering Interactive Computing Systems, pp 152–157
47. Perera C, Zaslavsky A, Christen P, Georgakopoulos D (2013) Context aware computing for the internet of things: a survey. IEEE Commun Surv Tutor 16(1):414–454
48. Pu P, Chen L, Hu R (2011) A user-centric evaluation framework for recommender systems. In: Proceedings of the Fifth ACM Conference on Recommender Systems, pp 157–164
49. Smirnov AV, Kashevnik AM, Ponomarev A (2017) Context-based infomobility system for cultural heritage recommendation: tourist assistant—tais. Pers Ubiquit Comput 21:297–311
50. Stefanidi Z, Margetis G, Ntoa S, Papagiannakis G (2022) Real-time adaptation of context-aware intelligent user interfaces, for enhanced situational awareness. IEEE Access 10:23367–23393
51. Stephanidis C (2001) Adaptive techniques for universal access. User Model User Adap Inter 11:159–179
52. Stephanidis C, Paramythis A, Sfyrakis M, Stergiou A, Maou N, Leventis A, Paparoulis G, Karagiannidis C (1998) Adaptable and adaptive user interfaces for disabled users in the Avanti project. In: Intelligence in Services and Networks: Technology for Ubiquitous Telecom Services: 5th International Conference on Intelligence in Services and Networks, IS&N'98 Antwerp, Belgium, May 25–28, 1998 Proceedings 5. Springer, pp 153–166
53. Stumpf S (2019) Horses for courses: making the case for persuasive engagement in smart systems. In: Joint Proceedings of the ACM IUI 2019 Workshops, vol 2327. CEUR
54. Tahir R (2015) Analyzing the intelligence in user interfaces. In: 2015 SAI Intelligent Systems Conference (IntelliSys). IEEE, pp 674–680
55. Tan H-Z, Zhao W, Shen H-H (2018) Adaptive user interface optimization for multi-screen based on machine learning. In: 2018 IEEE 22nd International Conference on Computer Supported Cooperative Work in Design (CSCWD). IEEE, pp 743–748
56. ThoughtWorks (2022) ThoughtWorks Technology Radar, vol 27. https://www.thoughtworks.com/content/dam/thoughtworks/documents/radar/2022/10/trtechnologyradarvol27en.pdf. Accessed 19 Jun 2023
57. Tsandilas T, Schraefel M (2005) An empirical assessment of adaptation techniques. In: CHI'05 Extended Abstracts on Human Factors in Computing Systems, pp 2009–2012
58. Turner, C.J., Ma, R., Chen, J., Oyekan, J.: Human in the loop: Industry 4.0 technologies and scenarios for worker mediation of automated manufacturing. IEEE access 9, 103950–103966 (2021)
59. Völkel ST, Schneegass C, Eiband M, Buschek D (2020) What is "intelligent" in intelligent user interfaces? A meta-analysis of 25 years of IUI. In: Proceedings of the 25th International Conference on Intelligent User Interfaces, pp 477–487

60. Wallace J (2020) A holistic UX methodological framework for measuring the aspects of how dynamic, adaptive and intelligent a software solution is and make recommendations for improvement
61. Yang Q (2018) A novel recommendation system based on semantics and context awareness. Computing 100(8):809–823
62. Zhou J, Sun J, Chen F, Wang Y, Taib R, Khawaji A, Li Z (2015) Measurable decision making with GSR and pupillary analysis for intelligent user interface. ACM Trans Comput Human Interact (ToCHI) 21(6):1–23
63. Zhou X, Peng X, Xie T, Sun J, Ji C, Liu D, Xiang Q, He C (2019) Latent error prediction and fault localization for microservice applications by learning from system trace logs. In: Proceedings of the 2019 27th ACM Joint Meeting on European Software Engineering Conference and Symposium on the Foundations of Software Engineering, pp 683–694

The Future of Midwife Training: Towards a Virtual Reality Haptic Obstetric Simulator with Two Points of Contact

Fernando Luján Millán, Pascual González López, Ana Belén García Bravo, Jonatan Martínez Muñoz, Arturo S. García Jiménez, and José Pascual Molina Massó

Abstract This chapter describes the development, guided by an exploratory process, of a virtual reality obstetric simulator based on the VITAKI toolkit and a Leap Motion device to provide, respectively, vibrotactile haptic feedback and two-finger tracking, which midwives use to assess the cervix and foetus in the moments prior to delivery. With exploratory iterations of this process, or alpha versions, it is found that different degrees of cervix consistency can be associated with different values of motor vibration speed, that cervical dilatation can be assessed using two fingers and vibration, and that it is even possible to locate and distinguish with vibration such small shapes as those of the anterior (diamond-shape) and posterior (triangular) fontanels of the foetus. In the latter case, however, the evidence shows the need for a support surface to recognise such small shapes, something to oppose or force. Even so, compared to previous work, the simulator stands out by adding an extra point of contact, and gives rise to a possible further development of this work combining a force feedback device with vibrotactile feedback.

F. Luján Millán · P. González López · J. Martínez Muñoz · A. S. García Jiménez · J. P. Molina Massó (✉)
Instituto de Investigación en Informática de Albacete (I3A), Universidad de Castilla-La Mancha (UCLM), Albacete, Spain
e-mail: JosePascual.Molina@uclm.es

P. González López
e-mail: Pascual.Gonzalez@uclm.es

A. S. García Jiménez
e-mail: ArturoSimon.Garcia@uclm.es

A. B. García Bravo
Servicio de Salud de Castilla La Mancha (SESCAM), Albacete, Spain
e-mail: abgarciab@sescam.jccm.es

S. Sayago et al. (eds.), *Future Perspectives on Human-Computer Interaction Research*,
https://doi.org/10.1007/978-3-031-71697-3_8

1 Introduction

One of the techniques that midwives use in their profession is the digital vaginal examination, which is used to determine the woman's labour stage and, more importantly, to determine how the foetus is presenting and thus to know whether the delivery can be eutocic (normal delivery, no instrumentation is required) or, on the other hand, an instrumental delivery or even a caesarean section is necessary. In the case of instrumental delivery, a good examination is of utmost importance in order not to harm the foetus with the instruments used.

The teaching and learning of this technique are based, on the one hand, on theoretical knowledge of the anatomy of the woman and the foetus and, on the other hand, on practice with silicone obstetric simulators and real practice with pregnant women. Figure 1 shows an example of a silicon model. A simpler one can be found in [1], which is box where different parts representing specific cases are placed at the back, and a hole at the front of the box allows the fingers to be inserted to perform the examination of the simulated case. This simple simulator includes, among the interchangeable parts, the head and genital organs of the foetus, and four cervixes in different stages. Silicone models, even the simplest, are expensive and provide only a limited number of cases to practice.

Compared to physical silicone simulators, Virtual Reality (VR) solutions based on tactile and kinaesthetic feedback devices (haptic devices) can offer many more advantages, such as the possibility of recreating an unlimited number of cases, personalised monitoring of the student, carrying out examinations under the supervision of a teacher or facilitating self-assessment, among others. In this sense, the LoUISE research group has been developing different VR obstetric simulators for some time with the dual aim of, on the one hand, facilitating the learning of this technique for

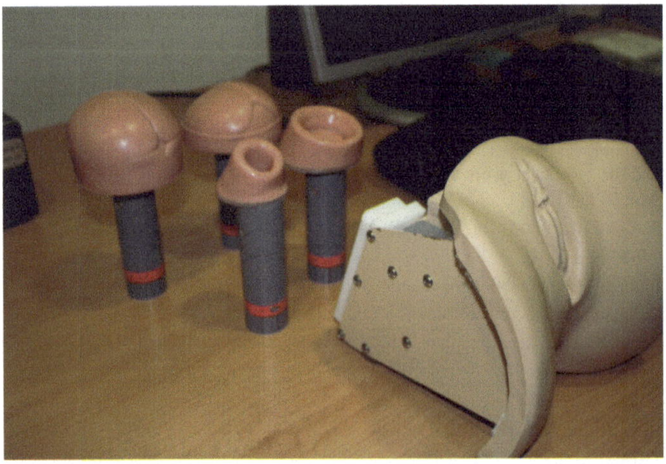

Fig. 1 Silicon obstetric simulator used by the midwifery teaching unit of the Complejo Hospitalario Universitario de Albacete

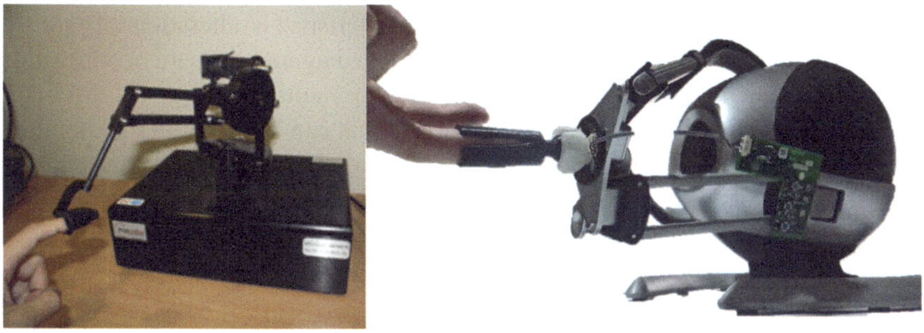

Fig. 2 Phantom (left) and Falcon devices (right)

future midwives in a simulated and controlled environment and, on the other hand, contributing to reducing the need for real practice with pregnant women.

Previous work [18, 20] has shown an obstetric simulator based on the Sensable Phantom device (now marketed by the company 3DSystems [2]), and another based on the Novint Falcon device [11] with a custom effector. Figure 2 shows these devices used.

The development of both simulators was assisted and supervised by a midwife who, as an expert in the field, validated the steps being taken. Of the two simulators, the one based on the Falcon device was tested with other midwives in addition to the previous expert, thus being able to obtain the opinions of more professionals. Overall, the impressions were good, but a common criticism was that there was a lack of the ability to examine with two fingers, which is the most common practice in this technique, but the two devices (Phantom and Falcon) only provide haptic stimulation to a single finger, the one inserted into the thimble.

In order to provide this missing but demanded functionality, two main solutions were planned. One was to make use of a grid of equal haptic devices, each providing feedback to one finger, for example two Falcons. The other solution was also to combine two haptic technologies, but this time different ones: one Falcon-like device would provide force feedback to one finger, while the other would receive a tactile stimulus from a vibrating device.

This chapter explores how a vibrating device can contribute to the obstetric simulator. However, before combining it with another force feedback device, what is proposed here is to investigate how far vibration technology can be used in this field by proposing a new simulator based solely on this haptic technology.

2 Related Work

Exploration by touch (palpation) is a tool widely used by healthcare professionals (both nursing and medical) that consists of pressing with the fingers an area of interest to locate and/or analyse something under the patient's skin, or to feel the presence or absence of anatomical and/or physiological characteristics or alterations. There are different palpation techniques, which can be used to diagnose the patient or to guide another operation, and may require a single finger or multiple fingers.

Many of the virtual touch and feel simulators that can be found in the literature make use of the more traditional haptic devices based on electric motors, such as the Phantom family of devices. References [7, 23, 25] compile many of these haptic simulators in their respective reviews in the medical field. Here, we will review those most relevant to the digital vaginal examination technique that is the subject of this research project.

Thus, Crossan et al. [6] presents a Virtual Reality simulator aimed at training in prostate cancer diagnosis. The prototype is composed of a haptic Phantom interface that provides feedback to the user's finger, a structure that restricts movements and an SGI workstation to render the patient's anatomy. In the field of veterinary medicine, the Horse Ovary Palpation Simulator (HOPS) [8] allows virtual palpation of a mare's ovaries also using a Phantom device. The same research group developed a simulator for rectal exploration in cows, using a Phantom Premium 1.5 inside a fibreglass model of a cow [4, 31]. In gynaecology and obstetrics, the simulators most relevant to our work are SIMone [17] and SITEG [16]. The former is a haptic simulator that recreates complicated delivery situations where the use of instruments may be required, such as forceps, an instrument with which the foetal head is grasped and pulled to assist the delivery of the foetus. The second allows the gynaecological examination to be simulated in its two phases, a visual one in which a speculum is used to observe the colour and texture of the vagina and cervix, and another in which the touch of a finger is used as an instrument to examine and look for consistencies that give away the presence of pathologies. For the latter, they use the smallest of the Phantom family, the Omni.

Scanning with several fingers manipulating simultaneously is challenging to implement in a medical simulator, so it is usually ignored and, when it is included, it is done in a way that greatly simplifies the manipulation [7]. However, there are also examples of this. Thus, in [3] a simulator for breast exploration using three fingers is presented, opposing a robotic hand to the user. Another example is the Virtual Haptic Back (VHB) project, aimed at creating a palpation training system for students of osteopathic medicine and physiotherapy, which used two PHANToM Premium 3.0 [12]. In [22], two haptic devices are also used simultaneously to train the palpation technique of a cat's abdomen.

Finally, in terms of vibrotactile feedback, in [15] we already demonstrated that it was possible to recognise three-dimensional geometric shapes with a glove equipped with several vibrotactile actuators, the same technology used in the present work taken to the field of application detailed below.

3 Palpation of the Cervix and Fontanels in Obstetric Exploration

The complexity of human birth [9] has an evolutionary connotation, as the bony canal was modified by bipedalism, leaving behind the birth canal of the quadrupedal mammal, making the birth canal of the bipedal mammal more irregular and narrower. The foetus does not pass through the three narrows of the obstetric pelvis in a straightforward manner; indeed, its passage through the bony birth canal is an intelligent obstacle course. The foetal skull is malleable since the parietal bones can slide over the frontal and the occipital bones in a process called moulding. This process allows the skull to adapt to the birth canal. The foetus must use its movements to find a way of opposing the smallest diameter it can present with its flexion to the largest diameter of the maternal pelvis in each strait.

Accommodation is the process by which the foetal head adapts to enter the pelvic cavity of the mother. This process is conditioned by both the diameter of the maternal pelvis and the diameter of the presentation. The latter varies according to the position of the head relative to the mother's pelvis. When the foetus has its head well flexed, chin to chest, the diameter of adaptation to the pelvis is the smallest, the so-called suboccipitobregmatic diameter, which surrounds the crown of the head passing through the greater fontanel or bregmatic fontanel, and measures 9.5 cm. But other positions of the foetus can complicate delivery, as is the case of presenting the largest diameter, which is the mento-occipital diameter, which passes through the crown of the head and the chin, and measures 13.5 cm.

As the foetus progresses down the birth canal, it descends through the so-called four Hodge planes (four parallel planes), starting at Hodge-1 (plane on the pelvic inlet) and ending to Hodge-4. Even with the smallest diameter, the foetus cannot descend if the cervix does not widen sufficiently. The cervix is the lower fibromuscular portion of the uterus that projects into the vagina, forming the endocervical canal that joins the external cervical with the uterine cavity. Although the cervix is usually 3–4 cm long and about 2.5 cm in diameter, during the labour progress it will become effaced (i.e. shortened in length) and dilated (increased in diameter). It will also change its consistency from hard to soft, and its position from the back of the vagina to the front, i.e. facing the cervix towards the exit.

Dilatation, effacement, consistency, position and plane are the five signs of labour progress that midwives assess, score and add together on the partograph to obtain what is known as Bishop's index (Fig. 3). And the tool they use to make this assessment is their fingers, normally inserting two fingers into the pregnant woman's vagina. For example, depending on the depth, they can determine the plane, with the fingertips they touch and assess the consistency of the cervix, and with one or two fingers they estimate its dilatation. For instance, if they can insert two fingers into the cervix, the dilatation is around 3 cm.

Using the same tool, finger touch, midwives also assess the presentation of the foetus as soon as they can touch it through the endocervical canal. In particular, by palpating with their fingers, they look for anatomical references in the foetus that

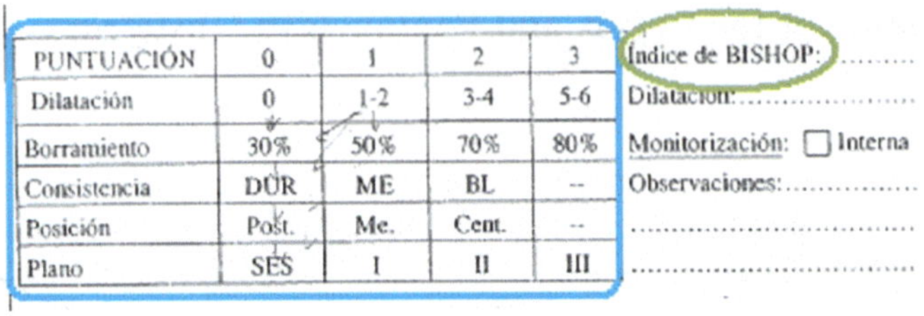

PUNTUACIÓN	0	1	2	3
Dilatación	0	1-2	3-4	5-6
Borramiento	30%	50%	70%	80%
Consistencia	DUR	ME	BL	--
Posición	Post.	Me.	Cent.	--
Plano	SES	I	II	III

Índice de BISHOP: ....
Dilatación: ....
Monitorización: ☐ Interna
Observaciones: ....

Fig. 3 Calculation of Bishop's index on a partograph (text is in Spanish)

give them clues or certainty about its presentation. One of the most important of these is the fontanels. Thus, between the bones of the foetal skull, not yet welded together to allow adaptation to the birth canal, there are grooves or sutures of a softer consistency, which converge in larger membranous spaces known as fontanels:

- Between the frontal and parietal bones, in the anterior part, where the coronary and sagittal sutures meet, there is a diamond-shaped fontanel called the anterior or bregmatic fontanel or bregma.
- Between the parietal bones and the occipital bone in the posterior part, where the sagittal and lambdoid sutures meet, a triangle-shaped fontanel is drawn, which is called posterior or lambdoid fontanel or lambda.

From a dilatation of 3 cm it would be possible to palpate the cranial vault. Figure 4 illustrates how the midwife, using the digital vaginal examination technique, tries to locate the fontanels. For example, if the foetus has the aforementioned suboccipitobregmatic diameter, the midwife should find the smaller (posterior, triangular) fontanel in her examination. On the other hand, if the foetus has the mento-occipital diameter, also mentioned above, then the midwife would only palpate the larger (anterior, rhomboidal) fontanel, which would already indicate a complicated presentation, and which she would confirm by touching the foetal face.

Fig. 4 Palpating the fontanels

4 Hardware and Software

For the development of this simulator, we relied on our vibrotactile solution VITAKI, accompanied by a Leap Motion device and carrying out the integration and programming in Unity [29]. This solution, a priori, entails a series of considerations:

- Haptic feedback: The force feedback provided by the Phantom and Falcon devices in previous work is replaced here by vibro-tactile stimuli. Developing a new obstetric simulator with this constraint represents a major challenge, requiring ingenuity in its design, and necessitating tests to validate what can be simulated and to what extent. For example, vibrating motors have the advantage that they can be placed anywhere on the hand. However, the best position for the stimuli to be simulated and the most practical way to attach it to that location must be determined.
- Tracking the position and orientation of the fingers (hand/finger tracking): The Leap Motion device will be in charge of locating and tracking the user's hand in real space in order to transfer its movements to the virtual simulation. Rather than the hand, what we are interested in is knowing the position of the index and middle fingers, which are the ones that the midwives insert when examining, but this should not be a problem as Leap Motion not only tracks the hand as a whole but also each of the individual fingers. However, it should be noted that Leap Motion tracks from a fixed point of view, so it will need to be well positioned, and it may still happen that when the hand is rotated during an examination the device loses sight of the fingers it was tracking. In addition, tracking could be impaired if other objects are introduced into the hand capture space, as Leap Motion is a computer vision-based device that is sensitive to the image captured by its cameras. This, as with VITAKI, requires testing to determine the limits of the solution.

4.1 VITAKI

VITAKI is a toolkit developed by Jonatan Martínez in his doctoral thesis [14] that facilitates the introduction of vibrotactile haptic feedback in any project through small vibrating motors, thanks to its versatility in adapting it to the needs of each project and its ease of programming (in C) with it. VITAKI is based on Arduino and Bluetooth and, in addition to the Arduino board itself and the Bluetooth connection module, it has a switch to turn it on, two LEDs that indicate its status—one red and one yellow—, a USB port to charge the device and, finally, ports to connect up to nine vibrating motors according to the needs of the project (Fig. 5).

The operation of VITAKI is simple: once the communication connection is established, the vibration data is sent continuously, and if at some point it stops being sent (after a certain period of time) then all the motors are stopped. This is done because, on the one hand, sending data continuously minimises latency (the motors

Fig. 5 VITAKI control unit and one actuator

take a short time to start up) and, on the other hand, it prevents the vibrators from continuing to act indefinitely in the event of a loss of communication.

In order to communicate with VITAKI from the simulator, a script called "VitakiController" is created. It makes use of Unity's "SerialPort" class, which provides a framework for synchronous and event-driven I/O, access to connection and breakpoint states and access to serial controller properties. To create the SerialPort object, it is necessary to enter a String variable with the name of the port to which the VITAKI is connected. Once connected, the communication is done by writing in a 32-byte buffer the speed values corresponding to each motor, although only 18 of these bytes are used, 2 bytes for each of the 9 motors supported by VITAKI. The script is completed with functions to assign specific speed values to each motor, which for this simulator will correspond to specific fingers, as well as to read the state of VITAKI. The function that is responsible for continuously sending data to the motors so that they do not stop is called from within the Update function, a function that in Unity is executed once per frame.

4.2 Leap Motion

Leap Motion [28] is an optical tracking system based on stereoscopic vision that consists of three infrared light emitters and two infrared cameras. Thus, the Leap Motion device captures two images (one per camera) and the driver is in charge of finding out the position of the fingers thanks to the small differences between the two images. The Leap Motion driver, through its API, then delivers the positions of the fingertips in Cartesian space. These positions are relative to the centre point of the device, which corresponds to the position of the infrared emitter of the medium.

The working range of the Leap Motion device is approximately 80 cm, limited by the time it takes for the infrared light to propagate through space, reflect off the hand and be captured by the cameras. The field-of-view angle is 150° across the device's width, and 120° in depth, as shown in Fig. 6. This provides sufficient working space for our obstetric simulator.

In addition to its physical characteristics, Leap Motion also offers support for development with Unity, which makes it easy to fit into simulator development. Thus, it provides objects ("Game Objects" in Unity) such as the Hand Model Manager, which is a sibling of the main camera and is the parent object of all its hand model types, such as Capsule Hands and Rigged Hands, which can be seen in Fig. 7. For this simulator, the Rigged Hands model has been chosen because, although the appearance should not matter as the digital vaginal examination is performed blindly guided only by the touch of the fingers, one of the advantages of the virtual simulator is the possibility to validate on screen where the fingers are and what they are touching, and in this sense, the Rigged Hands model is more realistic.

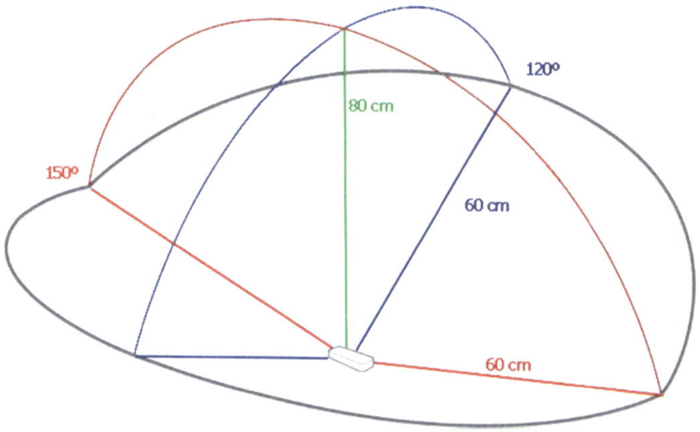

Fig. 6 Field of view and range of Leap Motion

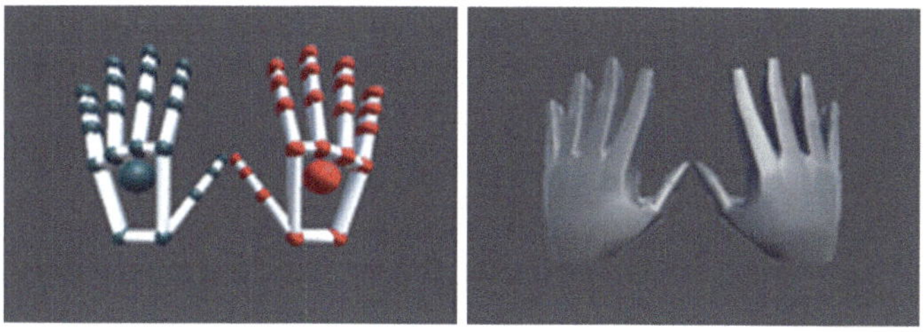

Fig. 7 Left: Capsule hands; Right: Rigged hands

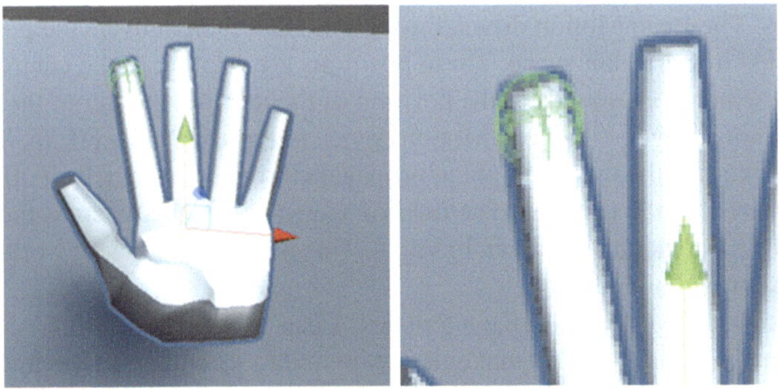

Fig. 8 Capsule collider in the rigged hands model

Similarly, by taking advantage of Unity's physics simulation engine, and in particular object collision detection, we can add specific components to the Rigged Hands model to detect when the user's fingertips touch other objects. Figure 8 shows, on the index fingertip of the hand model, the capsule-shaped geometry of the Capsule Collider.

5 Methodology: The Inventor Lifecycle

For this work the methodology "The Inventor lifecycle" has been followed, which the author presents as "a reasonable lifecycle for exploring an area that is new to oneself and plans to discover new things about how to use the tools and framework, possibly developing some completely new features as well" [24].

The process of this methodology is shown in Fig. 9. It consists of two main loops, one for alpha and one for beta versions. In alpha iterations, we do not know exactly what features our system will have, so we are allowed to change them as we progress in the process of exploring the problem and its solution. As the deadline approaches, both the design and the features of the product are frozen, and we enter the beta loop where we focus mainly on testing and debugging the software until the final version of the product is released.

This methodology or life cycle, therefore, adapts very well to the problem addressed here, exploring the limits of the technology and checking that it is viable for our objective. It allows us to raise hypotheses and, through attempts to prove them, to find out the limits or new features of the working tools.

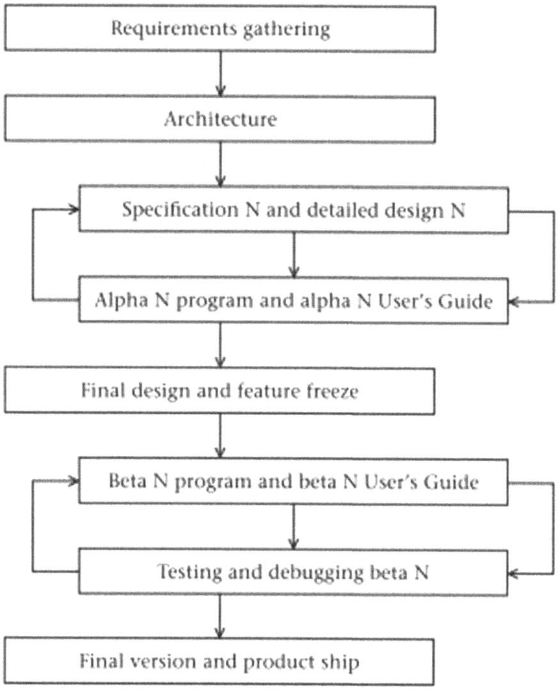

Fig. 9 The inventor lifecycle (picture taken from [24] with permission of the author)

6 Alpha Versions

This section describes some of the main alpha versions that have been created for the development of the project. Each alpha started with an objective associated with one or more requirements and, when the iteration was finished, it was evaluated in order to tackle the next alpha. As it is an exploratory process, the requirements are open to be changed, eliminated or even to create new requirements. At the end of these iterations, the resulting requirements are compiled and beta versions are created.

6.1 Integration of VITAKI and Leap Motion in the Simulator

One of the first questions to be solved was how many vibrating motors to place on the fingers and how to attach them to the fingers. Starting with the latter, two possible solutions were tested:

- Velcro Attachment: The actuator is placed on the fingertip and attached by wrapping a strip of Velcro around the finger. It is convenient for testing with different users in the same period of time, as it is easy to put on and take off. However, it has some drawbacks: on the one hand, it prevents the index finger from being

completely joined to the middle finger, which midwives have been known to use as a measure to assess a 3 cm dilation, the minimum would be about 4 cm; on the other hand, the cable connecting the motor to the VITAKI controller confuses the Leap Motion in its task of detecting the fingers of the hand.
- Latex Glove: The actuators are placed on the index and middle finger of a glove and the hand is carefully inserted so that the actuator is placed on the fingertip. This solves interference with Leap Motion finger tracking. In addition, the midwives perform the examination wearing gloves, thus adding realism to the simulation. The drawback is that care must be taken when removing and putting on the glove not to pull the wires too much, as they could break.

On the other question—number and location of vibrators per finger—it was initially proposed to place two vibrators on each fingertip, one on the fingertip and one on the side, assuming that the one on the fingertip would be useful for assessing compliance or locating fontanels and the one on the side for estimating dilatation. However, in the tests performed it was found that the stimulus of the actuator placed on the fingertip completely eclipsed the other. Even sending mild stimuli to the fingerprint and strong stimuli to the lateral the user thought that the vibrating actuator was the one on the fingerprint. Therefore, it was decided to leave only one vibrator per finger, placed in both on the fingerprint.

With the realism provided by the latex glove, it is considered whether it is also possible to imitate the silicone models by providing a front into which the user must insert their fingers, which in addition to providing a point of support during the examination would also limit the movement of the user's hand, which would otherwise remain free in space. The question in this case is whether something like this can also be integrated with Leap Motion. With cardboard, a simple front is constructed that fulfils this support function and also accommodates the Leap Motion device (Fig. 10, left and centre). However, in various tests it was found that it interfered with the Leap Motion capture process, so the idea was discarded. Instead, it was decided to create a virtual front end that, again imitating the silicone model, guides the user through vibration to the hole where the fingers should be inserted (Fig. 10, right).

6.2 *Simulation of Consistency with Vibration*

One of the greatest challenges of this work is to simulate the tactile feedback provided by the different tissues that are palpated in an obstetric exploration with a totally different stimulus, such as vibration. This tactile feedback is important, as has been explained, to assess the consistency of the cervix, or to distinguish between the bones of the skull and the sutures and fontanels. Therefore, in this alpha iteration, we seek to clarify whether there is any relationship between hardness and vibration, and what it is.

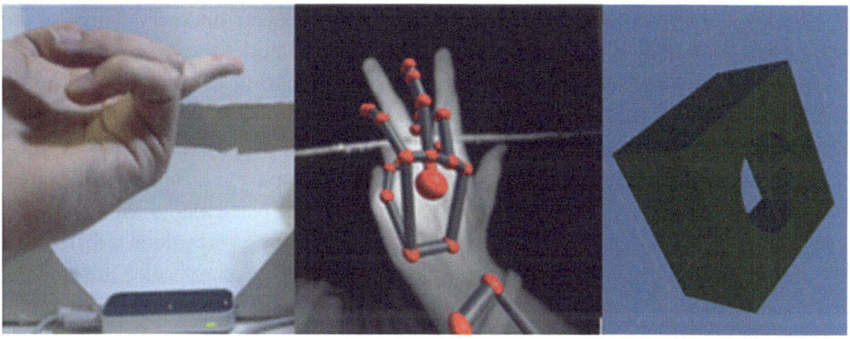

Fig. 10 Front end build with cardboard (left and centre) and virtual front end (right)

For this purpose, a test environment was prepared consisting of six virtual cubes, to each of which a vibrator speed value was associated (Fig. 11). Participants in this test had a vibrator placed on their finger, and thanks to Leap Motion tracking, each time they brought their finger close to one of the virtual cubes, the finger actuator vibrated. Two groups of cubes were prepared, one with lower velocity values, from 6 to 15, and the other with values up to 30. Each cube had a different value except for two that had the same value. Five different individuals participated in the test, 3 men and 2 women, aged between 20 and 60 years. None of them were familiar with these technologies and only one of them was a midwife.

Participants in this test were asked to indicate which of the cubes seemed harder, which seemed softer and, if possible, to order them by hardness. All participants associated the weak stimuli with soft objects and the strong stimuli with hard objects. When sorting the cubes, they all did so in the same way, although only one of

Fig. 11 Consistency simulation test with vibration (text is in Spanish)

them realised that there were two that vibrated with the same intensity. Three of the participants commented that they found high velocity values (above 20) annoying.

Continuing with this question, the next test sought to determine the minimum difference between different speed values that the user could distinguish. With the vibrator placed on the participant's finger, two impulses of 3 s each were sent, for a total stimulus of 6 s. The stimuli could be the same or have the minimum difference allowed by VITAKI, and they were repeated 9 times. The participants were the same as in the previous test. The results were that, with low motor speed values, a difference of 1 unit in the value sent to the motors was enough for the user to notice the change. On the other hand, it was not for high motor speed values. The latter could be due to the numbness that these values produce in the finger.

6.3 Determination of Dilatation with Vibration

Obstetric simulators based on force feedback devices—Phantom and Falcon—had the limitation of offering a single point of contact, the tip of a finger, with the virtual model. It is in the assessment of cervical dilatation where the ability to palpate with a second finger is most lacking because, although it is possible to perform an assessment with a single finger, two fingers make it possible to estimate the diameter directly from the distance between them.

This alpha version addressed two issues. On the one hand, since it is intended to measure a diameter, it is important that the centimetres measured in reality correspond to the same centimetres in the virtual model. On the other hand, with the system correctly calibrated, we wanted to test whether it was possible to estimate the diameter of a virtual cervix using vibration as tactile feedback.

The first question was solved by using the user's own abduction of the index and middle fingers. So, before starting, the user is asked to open them by 10 cm, Leap Motion captures this and a calibration function adjusts the measurements so that this opening corresponds to 10 cm in the virtual world as well.

For the second question, we tried to use Unity's collision detection and also measuring distances. Thus, in the latter case, a script controls the distance between the fingers and if it reaches the dilatation diameter, it sends a pulse to the vibrating motors of the fingers. Figure 12 shows the interface of this test with a dilatation of 10 cm, validated by the midwife collaborating in the project.

6.4 Palpation of Fontanels with Vibration

In our previous work with Phantom and Falcon, it was demonstrated that it was possible to palpate with these devices the fontanels of the head of a virtual foetus and to distinguish between the anterior (diamond-shape) and posterior (triangular) fontanels, although not without technical problems at the confluence of surfaces of

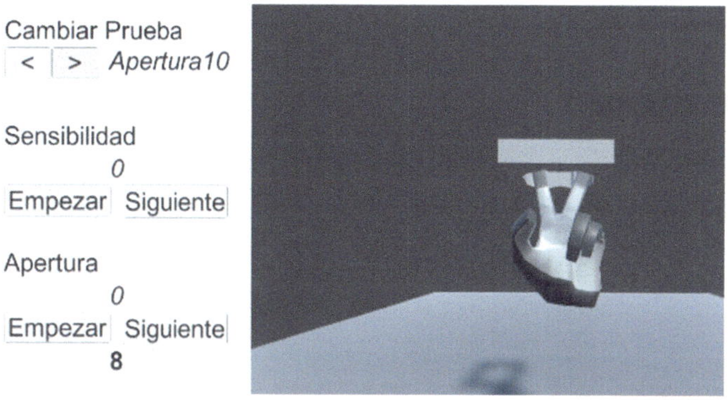

Fig. 12 Dilatation assessment test with vibration (text is in Spanish)

different hardness. For this other simulator, it has already been proven that different vibrations with different degrees of consistency can be assigned, as could be here the difference between the bones of the cranial vault and fontanels. The question is whether, in addition, it is possible to recognise a shape with vibrotactile feedback.

It could be argued that, based on the results of a previous work in which we already studied shape recognition with vibration [15], this test would not be necessary, but there is a considerable difference in size. Compared to the 3D figures of about 25 cm in that work, the dimensions of the fontanels are much smaller, from 1 to 3 cm.

For this test, a rectangular object is prepared with a geometric figure inside that the participant must discover with vibrotactile feedback (Fig. 13). The test was performed with three people, between 21 and 24 years of age, among whom this time the midwife collaborating in this work was not present. The first of them failed to recognise any figure before interrupting the test due to arm fatigue. None of them managed to guess the shape of the hidden figures.

It was then decided to modify the test by placing the Leap Motion 15 cm away from a wall, so that the wall would coincide with the rectangular object containing the shape to be discovered. The test then went from guessing the shape in the air to guessing it on a surface. With the same three participants as before, all three now guessed the shapes correctly after a short period of exploration. This is in line with the result of another paper [13] in which users were able to distinguish small 2D geometric shapes with vibrotactile feedback by following their outline on a table. Following this, the claim to simulate a realistic cranial vault is abandoned for a simpler but identifiable model (Fig. 14).

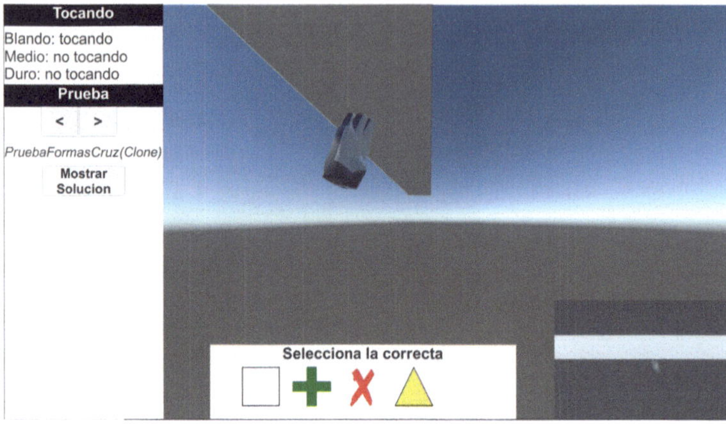

Fig. 13 Shape recognition test with vibration (text is in Spanish)

Fig. 14 Simple model for the posterior fontanel

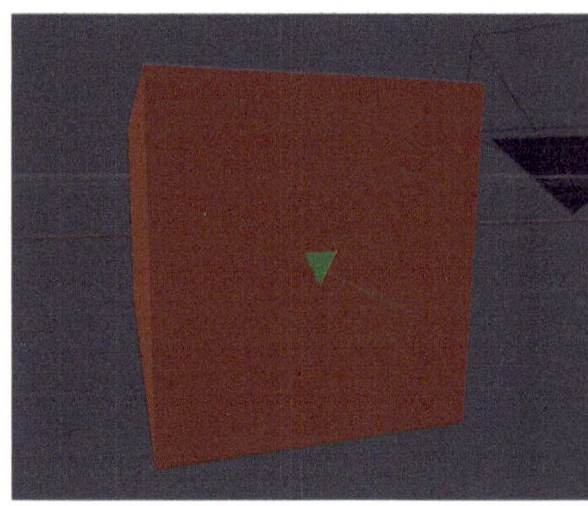

7 Beta Version

Based on all previous tests, the first fully functional beta version is built (Fig. 15). This version includes a menu with the options to create a new case, save it, calibrate the system or exit (Fig. 16). For the configuration of the case to be simulated, a form is used based on the partograph with which the midwives are already familiar, as shown in Fig. 3. During the simulation, the user can observe the case to be examined from two points of view, from behind his hand (main) and from the camera associated with Leap Motion (image in the lower right corner). Once the case has been evaluated, the user then enters his answer.

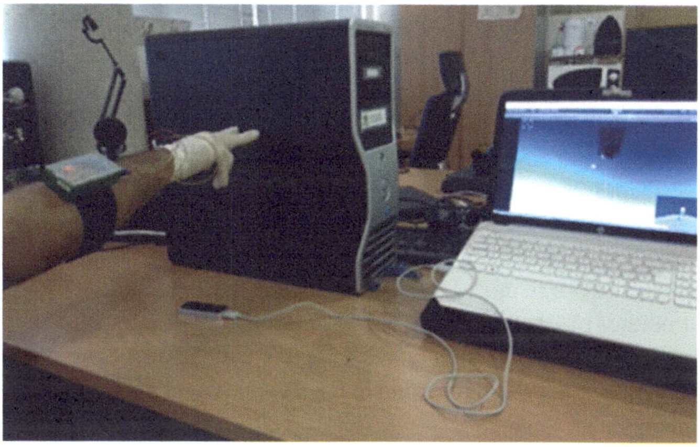

Fig. 15 User testing the beta version

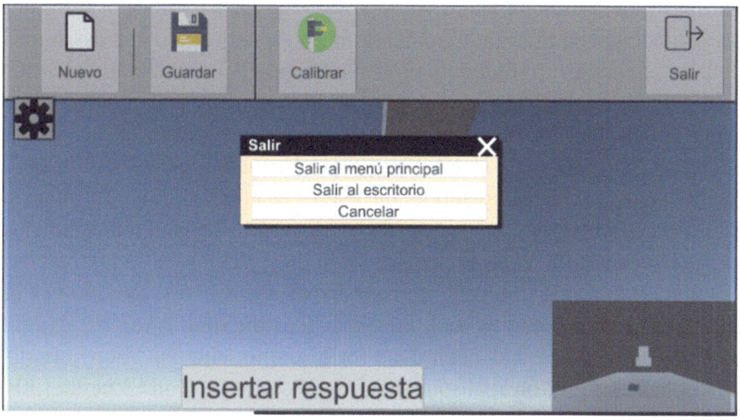

Fig. 16 Screenshot of the beta version interface (text is in Spanish)

8 Conclusions

This chapter has explained how midwives use their fingers to assess, by touch, five signs of labour progress (dilatation, effacement, consistency, position and plane), and also to look for anatomical references (especially the fontanels) in the foetus to reveal its presentation and to anticipate possible complications. Compared to traditional training in this technique of digital vaginal examination, virtual reality can offer many more advantages.

Directed by an exploratory method, the limits of vibrotactile haptic feedback technology have been explored in constructing an obstetric simulator to train this technique. To this end, several alpha versions have been created focussing on three key aspects: on the one hand, it has been shown that users can associate different vibrations to different degrees of hardness, useful for simulating the consistency of the cervix or distinguishing between bone and fontanel; on the other hand, it has also been shown that it is possible to measure a diameter with two fingers and vibration, necessary for assessing dilatation; finally, it is also possible to use vibration to recognise shapes as small as fontanels. However, limits have also been found in this exploration, such as the difficulty of recognising these shapes without a surface to rest on. In other words, this is where the force feedback of the previous Phantom and Falcon-based work is most lacking. Despite of that, the current simulator has a feature that neither of the two previous ones had, which is precisely the interaction with two points of contact. With what we have learned, we plan to continue working on the construction of a two-finger simulator, combining vibration and force feedback or two force feedback devices.

Nevertheless, the problem addressed here remains an interesting challenge for further work and progress, given the intrinsic difficulty of learning the palpation technique, and the vital importance of correctly judging the labour progress and presentation of the foetus in actual work. In the future, a number of different technologies will need to be brought together as an ecosystem to aid and assist midwives through their careers, from student to professional practice, accelerating learning and reducing the likelihood of misjudgement in real labour. Currently, there are a variety of commercial simulators aimed at doctors, nurses and midwives, as for example Oxford Medical Simulation [21], UbiSim [27] or Virtual Medical Coaching [32]. All of them allow cases to be set up and let the user—whether student or professional—get immersed in them using consumer market virtual and mixed reality sets, such as the Meta Quest and HTC Vive. However, while these devices allow interaction with virtual mannequins using controllers or the hands themselves, they do not provide the haptic feedback required by techniques such as the digital vaginal examination [5]. The solution so far, as has been done for example with the Microsoft Hololens glasses, has been to rely on real mannequins (Victoria [10] and Lucina [30]). The augmented reality technology in those examples allows students to see the anatomy of the woman and foetus as if they had X-rays, but again the cases are limited to the mannequin. In the future, the solution must involve improving tactile simulation through better haptic interfaces, with new technologies that could be tested in our simulator, such as the electro-stimulation recently described in [26], which could be considered as a substitute for the vibrotactile one. Beyond that, these technologies should be part of a whole ecosystem, even assisting in real births, which may soon become a reality with sensor gloves such as those described in [19], created to help perceive neonatal skull sutures.

Acknowledgements Grants PID2020-115220RB-C21 and PID2023-149753OB-C21, funded by MCIN/AEI/https://doi.org/10.13039/501100011033, and 2022-GRIN-34436, funded by Universidad de Castilla-La Mancha (UCLM), all also funded by "ERDF: A way to make Europe". The authors would like to thank the Midwifery Teaching Unit of the Complejo Hospitalario Universitario de Albacete (CHUA) for their invaluable collaboration.

References

1. 3BScientific. Fetal monitoring and labor progress model set. https://www.3bscientific.com/es/en/fetal-monitoring-and-labor-progress-model-set-1005579-w43045-79851,p_895_4859.html
2. 3D Systems. Haptic devices. https://www.3dsystems.com/haptics
3. Alhalabi MO, Daniulaitis V, Kawasaki H, Hori T (2005) Medical training simulation for palpation of subsurface tumor using HIRO. Eurohaptics Conference, 2005 and Symposium on Haptic Interfaces for Virtual Environment and Teleoperator Systems, 2005. World Haptics 2005:623–624
4. Baillie S, Crossan A, Brewster SA, May SA, Mellor DJ (2010) Evaluating an automated haptic simulator designed for veterinary students to learn bovine rectal palpation. J Soc Simul Healthcare 5(5):261–266
5. Ballit A, Hivert M, Rubod C et al (2023) Fast soft-tissue deformations coupled with mixed reality toward the next-generation childbirth training simulator. Med Biol Eng Comput 61:2207–2226
6. Burdea G, Patounakis G, Popescu V, Weiss RE (1999) Virtual reality-based training for the diagnosis of prostate cancer. IEEE Trans Biomed Eng 46(10):1253–1260
7. Coles TR, John NW, Meglan D (2011) The role of haptics in medical training simulators: a survey of the state of the art. IEEE Trans Haptics 4(1):51–66
8. Crossan A, Brewster S, Reid S, Mellor D (2002) Multi-session VR medical training: the HOPS simulator. People and computers XVI-memorable yet invisible. Springer, London, pp 213–225
9. Dörr PJ et al (eds) (2017) Obstetric interventions. Cambridge University Press, Cambridge
10. Gaumard. Obstetric MR. https://www.gaumard.com/obstetric-mr
11. HapticsHouse, Novint's Falcon Haptic Device. https://hapticshouse.com/pages/novints-falcon-haptic-device
12. Howell JN, Conatser RR, Williams RL, Burns JM, Eland DC (2008) Palpatory diagnosis training on the virtual haptic back: performance improvement and user evaluations. J Am Osteopath Assoc 108(1):29–36
13. Martínez J, García AS, Molina JP, Martínez D, González P (2013) An empirical evaluation of different haptic feedback for shape and texture recognition. Vis Comput 29(2):111–121
14. Martínez J, García AS, Oliver M, Molina JP, González P (2014) Vitaki: a vibrotactile prototyping toolkit for virtual reality and video games. Int J Human-Comput Interact 30(11):855–871
15. Martínez J, García AS, Oliver M, Molina JP, González P (2016) Identifying 3D geometric shapes with a vibrotactile glove. IEEE Comput Graphics Appl 36(1):42–51
16. Moraes RM, Souza DFL, Valdek MCO, Machado LS (2006) A virtual reality based simulator for gynecologic exam training. ITHET 2006:786–791
17. Obst T, Burgkart R, Ruckhäberle E, Riener R (2004) The delivery simulator: a new application of medical VR. Medicine meets virtual reality 12: building a better you: the next tools for medical education. Diagn Care 98:281–287
18. Oliver J, Martínez J, García AB, García AS, González P, Molina JP (2022) Desarrollo con la metodología TRES-D de un simulador obstétrico basado en el dispositivo háptico Phantom. In: En Actas del XXII Congreso Internacional de Interacción Persona-Ordenador, pp 26–33
19. Opie J, Jaufuraully S, Salvadores-Fernandez C, Bagchi B, Desjardins A, Tiwari M, Blandford A (2023) The future of neonatal skull suture detection. In: Proceedings of the 2023 CHI Conference on Human Factors in Computing Systems (CHI '23), April 23–28, 2023, Hamburg, Germany
20. Ordoño C, Molina JP, García AB (2022) Desarrollo y evaluación de un simulador de RV para la valoración obstétrica de cérvix y fontanelas. Interac Rev Digital AIPO 3(2):137–148
21. Oxford Medical Simulation. https://oxfordmedicalsimulation.com/
22. Parkes R, Forrest N, Baillie S (2009) A mixed reality simulator for feline abdominal palpation training in veterinary medicine. Stud Health Technol Inform 142:244–246

23. Ribeiro ML, Lederman HM, Elias S, Nunes FL (2016) Techniques and devices used in palpation simulation with haptic feedback. ACM Comput Surv (CSUR) 49(3):1–28
24. Rucker R (2003) Software engineering and computer games. Addison-Wesley
25. Talhan A, Jeon S (2017) Pneumatic actuation in haptic-enabled medical simulators: a review. IEEE Access 6:3184–3200
26. Tanaka Y, Shen A, Kong A, Lopes P (2023) Full-hand electro-tactile feedback without obstructing palmar side of hand. In: Proceedings of the 2023 CHI Conference on Human Factors in Computing Systems (CHI '23), April 23–28, 2023, Hamburg, Germany
27. UbiSim. https://www.ubisimvr.com/
28. Ultraleap. Leap Motion Controller. https://www.ultraleap.com/product/leap-motion-controller/
29. Unity Technologies. Unity. https://unity.com/
30. University of Bradford (2023) Midwifery students benefit from new high-tech simulation equipment. Press release. Published: Tuesday 6 June 2023. https://www.bradford.ac.uk/news/archive/2023/midwifery-students-benefit-from-new-high-tech-simulation-equipment.php
31. Virtual Cow. https://www.virtalis.com/systems/haptic-cow-haptic-horse
32. Virtual Medical Coaching. https://www.virtualmedicalcoaching.com/

Flipping the Reality of Young Children's Technology Through the 4Cs: Create, Connect, Communicate, and Control

Juan Pablo Hourcade and Flannery Currin

Abstract The advent of mobile touchscreen devices lowered barriers to enable young children to use computing devices. However, the new opportunities afforded by these devices have been eclipsed by its most common uses, which often involve unimaginative and isolating experiences, and sometimes include dark patterns that induce compulsive use and disregard privacy. To flip this reality, we build on the 3Cs approach to young children's technologies (create, connect, and communicate), and propose a 4th C: control. We argue for more technologies to give children and caregivers control over their activities, time, data, and decision-making. In this book chapter, we provide a historical and child development perspective to motivate our approach, present its characteristics, illustrate it with examples, and discuss challenges and opportunities.

1 Introduction

Computer science became a field independent from its parent disciplines, mathematics and electrical engineering, in the 1960s. The path to independence was not without controversy with the nascent field having to justify being its own discipline. This was the context in which future Turing Award winners, Newell, Perlis, and Simon, sought to defend the field as its own area of study in 1967 in an article titled *What is Computer Science?*, published in *Science* [1]. In the article, they defined computer science as "the study of the phenomena surrounding computers" [1].

Around the same time, Louis Fein, who had coined the term *computer science* in 1961 [2], addressed a related concern of why society should dedicate resources to study computer science. His perspective may be best summarized through a quote from a 1965 article in *Time* magazine, "What the hell are we making these machines

J. P. Hourcade (✉) · F. Currin
Department of Computer Science, The University of Iowa, Iowa City, IA, USA
e-mail: juanpablo-hourcade@uiowa.edu

F. Currin
e-mail: flannery-currin@uiowa.edu

S. Sayago et al. (eds.), *Future Perspectives on Human-Computer Interaction Research*,
https://doi.org/10.1007/978-3-031-71697-3_9

for, if not to free people?" (1965). In other words, Fein's promissory note for investments in computer science was a future where people would be freer. It was a promise of broad positive societal impacts.

Moving forward 60 years, the phenomena surrounding computers has expanded tremendously, with a recent addition being widespread use of computers by 2–5-year-old [3]. It is unclear though, whether this expansion has had an overall benefit on young children and society given the unimaginative and isolated characteristic of prevalent uses of technology by young children [3] and serious concerns about privacy [4] and compulsive use [5, 6].

In 2017, already concerned about the trends brought about by young children's use of mobile touchscreen devices, a group of child–computer interaction researchers proposed a novel approach to technologies for young children that contrasted with prevailing approaches. They argued that more of the activities supported by technologies for this age group should involve **c**reativity, **c**ommunication, and a **c**onnection with the social and physical environment around children (3Cs) [7].

In this book chapter, an extended version of a previously published paper [8], we second their call and add a fourth C to address challenges related to privacy and compulsive use of technologies: control. Our contributions include a contextual and interdisciplinary motivation for the 4Cs approach, guidelines for technologies to follow the 4Cs approach, a clear description of how it can be brought to practice including examples of existing technologies, and a discussion of opportunities and challenges ahead.

In the following sections we first provide historical context for the latest changes in computing to establish how the current landscape differs from historical trends. We also discuss child development and how it could be affected by dark patterns in computing. We follow this discussion with a summary of the 3Cs approach, describe the 4th C (control) and how it can be applied to technologies, provide examples of 4Cs technologies already in use, and discuss broader implications for child-computer interaction.

2 Historical Context of Human Factors Developments in Computing

Various times have been proposed as the beginning of the human–computer interaction (HCI) field, whether related to the first CHI conference in 1982 [9], the beginning of the Software Psychology Society in 1976 [9], Engelbart's "Mother of All Demos" in 1968 [10], or Sutherland's work on Sketch Pad in the early 1960s [11]. These events tend to be related to personal computing and the evolution of graphical user interfaces. We argue that more broadly, human factors have been involved in many major changes in computing, from the inception of digital computing to this day. Below, we provide a few examples to illustrate how these changes have broadened the use of computing by more people, even at the cost of higher execution times, and expanded the applications of computing. In other words, these changes have played a key role in expanding the "phenomena surrounding computers". We present these changes to illuminate the difference between the latest developments in computing and prior ones in terms of user control and the promise to "free people".

One of the first obvious examples of changes in computing related to human factors was the switch from implementing algorithms through hardware to implementing them primarily through software. The ENIAC, the first electronic computer to run in the United States (and the only one for five years), initially had to be programmed through rewiring [12]. This literally involved running wires between electronic components. It was not until 1948 that the first bit of software was written and implemented, based in part on ideas laid out by John von Neumann in 1945 [13]. This change gave computer users more control, by adding flexibility, lowering cost, and saving time, which made slower execution times worth it while keeping the option to implement algorithms through hardware when it made sense.

About ten years later, another change was from programming primarily through assembly language to using human-like high-level programming languages. The first meeting to discuss these emerging languages happened in 1956 [14]. They were designed to provide ways of programming computers that were closer to the domains addressed by the programs, rather than forcing low-level interactions with computers. Programming in these languages did not yield more efficient code than writing in assembly language. It slowed down execution. They became the default choice for programming because they significantly expanded who could program computers and the application areas where computers could be useful and practical, giving more people control over computers.

Moving to the 1960s, another major change in computing was the broad adoption of operating systems, such as IBM's OS/360, which went beyond the batch-processing systems that started in the 1950s to enable programming once for a wide variety of hardware configurations, as opposed to programming the hardware directly [15, 16]. When considering this tradeoff of the convenience of programming once at a higher level with slower execution speeds, over potentially programming multiple times at a lower level for faster execution speeds [16], the former has won. Adding this extra software layer again gave users more control over computers by having specific configurations not impact human processes even at the cost of longer execution times.

Perhaps one of the changes that HCI researchers and professionals are most familiar with is the one from the use of command-line user interfaces to graphical user interfaces (GUIs) for non-technical users. This change started with the ideas from Sutherland [11] and Engelbart [10] mentioned above, continued with developments at Xerox PARC during the 1970s [17, 18], and broadly used operating systems starting in the 1980s [19] and took hold during the 1990s [20]. Again, expert users can often be more efficient using the command-line than a GUI, as demonstrated by many system administration (e.g., [21]) and programming-related tasks (e.g., [22]) still being performed through command-line user interfaces, but GUIs broadened access to more users. The World Wide [23] borrowed many of the nascent ideas from HCI and GUIs (e.g., [24]) for a simple, consistent, and flexible user interface that appealed to an even broader set of users. GUIs, in particular, gave more users control over computers [25], and significantly lowered the time that had to be dedicated to learning how to use computers. For example, training to learn to use very basic features of WordPerfect (e.g., starting the program, using menus, editing text, opening and saving a file, printing), a popular word processor in the early 90s, could last five-and-a-half hours [26], whereas no similar training is expected for similar software (e.g., Google Docs) nowadays.

In the late 2000s, the release of Apple's iPhone [27] provided the first highly usable mobile touchscreen user interface, so usable that even frogs [28] and bearded dragons [29] can make intentional use of them. This unprecedented broadening of access also included, for the first time, young children [30], who prior to these devices being available, faced barriers to using a mouse and keyboard [31].

The latest changes in computing are related to the ubiquity of computing provided by mobile computing, high-speed Internet access, and smart devices, combined with the massive ability to capture, store, and process data. These changes further broaden the impact of computing and where it is available. Consider how computers affect our cognitive processes: changing how we perceive the world, what we need to remember, what we pay attention to, how we learn, and how we make decisions. Newell, Perlis, and Simon's "phenomena surrounding computers" [1] has become incredibly broad.

There is something different about this latest set of changes, though. They have come at an unprecedented cost in terms of control over our privacy, our information, and our relationship with computers, due to prevailing business models [32]. This lack of control for young children begins even before they have their own social media accounts as parents, teachers, and other adults negotiate appropriate sharing of children's information online [33, 34]. Is our current relationship with computing setting us free, per Fein's promise (1965)?

3 Relationship Between Young Children's Development and Computing

Child development is a dramatic process, particularly during the first few years of life. Changes in reaction time [35] (the inverse of information processing speed) provide a sense of the pace of development (see Fig. 1).

While there has long been debate over the relative impact of nature versus nurture on human development, more recent views point to the interaction of genetics and the environment over time to affect development [36]. Gottlieb's perspective, shown in Fig. 2, illustrates bidirectional influences from genetic to neural activity, to behavior, to the environment, and back [36]. It is easy to understand the top layer: our behavior can change the environment and the environment can change our behavior. But behavior is driven by neural activity, and neural activity is affected by the outcomes of our behavior. Likewise, gene expression impacts neural activity, and there is evidence that neural activity can in turn affect gene expression [36]. Note that gene expression

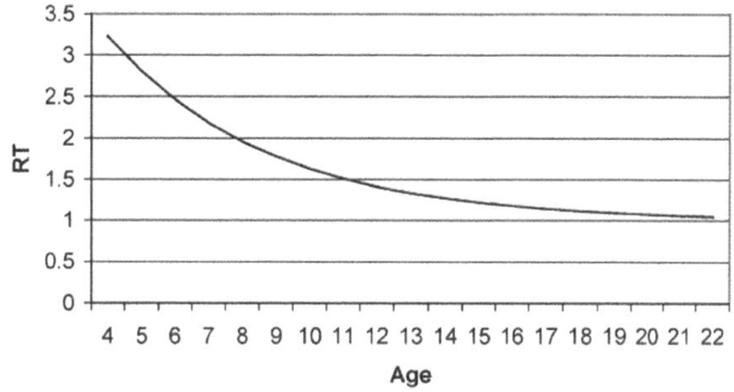

Fig. 1 Reaction time by age in years [35]

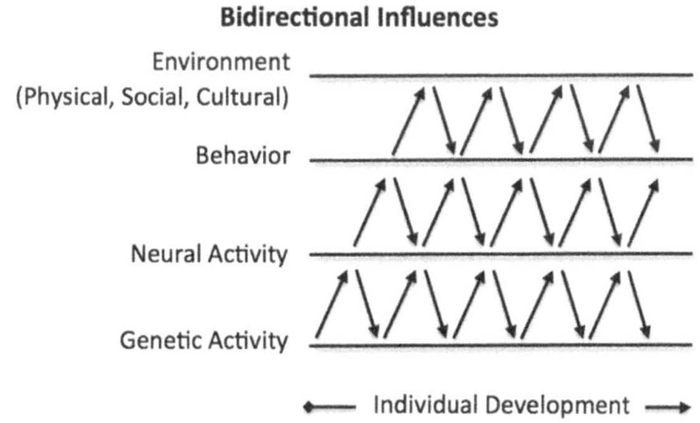

Fig. 2 Bidirectional influences between the environment and genetic activity [36]

is not the same as DNA, it refers mainly to using information from a gene to produce RNA molecules and proteins [37]. Gottlieb's views fall within a systems perspective of development that developmental psychologists have increasingly embraced by since the 1990s [38–42].

How are Gottlieb's views relevant to the relationship between young children's development and computing? Computers are increasingly mediating children's interactions with the environment. As more of children's time is spent using computers, this use, according to Gottlieb's bidirectional influences, should have an impact on their behavior, neural activity, and gene expression. These effects are likely to have a greater impact on young children, whose neural structures are changing quickly [35]. In other words, the concern is about how digital media can impact young children's cognitive development [43].

This concern is due to the steady increase in young children's use of mobile devices. In the United States, for example, a survey conducted right before the COVID-19 pandemic found that about half of 2–4-year-old children and two-thirds of 5–8-year-old own a mobile device [3]. The same survey found an average use of about one hour a day for 2–4-year-old children, most commonly to watch videos (37 min a day) and play video games (10 min a day) [3]. Only 28% of 2–4-year-old children accessed media with a parent most of the time [3], despite evidence joint media engagement is more beneficial for children's development than solitary media consumption [44]. Lower-income children 8 years old and under spent more than three times as much time on mobile devices as their higher-income peers [3], indicating technology use is likely to have disparate impacts on children of different socioeconomic backgrounds. In other words, the use of these devices by young children mostly involves unimaginative and solitary consumption of media and typically does not involve creativity, communicating with others, or connecting with the surrounding physical space. The impact of these experiences on children will largely depend on the quality of the media they access (e.g., is it educational or for entertainment purposes), the amount of time spent on it, and the social context in which it is used (e.g., with parents or individually) [43].

4 Dark Patterns in Young Children's Technology

Part of what is likely behind the rise in the use of mobile devices by young children is the business model behind most apps, which involves providing a free app in exchange for personal information [32]. Children's apps are no exception with a recent study finding that 67% of the top 1000 children's apps for Android and iOS transmit location, with close to half including location and IP address in the ad bid stream, and about 40 percent have access to potentially personal information, such as photo or video files [4].

The additional challenge is that this business model also incentivizes app designs that lengthen use, allowing apps to deliver more advertisements and gather more data. In other words, this business model leads to addictive designs [32]. Dark patterns related to incentives for compulsive use have previously been identified as widespread in popular children's mobile games [5, 6]. Many popular games targeting children combine designs for compulsive use with in-app purchases to enhance the gameplay experience and advertisement that is difficult to dismiss and is often for products young children should not use (e.g., for social media sites for users aged 13 and older) [6].

A recent analysis of data from the 2018–2020 United States National Survey of Children's Health found more than 70 percent of children under the age of 6 had more than an hour of screen time per day while more than 80 percent of children aged 6–17 had more than two hours of screen time [45]. Preschool children's screen time was positively associated with developmental and behavioral problems, such as developmental delay, speech disorders, learning disabilities, autism spectrum conditions, and attention deficit hyperactivity disorder [45]. While these relationships are correlational, not causational, there were significant dose–response relationships (i.e., screen time over a certain threshold was significantly correlated with higher incidence of developmental/behavioral problems) [45], which should be a cause of caution and concern.

Altogether, we posit the current status of young children's use of technology features not only unimaginative and isolating experiences, but also a lack of children's control over activities and decision-making (given the most common uses), time (given designs for compulsive use), and data. Going back once again to Fein's promise (1965), can we say that these uses of computers are setting children free?

5 Proposing the 4Cs for Young Children's Computing

While it is easy to criticize the current context of young children's interactions with computers, it is more difficult but necessary to use creative imagination to invent better futures [46]. We propose to use an existing approach proposed a few years ago, the 3Cs [7], and add one more component to bring it up to date with what we know about young children's current interactions with computing.

5.1 The 3Cs: Create, Connect, and Communicate

The 3Cs approach to preschool children's use of technologies calls for more children's technologies to support creativity, a connection with the social and physical environment around children, and face-to-face communication with other children and caretakers [7]. The inspiration behind the activities to be supported came from Vygotsky's sociocultural approach to child development and some of its successors [47, 48]. It was also inspired by Papert's perspectives on learning [49]. Both elevate social, creative activities, with Vygotsky in particular putting an emphasis on the role of language and tools [47, 48].

The key characteristics of activities proposed in the 3Cs approach and how they contrast with non-3Cs activities are summarized in Table 1 [7]. The non-3C activities reflect to a great degree the current state of the most common uses of technology by young children: social isolation, a primary focus on the device, experiencing media created by others, limited customization, instant gratification, and the leveraging of children's interests to keep them glued to the technology. The 3Cs approach seeks to flip this narrative by calling for technologies that do the exact opposite: facilitate children's communication with adults and peers, help them connect with the physical and social surroundings, support creative activities, help plan activities, involve delayed gratification, and leverage children's interest to arrive at powerful ideas.

The concepts in the table make it clear that the 3Cs approach attempts to address many of the concerns about young children's current use of technology [7]. There is a strong emphasis on social aspects and the use of technology to facilitate beneficial activities rather than being the focus of activities.

One observation is that the 3Cs approach resembles in many ways more traditional child play activities that do not involve technology. The question then is, why bother using technology at all? The 3Cs authors answered with five areas where computer technologies could add value: bridging abstract and concrete thinking, linking children to their strong interests, enabling a wider range of entities to be

Table 1 Non 3Cs versus 3Cs activity characteristics [7]

Non 3Cs approach	3Cs approach
Social isolation	Communicate with adults and peers
Primary focus on device	Connect with social and physical environment
Experience media	Participate in creative activity inspired by media
Same experience for everyone	Tech facilitates adults and children planning their own activities
Instant gratification	Delayed gratification
Use interests to maintain engagement	Immerse children in their interests to arrive at powerful ideas

created and shared, providing additional communication channels, and scaffolding beneficial activities [7].

Note that the authors of the 3Cs approach did not necessarily call for all young children's technologies to follow the approach, but rather for a proper balance between the use of 3Cs and non 3Cs technologies [7].

5.2 *Adding a Fourth C: Control*

While the 3Cs approach has many components that address current concerns with young children's use of technology, it does not fully address the concerns we previously outlined in Sect. 4. On its own, it does not speak to dark patterns involving privacy risks and promoting compulsive use of technologies by taking away children's decision-making and attempting to control their activities. These dark patterns remove control from children and their caregivers over their data, their time, and their activities and decision-making. In fact, 3Cs technologies that do not involve control could capture children's creative expressions and their communication with loved ones without their permission.

Hence, we propose a fourth C to be added to the 3Cs: control. A focus on control is not new in human–computer interaction. One of Ben Shneiderman's golden rules is to "support [an] internal locus of control" [50]. He argued users should feel in control and initiate actions, and the system should behave as expected. This golden rule was inspired by experiences with software with poor usability in the early years of the human–computer interaction field. Similarly, Nielsen included "user control and freedom" as one of his 10 heuristics, which largely referred to the ability to undo actions. Our sense of control goes beyond Shneiderman's and Nielsen's to call for technologies that respect privacy and that do not attempt to manipulate behavior for profit.

Table 2 outlines the characteristics of 4Cs technologies that add on to those of 3Cs technologies presented in Table 1. The characteristics we propose go beyond technology itself to the activity surrounding the use of technology. This is consistent

Table 2 Characteristics of technologies that lack or include the 4th C (control)

Lack of control	Control
Activity not possible without tech	Tech as a scaffold to activity
Compulsive engagement with tech	Intentional disengagement from tech
Personal data collection as part of business model	Privacy-preserving data collection used to improve technology/make it function
Tech in control of activity	Adults and children in control of activity

with the view within child-computer interaction to "design the ecology, not just the technology" [51].

5.2.1 Remove Dependence on Technology

The first characteristic we propose is to move away from designing technologies such that they are a required component of activities and instead use technologies as a scaffold [52] to facilitate beneficial activities. The idea is to have more technologies designed to not be necessary in the long term. Rather, 4Cs technologies should help children gain skills or knowledge to participate in beneficial activities and no longer need to be used once children have achieved these goals. Another way of thinking about it is that instead of measuring a technology's success based on engagement (i.e., how long it is used), its success depends on children achieving developmental objectives and possibly outgrowing the technology.

In terms of control, this characteristic removes dependence on technology, at least in the long term, returning control to children and caregivers. For example, a technology could coach young children to develop their own developmentally appropriate stories [53], but no longer needs to be used once children are able to generate them on their own.

5.2.2 Control Over Time

The second characteristic we propose is to design activities that involve intentional disengagement from technology, instead of design for compulsive engagement. This concept builds on the 3Cs characteristic of activities inspired by media. The idea is for there to be just enough technology to facilitate beneficial activities (e.g., help plan or inspire them, provide occasional, on-demand support) and that these activities involve a focus on other children, adults, and non-electronic objects. The technology itself may prompt or provide incentives to move to activities where technology is not present or moves to the periphery, similar to Hiniker's approach to motivate non-use of distracting technology [54]. Success is based on the ability to inspire and support beneficial activities, rather than how much time is spent on the technology. It involves children and their caregivers having control over their time. For example, the technology we mentioned in the previous paragraph that coaches children to tell stories could prompt them to tell a story to parents or peers without using technology.

5.2.3 Control Over Data

Privacy is the focus of the third characteristic. Under a 4Cs approach, the only form of data collection acceptable is not connected to individual users (i.e., it is not personally identifiable), is freely consented to and revokable, and is an integral part of the activity and/or used solely to improve the technology. Such uses could include understanding which portions of the technology are being used, patterns of use, or information necessary for the system to function. Access to location, IP address, microphone, or camera use that is transmitted and processed remotely would therefore most likely not be part of a 4Cs technology (there could be exceptions if the data does not reveal identities). This is in contrast to technologies that are designed for the purpose of collecting data, sometimes for delivering targeted advertising, other times to just sell the data [4]. It is also in contrast to technologies that collect sensitive data, even if it is not for profit purposes, that could one day be exposed by malicious actors [55] or is simply collected and stored without children's or parent's consent [56].

This characteristic of a 4Cs technology gives children and adults control over information about them, in line with Livingstone et al.'s concerns [56]. For example, with adult and (if developmentally appropriate) child permission, a technology coaching children to tell their own stories could collect non-identifiable data indicating which parts of the technology are used and how to improve the system.

5.2.4 Control Over Activities and Decision-Making

The final characteristic goes back to Shneiderman's "internal locus of control" [50]. This aspect of the 4Cs is about who controls what happens in activities involving technologies. It is about giving meaningful choices to children and their caregivers rather than imposing ways of using a technology or manipulating children into using a technology in a particular way. It puts technology in a support role, providing users with options, and keeping them in full control. Others have explored the spectrum of full autonomy for technology to user control in robotics [57]. In the same space, Elbeleidy et al. [58] noted how little work in Human–Robot Interaction envisions a future with teleoperated robots (fully under human control) instead of fully automated robots. The full human control in this 4Cs characteristic gives children and their caretakers control over decision-making.

6 Examples of 4Cs Technologies

Given the contrast between 4Cs technologies and the overwhelming majority of digital technologies young children experience, it may be difficult to imagine how these could be designed and implemented. However, examples of 4Cs technologies do exist. They share a common thread of supporting social, flexible, creative, and physical activities. These activities often resemble activities without technology, but technology inspires, adds interest, lower barriers, or enables better support.

6.1 StoryCarnival: Set Up Make-Believe Play

The 3Cs paper described the early development of a system called StoryCarnival [7], which was inspired by the concept of the 3Cs. StoryCarnival is now publicly available at storycarnival.org. Pantoja et al. designed StoryCarnival to support social roleplay [59, 60] in the style of the Tools of the Mind approach to early childhood education [48]. This kind of roleplay, inspired by Vygotsky's ideas on play [47], is based on narratives, with preschool children planning roleplay such that they each play a character in the story space defined by a given narrative, using generic props (e.g., foam blocks) to stand for objects in the story, and not being limited by what happened in the story, but being able to expand on it [48].

Multiple large studies have provided evidence that play in the style of Tools of the Mind can help preschool children, in particular those from families with low socioeconomic status, develop executive function skills [61–65]. These skills are critical for goal-oriented behavior and involve self-regulation of behavior, emotion, and cognition [66]. They have been associated with academic success in mathematics and literacy [67–71]. In other words, these are meta-skills that can benefit children broadly. Hence, play in the style of Tools of the Mind arguably qualifies as an evidence-based beneficial activity for young children.

The main challenge with Tools of the Mind style play is that for it to be effective it requires a non-trivial amount of training for teachers in addition to in-class coaching sessions [64]. Pantoja et al. designed StoryCarnival to lower these barriers and make it easier to implement these activities [59, 72]. The design of StoryCarnival took place over 39 sessions at a preschool in the United States [59, 72]. In these sessions, researchers attempted to implement Tools of the Mind style play and identified key obstacles. They then designed, with feedback and ideas from 3 to 5-year-old children, technology supports to address these obstacles [59, 60].

The first obstacle they encountered was the lack of available narratives that suited groups of children roleplaying together. Not only did children lack media experiences in common (e.g., TV shows they watch at the same time), but the overwhelming majority of books for this age group tend to feature one or two main characters, which does not work well when four children want to play together, each playing a different character. They, therefore, created electronic stories for children to experience, similar to e-books, to set up roleplay. All stories include four characters of equal importance and present a situation to be resolved, provide examples on how each character can contribute, but leave the resolution open so children can roleplay how to complete the story (see Fig. 3). All stories can be printed, enabling a screen-free option. There are also story templates that allow children an extra degree of control over the stories' content, providing options for settings, characters, and objects or events in the stories. Currin et al. discuss in greater detail the design of StoryCarnival stories [73]. Experiencing these stories is typically the first activity during a StoryCarnival session.

The second obstacle, mainly about 3-year-old children, had to do with some difficulty planning play, in particular figuring out who would play what character. StoryCarnival has a character selection tool that reminds children of characters' roles and guides them in selecting which character they will play (see Fig. 4). It is also possible to print this part of StoryCarnival. This activity occurs after experiencing a story.

Fig. 3 Screenshot from a StoryCarnival story showing three characters

Fig. 4 Screenshot from StoryCarnival's play planner, including options to select characters, or have a selection be random (by selecting the dice)

After experiencing a story and planning play, children play with each other pretending to be characters in the story, using generic props to stand for objects. At this stage, the obstacle StoryCarnival researchers found was that some children would have difficulty joining play or could become disengaged. StoryCarnival addresses this problem through a tangible, teleoperated voice agent. The voice agent is a small box with artwork resembling a character that appears in many of the stories and has a Bluetooth speaker inside (see Fig. 6). The adult running the session (e.g., a teacher) can control the speech of the agent from a user interface that gives the option to select from a set of categories of speech (e.g., reminding a child what their character is supposed to do, giving praise, encouraging collaboration, asking for help), with multiple options per category, or type in text for the agent to speak (see Fig. 5). The system then uses text-to-speech synthesis to make the agent "speak" to children. An early version of the voice agent included a tablet app children could use to control the agent's speech during play, but Pantoja et al. found this led children to focus on the tablet screen rather than their peers or other play activities [72]. Pantoja et al. discuss the process of designing the first version of the voice agent [72], while Hourcade et al. discuss a more recent version (Fig. 6) [74].

Through its three components, StoryCarnival uses technology to set up and support social play, but the main activity supported by the system consists of children

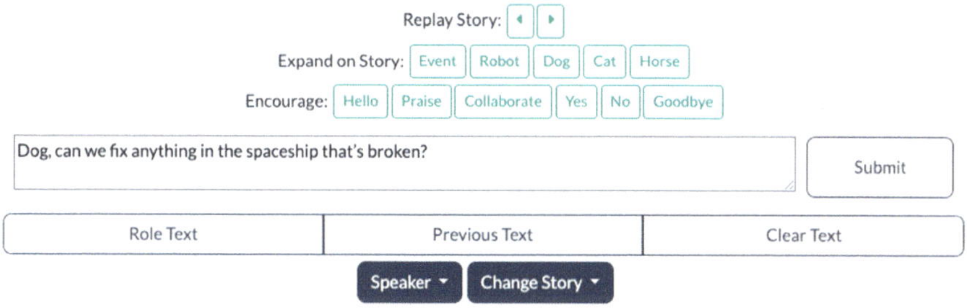

Fig. 5 Screenshot of user interface for controlling teleoperated voice agent

Fig. 6 Picture of StoryCarnival's tangible, teleoperated voice agent

engaging with each other and with the non-electronic physical space and objects around them. The portions of the system that can be experienced through a screen do not take much time during a session (typically about 5 min [75]) and are available in print. The rest of the session (20–25 min [75]) involves children playing with each other, with non-electronic objects, and optionally with the voice agent.

StoryCarnival supports the first C, creativity, by setting up an activity where children can creatively resolve a story by playing with each other and pretending to be characters in the story. In doing so, it does not provide instant gratification, but instead gratification is delayed and realized through the roleplay through which children resolve the story.

The activity also involves the second C by supporting children connecting with their social and physical environment, not only by playing with each other, but also by setting up play that involves moving around the location where play occurs and using non-electronic physical props. This involves having the primary focus of the activity, not on devices, but on people and the physical space around children.

The third C, communication, is incentivized by examples in the stories of the characters communicating and coordinating with each other. One of the key results from StoryCarnival so far is that it appears to help integrate shy children into play through its voice agent, which includes children communicating more often [75].

Finally, in terms of control, the system is designed to avoid privacy pitfalls (e.g., the agent does not collect any speech and is controlled by the adult facilitating the activity), enables children and caregivers to select the activity in which they would like to engage, and gives agency to children in resolving the story together. It also purposefully disengages children from screens, if used, after running the stories and play planner. More importantly, StoryCarnival is designed to get children to learn narratives and skills so they can engage in social roleplay, such that it should not be necessary in the long term.

6.2 Head up Games: Augmenting Traditional Social Games

Head Up games are designed in opposition to location-tracking augmented reality games like Pokémon Go in that they do not focus children's attention and interactions on screen-based interfaces [76]. Instead, handheld devices are used to add interactions or mechanics to traditional children's games which could include running or other activities that require focus on children's surroundings. The handheld devices sense proximity to other handheld devices, enabling, for example, a game of tag to include an invisible indication that someone has been tagged via vibration [77]. Soute et al. described a challenge in maintaining children's interest in Head Up games over time and suggested support for leveling the games could sustain children's interest [76]. Because children often improvise, negotiate, and iterate on game rules, Avontuur et al. explored using a simple GUI to allow children to set parameters to change the rules of a Head Up game (e.g., the number of teams, the number of home bases, etc.) [77]. They found children were able and motivated to adjust game rules using the interface and the presence of an adult facilitator (a camp counselor) helped to manage conflicts when children disagreed on the rules they wanted to play by [77].

Head Up games support creativity and control by enabling children to devise their own games (e.g., variations of the game of tag). There is delayed gratification in that children have to design the game before enjoying playing it. The activity's focus is primarily on other children and the physical environment, supporting connection, and children need to communicate and negotiate with each other to devise a rule set, too. The design also preserves children's privacy and there is a clear switch from designing the game with a screen to disengaging from technology to play the game. In addition, children may get ideas on how to design games and move on to create their own activities without the help of technology, in other words, technology can be a scaffold to learn new ways of playing.

6.3 Augmenting Traditional Playgrounds

Other work embeds technology and infrastructure within a specific environment, such as a playground, again making it unnecessary to track specific children's location. Lund et al. developed tangible tiles which could be used as building blocks to create interactive floors and walls and programmed to support different games (e.g., to turn all the tiles a specific color by pressing them) [78]. The Interactive Slide project used an infrared camera to track children's interactions with images projected on an inflatable slide without requiring full images of the children [79]. Tetteroo et al. [80] described the concept of interactive playgrounds as game spaces which would ideally partially contain play. In other words, play on an interactive playground should ideally make use of elements of the technology and infrastructure but also contain elements that do not rely on that specific environment (e.g., a make-believe pretense). That goal opens possibilities for a single play session on an interactive playground to inspire different-but-related play on traditional playgrounds, at home, or in other contexts.

In these augmented playgrounds, play is often social, supporting communication between children. It also directly involves children moving around and being in contact with the physical space around them. Some effort typically needs to be made before gratification is achieved (e.g., climbing a ladder to use a slide). If children were able to program or manipulate the environments, then they could customize experiences and have more control over them. These augmented playgrounds could be designed with privacy in mind, especially if they avoid using cameras or other sensors in a way that could identify children.

6.4 Social Play Things to Support Open-Ended Play

Interactive play objects which respond to simple interactions (e.g., a cylinder which changes color when rolled) can support children in open-ended play and inspire them to create their own games [81]. Frauenberger et al. designed three sets of interactive play objects they call Social Play Things with groups of neurodiverse children [82]. LightSpaces were magnetic pieces of fabric which lit up different colors when children squeezed primary color inputs (e.g., if one child was squeezing blue while another was squeezing yellow, the lights would turn green). The pieces of fabric could be attached to furniture or other objects. MusicPads were tiles which made sounds when pressed and could be used to create dancing games or puzzle games in which children tried to systematically figure out what each tile does. PictureStage was a lamp which could project children's drawings and recognized specific tagged cubes which prompted it to apply different effects to the projected image (e.g., inverting the colors). With these prototypes, children negotiated control of the technology and surrounding play activities within their groups. Critically, Frauenberger et al. described the importance of incorporating layers of technology such that play objects can function either with or without the technology layer [82]. For example, the magnetic fabric could be used in costumes or set designs without the lights and the tiles could be used as stepping-stones without producing any sound. This principle also applies to work in other areas as well: the Interactive Slide, for example, could still function as a slide without any augmentation [79].

These Social Play Things resemble possible components for augmented playgrounds, but for a smaller scale, indoor use. They enable children to be creative in how they are used, as they do not dictate how to conduct an activity. They are more fun to use in social settings that involve communication. They are also physical, inherently including a connection to the physical space around children. These devices also involve delayed gratification, as there is a planning and design phase to using them. By design, they keep children in control of the activities, preserve privacy, and enable children to use them without the digital aspects working.

6.5 Osmo: Tangibles on a Spectrum Toward 4Cs

Osmo [22] is a commercial product that is on the spectrum between non-4Cs and 4Cs technologies. With Osmo, young children use an app on a tablet that uses a camera to see how children manipulate non-electronic tangible items. These tangible items can be used, for example, to form letters to help children learn the alphabet [83], or play board games to learn mathematics [84]. The apps direct the activity and children interact with them by manipulating tangible items in front of the tablet.

How does Osmo do with respect to the 4Cs? While Osmo is mostly intended to be used individually by children, it can more easily afford collaboration than typical tablet apps. Children's focus is split between the tablet and tangibles. While media drives the experience, there is room for creativity, and the activities are educational. In terms of control, the app is a bit further from the 4Cs since many of the activities are not possible without the tablet, and the apps drive the activity. However, there is no design for compulsive engagement and the company's business model is based on the sale of its products rather than data collection.

Osmo is one example illustrating the 4Cs are not an all-or-nothing set of principles, but rather a framework for viewing the broad spectrum of children's technologies and weighing potential tradeoffs.

7 Discussion

The examples in Sect. 6 illustrate a broad range of ways in which 4Cs technologies can be implemented, making it clear the concept is not utopian, but possible. Also of note is that, as demonstrated by Osmo, there is a spectrum between 4Cs and non 4Cs technologies. What we argue for in this paper is not that young children only use 4Cs technologies, but that there be a balance in the technologies they use, and that the most harmful dark patterns discussed in Sect. 4 be avoided altogether. For example, we think it is quite reasonable for young children to watch educational media or play educational apps from reputable sources. At the same time, we propose that these activities can be balanced with others closer to the 4Cs.

Another way of thinking about our proposal is for technologies to attempt to incorporate as many of the 4Cs as possible. For example, even software designed for use on smartphones and tablets could aim to incorporate more of the 4Cs. Passive media experiences (e.g., videos) could be followed by prompts for activities that do not involve technology and involve creativity. Likewise, there could be prompts to engage others around children or look for things in the rooms where children are located.

There may also be some situations, where it is difficult to strictly follow the 4Cs. For example, some apps may need location to function appropriately but could still use the data only in ways that are necessary for the app to function and delete it as soon as it is no longer needed. Likewise, in many situations, it may not be practical to obtain consent to obtain data (e.g., in an augmented public playground). Again, minimizing data collection and retention to what is necessary for the technology to function is the key in these situations.

Alternative business models could avoid inappropriate ad content, designs for addiction, and abusive data collection practices. However, these do not come without challenges. Current technologies are more likely to include these negative aspects because they are free and are funded through ads and/or the sale of personal data, which provides incentives for addictive designs. One option for funding is to enable 4Cs technologies to be available freely, following the model of public broadcasting for radio and television. In fact, these organizations, which are already engaged oftentimes in freely providing high-quality educational media would be prime candidates for embracing the 4Cs approach. For other technologies, it could be that schools (e.g., for something like StoryCarnival) or cities (e.g., for augmented playgrounds) could adopt them.

The other alternative would be for parents to have to pay for technologies. In such a scenario, it may be difficult for 4Cs technologies to compete with free offerings. However, something akin to the certifications we see in food products could alleviate this challenge. For example, many people prefer to purchase food that is certified to meet certain criteria by third parties, such as being organic or fair trade. The certification process provides certain guarantees and moves the complexity of decision-making to something simpler. Instead of reading through (or taking the risk of ignoring) terms and conditions documents, parents could trust a certification by a third party that agrees with their priorities. The challenge with this approach is that it may not do much to help children from lower income families whose parents may not be able to afford certified technologies, just like they may not be able to afford organic food.

7.1 The Future of 4Cs Technologies

Despite the barriers to implementation and dissemination of 4Cs technologies, there are many opportunities for more 4Cs technologies. Part of the pattern with the technologies in Sect. 6 is that they ease, inspire, or support existing non-electronic, beneficial activities. One area of inspiration for future 4Cs technologies may therefore be similar activities for children that could also benefit from extensions. The extensions could be used to lower barriers to the activities, reduce the time it takes to set them up, get children more interested in them, and even get them to be even more beneficial. The challenge is how to make these technologies more broadly available, which may involve some level of flexibility in deployment and business models that are like Osmo's or the support of non-profits or government agencies, as mentioned above.

Another pattern in the 4Cs technologies we presented is that they tend to favor tangible interactions, as well as interactions with sensors and actuators that may be embedded in children's physical environments, or that they may carry (e.g., in the Head Up games) while keeping sensory resources primarily dedicated to the non-digital environment around them. The development of more sophisticated sensors and actuators could, therefore, enable the design of more powerful 4Cs technologies.

The 4Cs can also be a useful lens through which to think about how new developments in computing could benefit children and how to spot potentially harmful implementations. A timely example is generative artificial intelligence. Systems that could develop novel narratives to inspire beneficial activities for children could be tempting to use with young children. The 4Cs would emphasize that such technology be controlled by trusted caregivers, who may partner with such a system to ensure the quality and appropriateness of such narratives. A 4Cs approach would also curtail data collection that is often part of these systems. On the other hand, a non-4Cs use of generative artificial intelligence could deliver a never-ending stream of unknown quality media for kids that exacerbates current problems of addiction. Another non-4Cs use would take all the data children provide to a system or use children's creations to build its models without their permission.

The 4Cs view on privacy can also inform the relationship between data as a commodity, academic research, and industry. Increasingly, a non-trivial portion of academic research in computing relies on massive data collection often by third parties, which could include commercial toys or kits for young children. With a 4Cs approach, any such data collection would have to occur with parental consent and control over their data, with a preference for gathering as little data as possible to evaluate the technology, improve it, or make it function.

8 Conclusion

It is time to use our creative imagination to rethink technologies for young children. Current trends involve too many dark patterns leading to isolation, passive consumption, unimaginative uses, disconnection from physical spaces, compulsive use, and threats to privacy. The 4Cs provide a guide to a different approach. In this paper, we have motivated the 4Cs approach, described it, provided examples of actual technologies compatible with it, and discussed future threats and opportunities. Throughout most of the history of computing, the changes that broadened use and access preserved user control. It is time to get it back and ensure it is there for young children, too.

Acknowledgements This material is based upon work supported by the National Science Foundation under Grants Nos. 1908476 and 2040204, and a National Science Foundation Graduate Research Fellowship under Grant No. 000390183.

References

1. Newell A, Perlis AJ, Simon HA (1967) What is computer science? Science 157:1373–1374
2. Fein L (1961) The computer-related sciences (synnoetics) at a university in the year 1975. Am Sci 49:149–168
3. Rideout V, Robb MB (2020) The common sense census: media use by kids age zero to eight. Common Sense Media, San Francisco, CA
4. pixalate (2022) Mobile apps: Google vs. Apple COPPA scorecard (children's privacy). Pixalate
5. Fitton D, Bell BT, Read JC (2021) Integrating dark patterns into the 4Cs of online risk in the context of young people and mobile gaming apps. In: Human-Computer Interaction—INTERACT 2021: 18th IFIP TC 13 International Conference, Bari, Italy, August 30–September 3, 2021, Proceedings, Part IV. Springer-Verlag, Berlin, Heidelberg, pp 701–711
6. Fitton D, Read JC (2019) Creating a framework to support the critical consideration of dark design aspects in free-to-play apps. In: Proceedings of the 18th ACM International Conference on Interaction Design and Children. Association for Computing Machinery, New York, NY, USA, pp 407–418

7. Hourcade JP, Pantoja LS, Diederich K, Crawford L, Revelle G (2017) The 3Cs for preschool children's technology: create, connect, communicate. Interactions 24:70–73. https://doi.org/10.1145/3096461
8. Hourcade JP, Currin F (2024) The 4Cs for young children's technology: create, connect, communicate, and control. In: XXIII International Conference on Human Computer Interaction. Association for Computing Machinery, New York, NY, USA
9. Shneiderman B (1986) No members, no officers, no dues: a ten year history of the software psychology society. SIGCHI Bull 18:14–16. https://doi.org/10.1145/15683.15685
10. Doug Engelbart Institute (2022) 1968 "Mother of All Demos" with Doug Engelbart ans Team (1/3). https://www.youtube.com/watch?v=UhpTiWyVa6k. Accessed 26 Mar 2023
11. Sutherland IE (1964) Sketch pad a man-machine graphical communication system. In: Proceedings of the SHARE Design Automation Workshop. Association for Computing Machinery, New York, NY, USA, pp 6.329–6.346
12. Shustek LJ (2016) Programming the ENIAC: an example of why computer history is hard. In: CHM. https://computerhistory.org/blog/programming-the-eniac-an-example-of-why-computer-history-is-hard/. Accessed 26 Mar 2023
13. von Neumann J (1993) First draft of a report on the EDVAC. IEEE Ann Hist Comput 15:27–75. https://doi.org/10.1109/85.238389
14. Sammet JE (1972) Programming languages: history and future. Commun ACM 15:601–610. https://doi.org/10.1145/361454.361485
15. Mealy GH (1966) The functional structure of OS/360, Part I: introductory survey. IBM Syst J 5:3–11. https://doi.org/10.1147/sj.51.0003
16. Bullynck M (2018) What is an operating system? A historical investigation (1954–1964). In: De Mol L, Primiero G (eds) Reflections on programming systems: historical and philosophical aspects. Springer International Publishing, Cham, pp 49–79
17. Johnson J, Roberts TL, Verplank W, Smith DC, Irby CH, Beard M, Mackey K (1989) The Xerox Star: a retrospective. Computer 22:11–26. https://doi.org/10.1109/2.35211
18. Kay AC (2011) A personal computer for children of all ages. In: Proceedings of the ACM Annual Conference—Volume 1. Association for Computing Machinery, New York, NY, USA
19. Williams G (1984) Apple Macintosh computer. Byte 9:30–31
20. Sullivan K (1996) The Windows 95 user interface: a case study in usability engineering. In: Proceedings of the SIGCHI Conference on Human Factors in Computing Systems, pp 473–480
21. Calcatinge A, Balog J (2021) Mastering Linux administration: a comprehensive guide to installing, configuring, and maintaining Linux systems in the modern data center. Packt Publishing Ltd
22. CLI Commands|npm Docs. https://docs.npmjs.com/cli/v6/commands. Accessed 8 Feb 2024. Select From Our Wide Range of Kids' Educational Games—Osmo|Osmo. https://www.playosmo.com/en/shopping/kits. Accessed 10 Apr 2023
23. Berners-Lee T, Fischetti M, Berners-Lee T, Fischetti M (1999) Weaving the Web: the original design and ultimate destiny of the World Wide Web by its inventor. Harper, San Francisco, CA
24. Conklin J (1987) Hypertext: an introduction and survey. Computer 20:17–41. https://doi.org/10.1109/MC.1987.1663693
25. Fox S, Rainie L (2014) The web at 25 in the U.S. In: Pew Research Center: Internet, Science & Tech. https://www.pewresearch.org/internet/2014/02/27/the-web-at-25-in-the-u-s/. Accessed 9 Feb 2024
26. Carter WD, William D (1991) A comparison of instructor-led and interactive video training for the personal computer application WordPerfect. Oregon State University
27. Protectstar Inc (2013) iPhone 1—Steve Jobs MacWorld keynote in 2007—Full Presentation, 80 mins. https://www.youtube.com/watch?v=VQKMoT-6XSg. Accessed 26 Mar 2023
28. 덕표내川 (2011) African Bull Frog ant crusher. https://www.youtube.com/watch?v=WlEzvdlYRes. Accessed 26 Mar 2023
29. Insensis (2011) Bearded Dragon playing Ant Crusher. https://www.youtube.com/watch?v=WTpldq3myV0. Accessed 26 Mar 2023

30. Hourcade JP, Mascher SL, Wu D, Pantoja L (2015) Look, my baby is using an iPad! An analysis of Youtube videos of infants and toddlers using tablets. In: Proceedings of the 33rd Annual ACM Conference on Human Factors in Computing Systems. ACM, New York, NY, USA, pp 1915–1924
31. Hourcade JP, Bederson BB, Druin A, Guimbretière F (2004) Differences in pointing task performance between preschool children and adults using mice. ACM Trans Comput-Hum Interact 11:357–386. https://doi.org/10.1145/1035575.1035577
32. Montag C, Lachmann B, Herrlich M, Zweig K (2019) Addictive features of social media/messenger platforms and freemium games against the background of psychological and economic theories. Int J Environ Res Public Health. https://doi.org/10.3390/ijerph16142612
33. Cino D, DalledonneVandini C (2020) Why does a teacher feel the need to post my kid?": parents and teachers constructing morally acceptable boundaries of children's social media presence. Int J Commun 14:1153–1172
34. Ferrara P, Cammisa I, Corsello G, Giardino I, Vural M, Pop TL, Pettoello-Mantovani C, Indrio F, Pettoello-Mantovani M (2023) Online "Sharenting": the dangers of posting sensitive information about children on social media. J Pediatr. https://doi.org/10.1016/j.jpeds.2023.01.002
35. Kail R (1991) Developmental change in speed of processing during childhood and adolescence. Psychol Bull 109:490–501. https://doi.org/10.1037/0033-2909.109.3.490
36. Gottlieb G (1991) Experiential canalization of behavioral development: theory. Dev Psychol 27:4–13. https://doi.org/10.1037/0012-1649.27.1.4
37. Brody L (2022) Gene expression. In: Genome.gov. https://www.genome.gov/genetics-glossary/Gene-Expression. Accessed 27 Mar 2023
38. Ford DH, Lerner RM (1992) Developmental systems theory: an integrative approach. Sage Publications, Inc
39. Rutter M, Sroufe LA (2000) Developmental psychopathology: concepts and challenges. Dev Psychopathol 12:265–296
40. Bronfenbrenner U, Smelser N, Baltes P (2001) International encyclopedia of the social and behavioral sciences. Int Encyclop Social Behav Sci 10:6963–6970
41. Thelen E, Smith L (2006) Dynamic systems theories. In: Damon W, Lerner RM (eds) Handbook of child psychology, Vol. 1: theoretical models of human development
42. Gottlieb G, Wahlsten D, Lickliter R (2007) The significance of biology for human development: a developmental psychobiological systems view. In: Handbook of Child Psychology. Wiley Online Library
43. Anderson DR, Subrahmanyam K, on behalf of the Cognitive Impacts of Digital Media Workgroup (2017) Digital screen media and cognitive development. Pediatrics 140:S57–S61. https://doi.org/10.1542/peds.2016-1758C
44. Takeuchi L, Stevens R (2011) The new coviewing: designing for learning through joint media engagement. The Joan Ganz Cooney Center at Sesame Workshop
45. Qu G, Hu W, Meng J, Wang X, Su W, Liu H, Ma S, Sun C, Huang C, Lowe S, Sun Y (2023) Association between screen time and developmental and behavioral problems among children in the United States: evidence from 2018 to 2020 NSCH. J Psychiatr Res 161:140–149. https://doi.org/10.1016/j.jpsychires.2023.03.014
46. Gabor D (1963) Inventing the future. Secker & Warburg, London
47. Vygotsky LS (1967) Play and its role in the mental development of the child. Sov Psychol 5:6–18
48. Bodrova E, Leong DJ (2007) Tools of the mind: a Vygotskian approach to early childhood education, Second Edition. Pearson, Upper Saddle River, NJ
49. Papert S (1980) Mindstorms: children, computers, and powerful ideas. Basic Books, Inc, New York, NY
50. Shneiderman SB, Plaisant C (2005) Designing the user interface 4th, edition. Pearson Addison Wesley, USA
51. Hourcade JP (2022) Child–computer interaction, Second Edition. Self, Iowa City, IW

52. Sharma P, Hannafin MJ (2007) Scaffolding in technology-enhanced learning environments. Interact Learn Environ 15:27–46. https://doi.org/10.1080/10494820600996972
53. CDC (2023) What developmental milestones is your 5-year-old reaching? In: Centers for Disease Control and Prevention. https://www.cdc.gov/ncbddd/actearly/milestones/milestones-5yr.html. Accessed 13 Feb 2024
54. Hiniker A, Sobel K, Suh H, Sung Y-C, Lee CP, Kientz JA (2015) Texting while parenting: how adults use mobile phones while caring for children at the playground. In: Proceedings of the 33rd Annual ACM Conference on Human Factors in Computing Systems. Association for Computing Machinery, New York, NY, USA, pp 727–736
55. Chin K (2023) Biggest data breaches in US history. UpGuard. In: UpGuard. https://www.upguard.com/blog/biggest-data-breaches-us. Accessed 31 Mar 2023
56. Livingstone S, Stoilova M, Nandagiri R (2019) Children's data and privacy online: growing up in a digital age: an evidence review. http://www.lse.ac.uk/my-privacy-uk. Accessed 13 Feb 2024
57. Beer JM, Fisk AD, Rogers WA (2014) Toward a framework for levels of robot autonomy in human-robot interaction. J Human-Robot Interact 3:74. https://doi.org/10.5898/JHRI.3.2.Beer
58. Elbeleidy S, Mott T, Williams T (2022) Practical, ethical, and overlooked: teleoperated socially assistive robots in the quest for autonomy. In: Proceedings of the 2022 ACM/IEEE International Conference on Human-Robot Interaction. IEEE Press, pp 577–587
59. Pantoja LS, Hourcade JP, Diederich K, Crawford L, Utter V (2017) Developing StoryCarnival: exploring computer-mediated activities for 3 to 4 year-old children. In: Proceedings of the XVI Brazilian Symposium on Human Factors in Computing Systems. Association for Computing Machinery, New York, NY, USA
60. Pantoja LS, Diederich K, Crawford L, Hourcade JP (2019) Voice agents supporting high-quality social play. In: Proceedings of the 18th ACM International Conference on Interaction Design and Children, IDC 2019 314–325. https://doi.org/10.1145/3311927.3323151
61. Diamond A, Barnett WS, Thomas J, Munro S (2007) Preschool program improves cognitive control. Science (New York, NY) 318:1387–1388. https://doi.org/10.1126/science.1151148
62. Diamond A, Lee K (2011) Interventions shown to aid executive function development in children 4 to 12 years old. Science 333:959–964. https://doi.org/10.1126/science.1204529
63. Mottweiler CM, Taylor M (2014) Elaborated role play and creativity in preschool age children. Psychol Aesthet Creat Arts 8:277. https://doi.org/10.1037/a0036083
64. Blair C, Raver CC (2014) Closing the achievement gap through modification of neurocognitive and neuroendocrine function: results from a cluster randomized controlled trial of an innovative approach to the education of children in kindergarten. PLoS ONE 9:e112393. https://doi.org/10.1371/journal.pone.0112393
65. Blair C, Raver CC (2015) School readiness and self-regulation: a developmental psychobiological approach. Annu Rev Psychol 66:711–731. https://doi.org/10.1146/annurev-psych-010814-015221
66. Dodzik P (2017) Behavior rating inventory of executive function, second edition. J Pediatr Neuropsychol 3:227–231. https://doi.org/10.1007/s40817-017-0044-1
67. Bull R, Scerif G (2001) Executive functioning as a predictor of children's mathematics ability: inhibition, switching, and working memory. Dev Neuropsychol 19:273–293. https://doi.org/10.1207/S15326942DN1903_3
68. Espy KA, McDiarmid MM, Cwik MF, Stalets MM, Hamby A, Senn TE (2004) The contribution of executive functions to emergent mathematic skills in preschool children. Dev Neuropsychol 26:465–486. https://doi.org/10.1207/s15326942dn2601_6
69. Blair C, Razza RP (2007) Relating effortful control, executive function, and false belief understanding to emerging math and literacy ability in kindergarten. Child Dev 78:647–663. https://doi.org/10.1111/j.1467-8624.2007.01019.x
70. McClelland MM, Cameron CE, Connor CM, Farris CL, Jewkes AM, Morrison FJ (2007) Links between behavioral regulation and preschoolers' literacy, vocabulary, and math skills. Dev Psychol 43:947. https://doi.org/10.1037/0012-1649.43.4.947

71. Clark CA, Pritchard VE, Woodward LJ (2010) Preschool executive functioning abilities predict early mathematics achievement. Dev Psychol 46:1176
72. Currin FH, Diederich K, Pantoja LS, Cargo H, Franzone N, Geiger-Lee J, Hourcade JP (2023) Designing stories to inspire preschoolers' creative, collaborative roleplay. In: Proceedings of the 2023 ACM Conference on Information Technology for Social Good. Association for Computing Machinery, New York, NY, USA, pp 40–47
73. Pantoja LS, Diederich K, Crawford L, Hourcade JP (2019) Voice agents supporting high-quality social play. In: Proceedings of the 18th ACM International Conference on Interaction Design and Children. Association for Computing Machinery, New York, NY, USA, pp 314–325
74. Hourcade JP, Bakala E, Gerosa A, Currin FH (2023) Stories and voice agents to inspire preschool children's social play: an experience with StoryCarnival: inspiring preschool children's social play. In: Proceedings of the 22nd Annual ACM Interaction Design and Children Conference. Association for Computing Machinery, New York, NY, USA, pp 543–547
75. Currin FH, Diederich K, Blasi K, Dale Schmidt A, David H, Peterman K, Pablo Hourcade JP (2021) Supporting shy preschool children in joining social play. In: Interaction design and children. ACM, Athens, pp 396–407
76. Soute I, Markopoulos P, Magielse R (2010) Head up games: combining the best of both worlds by merging traditional and digital play. Pers Ubiquit Comput 14:435–444. https://doi.org/10.1007/s00779-009-0265-0
77. Avontuur T, de Jong R, Brink E, Florack Y, Soute I, Markopoulos P (2014) Play it our way: customization of game rules in children's interactive outdoor games. In: Proceedings of the 2014 conference on Interaction design and children—IDC'14. ACM Press, Aarhus, Denmark, pp 95–104
78. Lund HH, Klitbo T, Jessen C (2005) Playware technology for physically activating play. Artif Life Robot 9:165–174. https://doi.org/10.1007/s10015-005-0350-z
79. Soler-Adillon J, Ferrer J, Parés N (2009) A novel approach to interactive playgrounds: the interactive slide project. In: Proceedings of the 8th International Conference on Interaction Design and Children. Association for Computing Machinery, New York, NY, USA, pp 131–139
80. Tetteroo D, Reidsma D, van Dijk B, Nijholt A (2012) Design of an interactive playground based on traditional children's play. In: Camurri A, Costa C (eds) Intelligent technologies for interactive entertainment. Springer, Berlin, Heidelberg, pp 129–138
81. Bekker T, Sturm J, Wesselink R, Groenendaal B, Eggen B (2008) Interactive play objects and the effects of open-ended play on social interaction and fun. In: Proceedings of the 2008 International Conference on Advances in Computer Entertainment Technology. Association for Computing Machinery, New York, NY, USA, pp 389–392
82. Frauenberger C, Kender K, Scheepmaker L, Werner K, Spiel K (2020) Desiging social play things. In: Proceedings of the 11th Nordic Conference on Human-Computer Interaction: Shaping Experiences, Shaping Society. Association for Computing Machinery, New York, NY, USA
83. Maldonado H, Zekelman A (2019) Designing tangible ABCs: Fröbel's sticks and rings for the 21st century. In: Proceedings of the 18th ACM International Conference on Interaction Design and Children. Association for Computing Machinery, New York, NY, USA, pp 326–333
84. Yi S, Yao Y, Maldonado H (2022) Studying interest during a pandemic: a case study of evaluating interest of young children through a tangible learning game. In: Interaction Design and Children. Association for Computing Machinery, New York, NY, USA, pp 604–610

Conclusion

Sergio Sayago, Montserrat Sendín, and Mercè Teixidó

Abstract To wrap up this book, this chapter recaps its main objective, presents a succinct summary of the key findings, and outline future research perspectives.

1 Objective and Summary

This book provides some future perspectives on Human–Computer Interaction (HCI) research towards the year 2030. HCI is a multidisciplinary field characterized by rapid evolution and continuously expanding boundaries. A multidisciplinary approach in HCI is due mainly to the continuous evolution of digital technologies and our changing relationship with them, and to our aspirations. As HCI scholars, we aim to understand, facilitate and improve the coexistence between people and interactive technologies in an increasingly digitalized society. From time to time, we believe that it is a useful intellectual exercise to take stock of the research conducted in a field. By drawing upon an extended and curated version of the best papers presented at the at the XXIII International Conference on Human–Computer Interaction held at the University of Lleida (Spain) in September 2023, the chapters of this book enable us to better understand the research conducted, identify gaps and missing areas, and ways of filling/addressing them, in a number of areas, including Human-Centred AI, Usability, Augmented and Virtual Reality, and User Centred Design.

Chapter 9 encourages us to rethink technologies for children in the future. Digital technologies tend to be thought of as being of benefit for children. Yet, there are, as

S. Sayago (✉)
Department of Computer Science and Digital Design, University of Lleida, Campus Universitari Igualada-UdL, Avinguda Pla de La Massa, 08, 08700 Igualada, Spain
e-mail: sergio.sayago@udl.cat

M. Sendín · M. Teixidó
Department of Computer Science and Digital Design, Escola Politècnica Superior, University of Lleida, Jaume II, 69, 25001 Lleida, Spain
e-mail: montse.sendin@udl.cat

M. Teixidó
e-mail: merce.teixido@udl.cat

S. Sayago et al. (eds.), *Future Perspectives on Human-Computer Interaction Research*,
https://doi.org/10.1007/978-3-031-71697-3_10

Chap. 9 argues, dark patterns such as incentives for compulsive use should draw our attention and receive increasing research efforts. Chapter 7 raises some open issues as far as adaptive human–machine interfaces are concerned, such as ethical and social implications, like human autonomy, job displacement and automation. Future developments and research in this area might well consider and address these issues. Chapters 4 and 5 deal with some challenges in building AI-enabled technologies that are more human-centred, which is a key issue nowadays, and there are reasons to believe that this will also be important in the future. Better explanations and putting the human-in-the-loop are crucial elements for trusting AI technologies and building better, more human-centred, ones. Although User-Centred Design and Usability has been with us for a long time in HCI, Chaps. 2 and 3 show us that there is still a lot of work to do in these areas. Usability is far from being dead in an era of UX. There is also room for thinking that we should go beyond placing the user at the centre in the context of the IoT and AI-powered technologies, since digital systems have evolved from being an user application to becoming an integral service where understanding the needs of the different agents (human and non-humans) involved is fundamental. Chapters 6 and 8 contribute to the continuous evolution of "user" interfaces, which are increasingly ubiquitous.

To wrap up this edited collection, it might be worth thinking about the relevance of the human presence in the development of AI systems since it will probably attract research attention in the year 2030 (and beyond). We can imagine a future where AI seamlessly integrates with our lives as a trusted partner, not just as a tool. This vision, which is being shaped by Human-Centred AI (HCAI), depicts a rapidly evolving field where prioritizing human needs and ethical considerations is crucial to ensure that AI development benefits all of humanity. Although HITL and HCAI have distinct focuses, they are often complementary approaches. HITL techniques can be used to develop HCAI systems that are not only user-centric but also reliable and trustworthy. As AI continues to evolve, the combined approach of HITL and HCAI will be crucial for responsible and beneficial AI development. However, there is still a lot of work on ethical issues surrounding AI. For example, Morgan Freeman has claimed unauthorized use of his cloned voice in a TikTok video. Similar cases, such as the one known about Scarlett Johansson, raise ethical and legal debates about the unauthorized use of a person's image or voice through AI and stress the importance of authenticity. Still, measures are needed to protect identity and establish clear legal rules on the use of AI in media, considering intellectual property and personal rights.

Overall, taking the contributions the chapters of this edited collection make to their respective research areas, along with other previous works, which have been discussed in Chap. 1, this book indicates that the only constant element in the evolutions of HCI is change; change in users, change in technologies, change in methodologies, change in issues related to our interaction with digital technologies, change in contexts of technology use and change in user interfaces. These changes present us with many future opportunities, such as an increasing evolution of "user" interfaces, going beyond user-centred design and human-centred AI, which will be explored towards the year 2030 and beyond.

SPRINGER NATURE

GPSR Compliance

The European Union's (EU) General Product Safety Regulation (GPSR) is a set of rules that requires consumer products to be safe and our obligations to ensure this.

If you have any concerns about our products, you can contact us on ProductSafety@springernature.com

In case Publisher is established outside the EU, the EU authorized representative is:

Springer Nature Customer Service Center GmbH
Europaplatz 3
69115 Heidelberg, Germany

The manufacturer's authorised representative in the EU is Springer Nature Customer Service Centre GmbH, Europaplatz 3, 69115 Heidelberg, Germany. If you have any concerns regarding our products, please contact ProductSafety@springernature.com

Printed and bound by CPI Group (UK) Ltd, Croydon, CR0 4YY
30/09/2026
02225592-0009